GERMANY

Publisher: Aileen Lau
Editors: Vivien Kim
                        Irene Khng
Assisting Editors: Aileen Lau
                        Catherine Khoo
Design/DTP: Sares Kanapathy
                        Brian Wyreweden
                        Sarina Afandie
Illustrations: Susan Harmer
Cover Artwork: Susan Harmer
Maps: Hong Li

 Published in the United States by
PRENTICE HALL GENERAL REFERENCE
15 Columbus Circle
New York, New York, 10023

ISBN 0-671-88284-8

Titles in the series:
Alaska - American Southwest - Australia - Bali - California - Canada - Caribbean - China -
England - Florida - France - Germany - Greece - Hawaii - India - Indonesia - Italy - Ireland -
Japan - Kenya - Malaysia - Mexico - Nepal - New England - New York - Pacific Northwest
USA - Singapore - Spain - Thailand - Turkey - Vietnam

USA MAINLAND SPECIAL SALES
Bulk purchases (10+copies) of the Travel Bugs series are available at special discounts for
corporate use. The publishers can produce custom publications for corporate clients to be
used as premiums or for sales promotion. Copies can be produced with custom cover
imprints. For more information write to Special Sales, Prentice Hall Travel, Paramount
Communications Building, 15th floor, 15 Columbus Circle, New York, NY 10023.

Printed in Singapore

GERMANY

Text by Stefan Baer

With contributions from:
Morten Strange

Project Editors:
Vivien Kim
Irene Khng

Prentice Hall Travel

New York London Toronto Sydney Tokyo Singapore

C O N T E N T S

C O N T E N T S

C O N T E N T S

C O N T E N T S

Classical traditions are preserved but art of the new age,

contemporary styles, concepts and media has emerged strongly in Germany today.

Celts, Teutons, Slavs, Bavarians, Swabians, Thuringians, Franks, Saxons,

Frisians... today simply healthy, smart and happy Germans.

Architecture and the decorative traditions reflect a refinement

Introduction

illkommen! (Welcome!) That is what the proverbial mat in front of the door says in Germany. And indeed, visitors from overseas will find that most Germans show much friendly interest and curiosity in them, the more exotic the better. They are observant and helpful towards anybody who looks lost or unsure about his bearings. The English find this solicitousness sometimes a bit much; but then they believe making your own mistakes and brushing against conformity to be one of the freedoms which make traveling in foreign countries pleasurable.

Healthy and wholesome German youths.

Getting around in Germany is very easy. Nothing is really far away, and there are no great distances. Racing down the autobahn may not be everyone's idea of a scenic drive, but at least you can do it if you want to. If you feel you must, you can drive through the whole length of the country in a day, from

1

Chapel of St Bartholomew on Koenigsee, Bavaria.

Flensburg in the north on the Danish border right down to Mittenwald, a popular ski resort in the Alps close to the Austrian border. Many Germans know at least a few words of English (although in former East Germany where it was obligatory in high school to learn Russian instead, things are a bit more difficult), and this – combined with an excellent road network and a good main-line train system – makes the centers of beauty and culture accessible without much effort. Trains tend to run on time; even if they are five minutes late, this is

spots: about the middle course of the Rhine with its string of castles ruined or spruced up and converted into hillside hotels, its steep vineyards producing renowned white wines and its legends from a medieval past; about the thick forests, trout-filled streams and cuckoo-clock attractions of the Black Forest where the traditional costumes with wide-brimmed black hats and blood-red pompoms are still worn at festivals and civic celebrations; about the step-gabled houses, twisting alleys and crenellated walls of Rothenburg in all its well-restored medieval splendor; about the lakes dotted with islands and fairy-tale castles and the sunny pastures of Upper Bavaria against a backdrop of the craggy peaks and mountain ranges of the Alps.

The casual visitor may have seen Cologne, Frankfurt, Munich, perhaps even Hamburg; most will have sped through the rolling Westphalian hills on an autobahn, bypassing the Lüneburg Heath to the north or the half-timbered medieval villages hidden in the Harz mountains, and know little about the brick Gothic churches of the Baltic seaboard or the subtle differences in taste between the charcoal grilled sausages of Franconia and Thuringia. Before the revolutionary events of autumn 1989, few western visitors – or West Germans, for that matter – would have penetrated further into East Germany than a day trip to its capital, East Berlin. Since reunification, five new regions await discovery, namely Mecklen-

reassuring, giving the lie to the cliché of awesome German perfectionism.

Sights, Sounds and Scenic Spots

First-time visitors will probably have heard or read about the favorite beauty

Rolling hills and 'black' forests of St Margen, Black Forest region.

The friendly smile of a fetching fraulein.

burg-Vorpommern, Brandenburg, Saxony, Saxony-Anhalt and Thuringia.

For a country with a modern infrastructure it is astonishing how little-known large parts of Germany are. The reasons for this are partly topographical, partly cultural and historical. For a long time it was definitely unfashionable for Germans to take their holidays in Germany. Instead they went sunbathing on the Spanish coast, sightseeing in Tuscany, gourmandizing in Provence. Only in the last few years has this tendency been reversed, have people come to realize the attractions of the simpler pleasures of hiking across the heath with its bracing air and wide vistas, mainly of sky and trees, of distant farmsteads and the rotor-blades of wind-driven generators. More and more Germans now rent a cottage in the foothills of the Alps, take their children for a holiday on a farm, spend a week in a family bed-and-breakfast on the slopes of the Harz or find a room with a view on the island of Rügen.

This renewed interest in *Heimat* (homeland, motherland) has its rewards for the foreign traveler as well. Much traditional architecture, be it churches, burghers' mansions or humbler dwellings are being sensitively restored, scenic walking paths are laid out and signposted, a great number of open-air museums of traditional buildings and lifestyles have been established, local festivals are being celebrated with more enthusiasm than ever before. Local tra-

Summer blossoms in a typical German garden.

ditions of craftsmanship and the more homely arts like cooking, preserving and cheese-making are being rediscovered or re-invented. All this works to reinforce the great diversity, the different colors and sounds, rhythms and manners that make up the character of Germany, so consciously modern yet at the same time in love with a romantic vision of its past.

MARTIN LUTHER

Prehistory of the German lands goes back more than half a million years. Human remains dating from between 500,000 and 150,000 BC have been excavated at several places. These inhabitants died out about 35,000 years ago, during the last Ice Age.

Before the Bronze Age (18,000 - 16,000 BC), some early tribes of unknown origin, the Celts, began to settle more or less permanently in an area from northern France to the Balkans, cultivating crops, domesticating animals and eventually establishing trade links with their neighbors. Between 800 and 100 BC, Indo-Europeans known as Teutons or Germanic tribes as well as Slavs migrated from the north and east, driving the Celts from their hilltop settlements and forcing them to flee westwards. These tribes, which made their mark on lands as far north as southern Scandinavia and as far south as the Lower Rhine and the Vistula, slowly acquired distinctive characteristics and regional identities.

In the 1st century BC, the Romans came to extend their empire northwards. They were briefly successful, establishing forts in strategic places like present-

Martin Luther Memorial beside ruins of Frauenkirche.

9

Caves of 300 million years at Iserlohn.

day Cologne, Trier, Mainz, Wiesbaden and Passau. In 53 BC, the great Roman general and statesman Julius Caesar led his troops along the banks of the Moselle, Neckar and Rhine, ending up in the misty, marshy British Isles; his description of this campaign, the *Gallic War*, was until recently a set text for German first-year Latin students. His book, together with *Germania* by the Roman historian Tacitus, are the main literary sources about the Germanic tribes' culture and custom, dress and appearance, forms of rule and religion. They still make splendid reading.

Because of ferocious resistance by the inhabitants, the Romans never established themselves far or firmly beyond the Rhine and the Main. There was much more Roman activity in southern Germany. Townships were founded, roads constructed, strong and valuable trade links established; some Roman emperors are known to have taken the waters at places like Baden-Baden and Wiesbaden, fashionable spas to this day. In AD 313, Emperor Constantine put an end to the persecution of Christians; Trier was established as the first bishopric on German soil and became a "Second Rome"; its Porta Nigra is the prime relic of the Roman period in Germany. About AD 400, the Romans withdrew from Germany; some Germanic tribes invaded Italy and eventually helped to destroy the last vestiges of the Roman Empire.

The Dark Ages

Beginning about AD 300, the invasion of the Huns from the east into central Europe signalled the permanent establishment of home ground for various distinct German tribes: the Bavarians in the south, Alemanns in Swabia, Thuringians in central Germany, Franks in the west and Saxons and Frisians in the north.

Over the next centuries, the country relapsed into a semi-barbarian stage, while the accumulated riches both physical and spiritual of classic Graeco-Roman civilization were laid waste and forgotten. Only on the outskirts of Europe, mainly in Ireland, was some classical tradition kept alive in church and

Chieftains and Pirates

When the Knights of the Teutonic Order drove them from their lucrative hunting-grounds in the Baltic and destroyed their lair on the island of Gotland in the early 1390s, some pirates managed to escape to East Frisia on the North Sea coast. Their leader was the dashing, bearded Klaus Störtebeker, who was probably born in Wismar and now made his headquarters at Marienhafe, a village some miles inland from the sea on the banks of a winding rivulet. In those days East Frisia was ruled by various clans, whose leaders were called *Häuptlinge* (chieftains). There were always feuds among the ruling clans, and the chieftains found the pirates useful as mercenaries, to kill or kidnap for ransom. Störtebeker's main interest, however, was to prey upon the ships of the Hanseatic League on their route through the English Channel. The Frisian coast was ideally suited for surprise attacks and quick escapes, as it was full of shoals and dangerous sandbanks which only the most experienced pilots could navigate.

Störtebeker, his companion Godeke Michels and their band of merry men seem to have set up shop at Marienhafe around the year 1394, and were doing a flourishing business in piracy for several years before the Hanse cities finally decided to get rid of this plague. In April 1400, war cogs from Hamburg, Bremen and Lübeck set sail for the Ems estuary and after a short wait, staged a lightning attack on three enemy ships, killing 80 pirates and taking the rest prisoners. Störtebeker and Michels together with a few companions managed to escape and soon set sail for Norway.

When their ship was sighted off the island of Helgoland, two war cogs from Hamburg set out in pursuit. After a wild chase and a furious sea battle, the pirates were overpowered, put into irons and taken to Hamburg. In October 1401, Störtebeker, Michels and 70 of their companions were condemned to death and executed on the Grasbrook meadow. Legend has it that Störtebeker asked to pardon as many of his men as he would be able to walk past after beheading; thus were eleven pirates saved, before the headless body stumbled and collapsed.

Almost 600 years have passed, and still Störtebeker's exploits are part of local legend and folklore; children learn about his courage and cunning at school, and visitors come to Marienhafe for a whiff of history and adventure. The Störtebeker Channel is still there, its banks overgrown with weeds and reeds, and so is the church tower that served as the pirates' lookout. And there is an iron ring fastened to the churchyard wall where Störtebeker tied up his ship.

monastery, and it took several centuries for Christianity to spread across Western Europe, bringing in its wake a gloss of civilization and culture. The most important center of this revival on German soil was the Benedictine abbey at Fulda near Frankfurt, founded in 744.

The culmination of this early renaissance was the reign of Charlemagne (*Karl der Große* in German), who was crowned emperor of all the Romans on Christmas Day AD 800 by Pope Leo III. After defeating the Saxons, he extended his empire to the Elbe river; his court at Aachen became a focal point of art and learning, vigorously emulating the Roman legacy. The emperors who followed, however, neither matched him in ability nor power, and in 823 his Frankish kingdom was split up; it had covered Europe from northern Germany to the Pyrenées, and from northern Italy to the east as far as today's Polish border.

It is only in the 10th century that one can really speak of the beginning of German history, because it was then

A medieval castle along the Rhine.

that a political entity roughly within the geographical limits of modern Germany arose. It was the creation of Otto I, the Great, who revived the imperial title and in 962 was crowned in Rome "King of the Franks and Lombards". His empire embraced the Bavarians, Franks, Frisians, Lombards, Saxons and Thuringians, and its official title "Holy Roman Empire" – to which the Germans added "of the German Nation" – spelled out its ambitions: to become, like classical Rome, the supreme power of the known world but infused by the spiritual light not of paganism, but of the Christian religion.

During the reign of Frederick I Barbarossa (r.1152–90) the dismemberment of the states of Henry the Lion, the Guelph Duke of Saxony and Bavaria who was married to a daughter of Henry II of England took place. His was the last great independent Germanic domain of the time. Until the end of the Holy Roman Empire in 1806, Germany remained a collection of small principalities and free cities under the imperial umbrella which over the centuries got more and more tattered.

Frederick I and II belonged to the famous Hohenstaufen dynasty; later the emperor tended to be a Habsburg, ruling in Vienna. During the long-drawn-out struggle between emperor and pope, great vassals such as the Wittelsbachs, Hohenzollerns and the Princes of Saxony each became, in fact, if not in theory, sovereign rulers within their own territories.

The fundamental law of the Holy Roman Empire, the *"Golden Bull"*, was in force from 1356 till 1806. It stipulated that the King of Germania was elected by a college of three ecclesiastical electors (the archbishops of Mainz, Trier and Cologne) and four lay electors (the palatine of the Rhine, the duke of Saxony, the margrave of Brandenburg and the king of Bohemia) and would subsequently be crowned king and emperor in Rome. As the might of the Holy Roman Empire declined, emperors were forced to seek alliances with rich cities

and powerful city leagues such as the Swabian and Hanseatic League. The Hanseatic League – the Hanse, for short – was founded in 1358 as a maritime and commercial organization linking more than 200 towns, with Lübeck as its administrative center.

Renaissance and Reformation

In 1432 Maximilian I, "the last of the German knights", became emperor; this marked the beginning of the hegemony of the Habsburg dynasty, which was to last for four centuries. Maximilian married Mary of Burgundy, who brought the Netherlands as a dowry into the marriage; in time, through marriage and other means, Bohemia, Hungary and Spain all came under Habsburg influence. The late 15th century was the golden age of Augsburg, thanks to the financial genius of Fugger the Rich and the Welser family. The early 16th century witnessed the flowering of Nürnberg as a European center of culture and science, with Albrecht Dürer as its foremost artist.

In 1517, Martin Luther (1483–1546), professor of theology and erstwhile Augustine monk, nailed 95 "theses" on the Wittenberg church door. It was common custom to use church doors as notice boards for important announcements, but what Luther had to say was to shake the Catholic Church in its very foundations. He was protesting against the sale of indulgences, bits of paper signed by some church authority which absolved the buyer from any number of sins committed in the past or future and shortened his years in hell. He denounced the pretensions of the priests to primacy in the spiritual domain and criticized the institution and hierarchical establishment of the Church.

Such criticism of the clergy using its power and influence for worldly and political ends had been going on for decades, if not centuries, but Luther – partly on account of his position and also of the dissension within the Church itself – caused considerable scandal throughout Germany. Although repeatedly warned and threatened and finally excommunicated, he refused to retract his accusations and so was exiled to the outer domains of the Empire. Under the hospitable roof of the Duke of Saxony he translated the Bible into the German language, making it more accessible to the people than the Latin version had been. In 1529 six princes and the representatives of 14 free towns united at Speyer to protest against the harsh treatment meted out to Luther; this group soon got stuck with the name "Protestants" and a new faith was born.

In 1555 the Peace of Augsburg laid down the precepts of *cuius regio, eius religio* – the state shall be supreme in its choice of the religious faith of its subjects. By the end of the 16th century almost four-fifths of Germany had peacefully converted to Protestantism.

At the same time, however, the Council of Trent (1545–63) brought about a revival of Catholicism, giving rise to the Counter-Reformation which was strongly supported by the emperor. Germany was split into opposing camps, often supported by the force of arms. In 1618 this conflict led to a revolt in Bohemia which spread and soon became a war between the states ruled by the Catholic House of Austria. Later Denmark and Sweden came to the assistance of the Protestant cause, while French troops moved in to gain territory at the expense of the Habsburgs. The campaigns were for the most part fought in Germany; the countryside was laid waste, major towns were sacked, and the economy and infrastructure ruined for decades. The whole exercise had been futile: when peace was declared in 1648, it merely re-established the equal rights of both faiths in Germany.

The Rise of Prussia

While other states within the Holy Roman Empire became weakened because of the sovereign ambitions of their princes, Prussia, led by a remarkable succession of able and far-thinking rulers, grew from strength to strength. In less than one hundred years it rose from an obscure principality in the northeast of the Baltic Sea to the second most powerful state in the Empire, after Austria.

Frederick II, the Great (r.1740–86), also known popularly as "the Old Fritz",

Goethe and Napoleon

At the request of a friend, Goethe sketched his meeting with Napoleon 16 years after the event.

2 October 1808

I was asked to present myself to the Emperor at eleven o'clock in the morning.

A fat chamberlain, a Pole, asked me to wait. All the others left the room.

I was presented to Savary and Talleyrand.

I was called into the Emperor's chamber.

At that moment Daru appeared and was immediately ushered in.

So I hesitated a bit.

Was called in again.

Entered.

The Emperor was sitting at a large round table, having breakfast; to his right, at a slight distance, stood Talleyrand; to his left and quite near was Daru, with whom he was conferring about the question of contributions. The Emperor signaled me to come closer. I stopped at a proper distance in front of him.

After he has looked me over, he said: "*Vous êtes un homme.*" I made a bow. He asked: "How old are you?"

"I am sixty."

"You have kept yourself well."

"You have written tragedies."

I confined my reply to the essentials.

Now Daru intervened; he, who had to cause so much sorrow, had taken some pains to flatter the Germans by acquainting himself with their literature.

He told the Emperor about my writings and added that I had also translated something from the French, namely Voltaire's "*Mahomet*". The Emperor commented: "It's not a good play!" and explained rather awkwardly that it was not proper for the vanquisher of the world to present himself in such an unfavorable light.

Then he turned the conversation to my "*Werther*", which he seemed to have studied very thoroughly. After some very just observations, he mentioned a particular passage and said: "Why did you do that? It's unnatural!" and then explained himself at length and ever so rightly.

I listened serenely and answered with an amused smile, that although I was not sure whether anyone else had raised objections to the passage in question, I thought he was quite right and that admittedly there was something artificial about it.

inherited a remarkably well-organized state possessing a standing army, a rare thing in those days. A paragon of enlightened despotism, he practiced enlightenment in private, despotism in public affairs, and fortified Prussia further by instituting a meticulous administration. He was a highly gifted and cultured monarch, a composer of some note, and a friend of such luminaries of the Enlightenment as Voltaire, Diderot and Rousseau; however, the main exponent of the Enlightenment in Germany, the dramatist and essayist G.E. Lessing (1729–81), found little favor with him.

Prussian bureaucratic discipline and high standards became a byword in Europe, and the characteristics of punctuality, administrative detailing and bureaucratic ethos of modern Germany trace their origin back to the 18th century.

France was the arbiter of taste in 18th-century Europe, and many of the smaller German states tried to emulate and imitate it, both in their lifestyles and in their artistic creations. The result of such ambitions often impoverished the populace, but has left lucky travelers today with a surprising number of beautiful small palaces and gardens as well as with some excellent libraries and art collections.

The Seven Years' War (1756–63), when even the combined might of Austria, France and Russia was unable to put an end to the political and military ambitions of Prussia, ended Austria's claims to supremacy for a hundred years. Frederick's only ally was England, bent as so often on keeping a balance of power within Europe.

After the French Revolution, the Napoleonic Wars (1803–15) broke apart the German princeling states. On his triumphant campaigns eastward, Napoleon secularized the Church's estates and amalgamated a number of principalities, which in many instances had been minute, to form medium-sized states such as Württemberg. Prussia, however, became a bulwark of resistance against the French invader. By the time Napoleon's troops struggled back after their defeat by a combination of Russian space and bad weather, Prussia led a war of resistance which broke out in 1813 as a battle of nations and ended in victory at Leipzig.

Industrialization and the Second Reich

After the defeat of Napoleon, a re-ordering of Europe took place at the Congress of Vienna (1814-15). It instituted in place of the defunct Holy Roman Empire a German Confederation of 35 autonomous states and free cities, which were represented by a diet which sat at Frankfurt under the presidency of Austria. Its antiquated constitution, cleverly devised by the Austrian chancellor, Metternich, clashed with the ideas of liberal Germans dreaming of an independent nation. The meeting of a German national parliament at Frankfurt in 1848-49, fol-

Herrenchiemsee Palace built by Bavarian King Ludwig II (1845–86) in Versailles style.

lowing the revolutionary flare-ups of 1848, produced no results. Instead, fear of unrest caused the authorities everywhere to promulgate reactionary laws. While liberal politics took a back seat, the economy prospered, and various regions of Germany experienced an in-dustrial revolution.

Within eight years after his appointment as Prussian Minister-President in 1862, Otto, Prince von Bismarck (1815–98), son of a Prussian landowner and erstwhile member of the Frankfurt parliament, succeeded in unifying Germany under Prussia with fire and sword. His main opponent was Austria, which wanted to regenerate the German Confederation by federating in a Greater Germany the countries between the North Sea and the Adria. Backed by a new generation of businessmen who had grown rich and powerful during the rapid industrialization, Prussia conducted a lightning campaign against her southeastern rival and won a decisive victory in 1866. Then Bismarck organized north Germany with a free hand, annexing Hanover, Hesse and Schleswig-Holstein for Prussia and forming from all the states north of the Main river the Northern Confederation.

The states of southern Germany, valuing their independence and more leisurely lifestyle, were reluctant to join Prussia's pan-German drive. But when the French emperor's ambitions seemed to be posing a threat to those southern states, Bismarck inflamed national pride on both sides of the frontier. France declared war, the southern states united and together with Prussia defeated the French in 1870. On 8 January 1871 the German Empire was declared in the Hall of Mirrors in Versailles, with William I as Emperor. Imperial Germany, increased by the acquisition of Alsace and Lorraine, remained, in theory, a federal state, but was, in fact, under Prussian domination.

The First Catastrophe

William II (r.1888–1918) had little liking for Bismarck and soon dismissed him from office in 1890, twenty years after the latter had almost single-handedly put together the "Second Reich", in some respects a successor to the Holy Roman Empire of the German nation. Germany was now a heavily industrialized country with a rapidly expanding population, if something of a political latecomer to the European concert of nations. William II, proud and nationalistic, was insensitive to the mistrust and resentment his forays into international politics created. After having made enemies of Russia and further antagonized Britain and France, an arms race ensued. So tense was the international atmosphere that when an Austrian archduke was assassinated in Serbia on 24 June 1914, it unleashed a storm. Within a week the major European powers were at war, with the United States of America joining the western allies in 1917.

After the German invasion of Belgium its army got bogged down in trench warfare in France. Four years and some 9 million dead later the war ended. While the German armies were crumbling against the combined strength of the allies, revolution broke out in various parts of Germany, partly inspired by the success of the Russian Revolution in 1917. On 11 November 1918 a Council of People's Representatives signed the armistice. Two days earlier, William II had abdicated and the Parliament at Berlin had declared Germany a republic. In August 1919 a new constitution was promulgated, ushering in a short-lived experiment in democratic statehood known as the Weimar Republic (1919–33).

Weimar, Hitler and a World War

At the Treaty of Versailles (June 1919) Germany was heavily penalized by the victors: the country was to be demilitarized, Alsace-Lorraine returned to France and huge reparations to be paid. These relatively harsh and humiliating terms were later used by ideologists to foster nationalist and separatist emotions among Germans. The Weimar Republic under its liberal socialist leaders was determined on the difficult task of re-establishing order, peace and prosper-

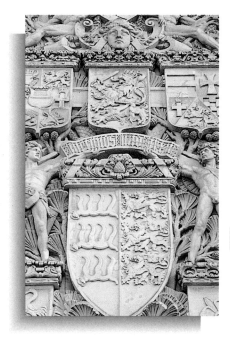

Wall detail from the neo-classical Reichstag building.

ity. Public opinion was deeply divided, giving rise to extremes of left and right radicalism and a plethora of small political parties in Parliament which often made it very difficult to pursue constructive politics. Nevertheless, German's economy slowly recovered and so did its international standing under the energetic, Francophile chancellor Stresemann.

In 1929 world depression hit Germany, causing huge unemployment, which in turn led to widespread violence and a radicalization of political life. In the elections of September 1930, the Nationalist Socialist Party led by Adolf Hitler became the second largest party in the Reichstag after the Social Democrats which, as the ruling party, was

Concentration Camp Museum at Dachau.

widely blamed for everything that went wrong. From this time on, the Nazis, thanks to an efficient organization and the use of violence, controlled the political life of the country.

In the elections of July 1932 they won a large majority, and in early 1933 Hitler became Chancellor. By the end of the year the Nazis were the sole political party, and on 12 December 1933 Hitler was acclaimed by popular plebiscite as Germany's *Führer* (leader, guide), with dictatorial powers.

The Nazis won popular support with a nebulous new ideology based on national identity, pride, purpose and racial superiority, but with the establishment of public order after the tumultuous Weimar years, and with jobs. Public

works on the new autobahns, housing construction, rearmament and military conscription cut unemployment from 26 percent in 1933 to 2 percent in 1938 (at a time when the US figure was still at 26 percent). Given this economic boost, big business was naturally supportive of the new regime.

The *Gleichschaltung* (bringing in line) of professional organizations and individuals met with little opposition. Lawyers and judges, doctors and professors, the media and the business community quickly adapted to the new order, the abolition of democratic principles and the curtailing of individual rights and freedoms. Among artists, many of the better ones either emigrated or withdrew into an inner emi-

A memorial outside an old concentration camp in Buchenwald.

gration. With some remarkable exceptions, leading members of the Protestant Church kept a low profile. The Catholic Church dropped its initial hostility towards Nazism after the concordat between the Reich and the Vatican (July 1933), which safeguarded the German Catholics' churches, property and schools in exchange for their abstention from politics.

Hitler survived several assassination attempts. The best known one was led by a group of German army officers and took place on 20 July 1944, just

Above the Hitler bunker in Berlin.

when the western allies were liberating Italy and France and the Soviet Union was on the counter-offensive. Over 200 people implicated in the plot were executed and some 7,000 others arrested.

Anti-Semitism had long been rife particularly in student fraternities, and even if many professors were dismayed by the cultural philistines running the country, they were quite ready to denounce Jewish or left-wing colleagues to further their own careers. A nationwide book-burning in May 1933 was targeted at all liberal thinkers and writers, which included many Jews. Persecution of Jews gradually grew in force and ferocity. As the Jewish writer and poet Heine had noted a century earlier: "They begin by burning books and end by burning peo-

ple." In the end, through concentration camps, slave labor and cold-blooded murder, the Third Reich witnessed the virtual extermination of Germany's Jews – some 6 million perished, roughly a third of the world's population of Jewry and gypsies and the persecution of other ethnic minorities.

Lack of interest and action by other governments assisted Hitler's aims; only protests were uttered when he rearmed Germany (1935), reoccupied the Rhineland which had been placed under French occupation (1936) and annexed Austria (1938). At a meeting in Munich in September 1938, Great Britain and France thought they could buy peace in Europe at the price of the annexation of the Sudentenland, an area

The Reichstag after the Second World War.

in Czechoslovakia with a predominantly German population. But the day of reckoning was only postponed: when on 1 September 1939 German tanks rolled into Poland, the Allies at last honored their undertakings and guarantees, and war was declared.

Denmark, Norway, Holland, Belgium, France, Yugoslavia and Greece were all defeated by Hitler's forces. In 1940 Germany, Italy and Japan concluded an Axis pact which aimed at instituting a new order in Europe and the Far East. When the effort to force Great Britain on her knees by aerial bombardment failed, Hitler turned eastward. In 1941 he tore up the non-aggression pact with the Soviet Union and made straight for Moscow, hoping that Japan would attack the USSR from the east. The Japanese, however, prevaricated and instead turned their attention to their real enemies – the American Pacific fleet. When they attacked Pearl Harbor on 7 December 1941, this almost immediately brought the United States into the war. Defeats in North Africa in 1942 were followed by the turning-point disaster at Stalingrad the next year, when the Russian winter and the vast size of the country combined, not for the first time, to repulse a foreign invader. However, the ultimate collapse did not occur before all major German cities and innumerable small towns had been ruthlessly bombed. With the war lost, Hitler committed suicide in his Berlin bunker on 30 April 1945.

Government

Ⅰn 1945, Germany lay in ruins. The people of Germany, war-weary, morally deeply shaken and concerned for an uncertain future, eked out an existence amid the rubble and debris of the collapsed Reich. Yet in the course of the next four decades, two very different Germanies emerged. In the west, the Federal Republic of Germany (FRG) developed into a stable and prosperous capitalist democracy; in the east, the German Democratic Republic (GDR) became economically the most productive state in the communist bloc and one of the Soviet Union's staunchest supporters and allies.

At previous conferences, the Allies – the United States, the Soviet Union, Great Britain and France – had already decided to divide the country into four zones of occupation. In the old German lands east of the rivers Oder and Neiße, the western frontier of Poland was moved westward while it lost territory in the east to the Soviet Union.

The colors of Germany flies bold and strong.

25

Rothenburg city hall, one of the many all over Germany.

The German Parliament building
rebuilt after the last war.

Socialism and Political Parties

In the Soviet-occupied zone, Moscow-trained German communists had already been flown into Berlin at the end of April 1945. In 1946 the Communist and Socialist Parties merged to create the Socialist Unity Party (SED) which soon brought all other political parties in this zone under its effective control. Then began a rapid program of expropriation, nationalization and land reform and a general shift to socialist policies, partly justified by the popular perception that pre-war capitalist structures in Germany had given rise to Nazism and its initial success.

Regional flags of Germany.

old Catholic Center Party, and its sister party in Bavaria, the Christian Social Union (CSU); the Social Democratic Party (SPD) with a strong anti-communist bias; and the Free Democratic Party (FDP), a joint venture of a range of liberal parties from different regions.

In addition there were (and are) several smaller parties representing specific regions, issues or constituencies. To this day, the main political battles are between the CDU and SPD, with the FDP joining now one, now the other in changing coalitions.

A generous notion of reconstruction on the part of the United States was given material expression in the Marshall Plan, announced in June 1947, which envisaged the economic and political rebuilding of Europe in directions that would strengthen America's new international role.

The administration of economic aid in western Germany required a currency reform, since the old Reichsmark was virtually without value. This reform of June 1948, being part and parcel of the establishment of a capitalist market economy underpinned by a democratic restructuring of the whole political and social framework, was unacceptable to the Soviets who retaliated by blockading all land access to Berlin for 11 months.

The last building block of a new western Germany was put into place when, after an assembly of delegates from the different regions had approved the new constitution, the Federal Re-

By 1949, the Soviet zone had undergone a major transformation in political, economic and social life, and the communist-dominated SED, backed by Soviet military administration, sabotaged any attempt at introducing genuine democracy in East Germany.

In the western zones the break with the past was not as dramatic. The denazification program, based on answers to a lengthy questionnaire, developed into a bureaucratic nightmare. By and large former Nazis, with the exception of major war criminals, were slowly reincorporated into West German life.

Three main political parties quickly established themselves: the conservative Christian Democratic Union (CDU), made up mainly of members from the

Former East German observation post in Staaken, Berlin.

public was formally founded in May 1949; the constitution, being regarded as provisional until unification with the Soviet-controlled zone, was called the *Grundgesetz* (basic law). In large measure as a direct response, the GDR was established in the Soviet zone a few months later, in October 1949.

One of the factors consolidating the existence of the two Germanies was the incorporation into a range of economic, political and military alliances in east and west respectively. In 1955 West Germany became a full member of NATO and two years later was among the founder members of the European Economic Community or Common Market, predecessor of today's EC. The GDR joined COMECON and the War-

saw Pact, the East European economic and military alliances dominated by the Soviet Union. The western Allies saw these alliances as a safeguard against the re-emergence of a nationalist Germany, while for German politicians the western orientation was a way of strengthening democratic processes at home and playing a part in the western concert of nations.

For almost four decades the two Germanies with their strong and mutually reinforcing ties to the bloc system of the two superpowers were the pawn and front line of the Cold War between the capitalist and communist worlds. Domestically this had the effect of providing relative stability to both countries throughout the years from 1949 to 1989.

Former East German guard.

An Economic Miracle

During the first ten years, the FRG experienced an "economic miracle". Government policies, billed as a "social market economy", meant that the state should guarantee or facilitate the conditions for economic growth as much as possible to market forces. The "social" qualification indicated a recognition of the need for certain provisions to protect the weaker members of society from the full ravages of unrestricted capitalism. During the 1950s economic policies were characterized by low taxes, high interest rates and profits, low wage increases for workers, a squeeze on domestic credit and the encouragement of investment.

With the recession of 1965-66 and growing disenchantment with the long-ruling CDU government, the party was forced into a "grand coalition" with the SPD, the erstwhile left-wing party which was now proposing a moderate management of capitalism with a human face.

The general sense of restlessness, of protest against the paternalism of the political leadership and the need for fresh air and experiments found its most vivid and powerful expression in the student movement of the late 1960s. This heady mixture of politics and culture, with demonstrations against the Vietnam war, with pop music and mini skirts, squatters' protest against speculative building and breezes of marijuana, provided inspiration to a whole generation.

On the crest of this wave of protest in 1969, a new period in West German history was inaugurated when the SPD managed to become the dominant party of government. Reforms were instituted, some old structures broken up, some cozy links between politicians and businessmen terminated, younger people appointed to important positions and new forms of dealing with the GDR explored. Various subcultures developed, searching for alternative lifestyles and giving rise to a proliferation of citizens' initiative groups concerned with local and regional issues.

The green movement originated in the 1970s; its basic tenet is ecological – a desire to conserve energy and protect

An enthusiastic effort in environment preservation.

the environment, a mistrust of modernism and especially of nuclear power, and a liking for a simpler and less materialistic way of life. This movement developed a higher profile in Germany than in any other European country. Members of *die Grünen* (the Green Party), founded in 1980, now sit in the German and European Parliaments, and the main thrust of their concerns has been co-opted by the three big political parties. (The radical right-wing Republicans are a more recent phenomenon; they have polled quite heavily in the south at the expense of the CDU.)

When a new worldwide recession in the late 1970s caused rising unemployment and the welfare state was beginning to be perceived as overstretched and heavily indebted, the SPD government became increasingly unpopular. In 1982, with the help of a few members of the FDP who changed their parliamentary allegiance, the CDU under Helmut Kohl was able to take over the reins of power. Unsentimental, determined, a clever tactician, a man of will more than vision, Kohl in spite of frequent setbacks and widespread unpopularity, has been astonishingly successful in keeping Germany politically and economically in the top league.

Cross Country

For exactly forty years, Germany was a divided nation. After the founding of

Villa Hammerschmidt, the official residence of the German Federal
President in Bonn.

Chipping and chiselling at the old Berlin Wall.

the GDR in 1949, many East Germans chose to vote with their feet. While the main border with West Germany was closed, it was still possible to cross from East to West Berlin and to leave from there for West Germany. Since most of the refugees were skilled younger males and members of the professions, this drain of manpower affected the GDR's economy. On 13 August 1961 the East-West border running through Berlin was secured by barbed wire, and more permanent walls of concrete were rapidly being erected, thus closing off the last means of the east-west escape. The psychological effect on East Germans seems to have been that people started coming to terms with a system they now had simply to accept.

A change in the relationship between the two countries began when the SPD came to power under the chancellorship of Willy Brandt. Brandt's *Ostpolitik*, his desire to see an easing of tensions and a facilitation of human contacts between the two Germanies met with considerable domestic opposition from the CDU/CSU, but he was able to push through a series of treaties and agreements which culminated in December 1972 in the "Basic Treaty" between the FRG and the GDR. From 1973 to 1989 intra-German relations were concerned less with the apparently receding, almost metaphysical question of potential reunification and rather more with the improvement of relations between the two countries. In human terms the beneficiaries were mainly pensioners, who were allowed to travel and settle in the West, and people imprisoned for "political offenses" (a vague term); quite a few writers and poets, who openly criticized the communist government, were expelled from the country or if they had been traveling abroad, were not allowed to return.

In the later 1980s extraordinary changes began to take place in eastern Europe. Under the reforming leadership of Gorbachev, who acknowledged how economically weak and politically overstretched the Soviet Union was, momentous changes were introduced to diffuse tension on the international as well as on the eastern bloc and domestic front. Poland, Hungary and Czechoslovakia were the first to bring to an end their respective Communist Parties' monopolies on power, while the GDR government reacted desperately with increasing repression.

In the summer of 1989, Hungary began to dismantle the fortified boundary with Austria. Some 20,000 East Germans holidaying in the country quickly took the opportunity to flee to the west where they were ecstatically welcomed. This started a kind of mass exodus; by the winter of 1989-90 up to 2,000 refugees arrived in West Germany each day, where problems about absorbing them soon became apparent.

One Germany

The position of the GDR government became highly precarious. Not only were its citizens leaving by the thousands, but within the country a vociferous discussion started and protest meetings took place, often initiated and guided by the Protestant Church. Early voices of reform tended to reject the West German system and demanded to move forward to some form of humane, truly democratic socialism; but these voices were soon drowned by others demanding complete unification. The GDR leadership tried to ride the waves by granting concessions and promising reforms, but to no avail. On 9 November 1989 a GDR spokesman admitted that newer, more far-reaching freedom to travel effectively meant that the Berlin Wall no longer served its former purpose. By midnight of the same day, people were dancing on the top of the Wall, helping each other over in both directions.

Elections held in the GDR in March 1990 resulted in a clear vote for rapid unification of the two Germanies; currency union took place on 1 July, and on 3 October 1990 reunification was formally established. East Germany was divided into five administrative regions, and the main West German political parties soon established themselves as the major political powers. The former SED under various new names still attracted a sizable number of votes and has representatives in all five new parliaments. All political, cultural and social institutions, nurseries and savings banks, museums and chain stores are now being cloned in the east, and economic reconstruction is going ahead apace.

The speed with which reunification took place meant that many aspects still may require improvement and important decisions made at the spur of the moment may need to be reviewed in time. It may take a long time for the two parts of Germany to assimilate perfectly and to grow together to become a physical and spiritual whole.

Patience, goodwill and money will be necessary in large amounts. For the foreseeable future, Germany is likely to concentrate on putting its new house in order and to improve relations with its eastern neighbors and will be wary of committing itself to new adventures and initiatives in the international field.

Germany's economy is characterized by a large number of medium and small firms which make for great flexibility and potential for innovation; a reputation for dependable and stylish products and a massive input of high tech; a highly skilled and conscientious workforce; and a reluctance to enter high-risk sectors.

This cautious approach is also evident in the business community's reaction to reunification. It shows little enthusiasm for a hands-on approach to tackle the east's primitive infrastructure or to invest in its ailing industries lumbered with obsolete machinery and crumbling factory buildings. While wages are being quickly – and artificially – adjusted to West German levels, unemployment is high and continually rising. Several thousand state companies have been privatized by the Treuhandanstalt, the governmental privatization authority; still, several hundred thousand disputes about ownership and compensation have

The BMW Building in Munich, a major corporate symbol of success.

Economy

37

High-tech German trains.

yet to be resolved. The almost complete collapse of trade with Eastern Europe is making the already difficult transition from a socialist economy to a social market economy even more difficult. West German entrepreneurs seem set to let the government sort out the more serious and costly problems first before they will move in to further unify the economic situation of west and east.

State Ownerships

For a country often held up as a prime example of the free-market economy, Germany has an array of links between government and business that is quite remarkable in their depth and extent.

State ownership and state holdings in business are extensive.

Underlying the official links, there is an intricate and powerful network of personal ties and overlapping interests. An easy switching between public office and business – although perhaps not as easy and common as in France – is yet evident at all levels of the political hierarchy, and many leading politicians have direct interests in business. It is, however, often only the foreigner who views such connections as liable to create conflicts of interest. Many Germans tend to regard them as mutually beneficial and essential to the smooth running and humming of the economy. The media, which could conceivably act as a watchdog over such matters, on the

Mercedes, international icon of success and symbol of top quality German engineering.

whole sees itself as part of the business establishment, and rarely questions the assumption that what is good for business is good for the country. Exceptions are magazines like *Stern* and *Der Spiegel*, which pride themselves on their investigative journalism.

It is hard to overestimate the hold of the banks, especially the big banks, on the business. The Bundesbank is the federal government's prime means of implementing monetary policy. It sees as its first duty the protection of the currency and, because of its unusual degree of independence, has occasionally clashed resoundingly with the government, which tends to be concerned with wider political aspects.

Banking still tends to be conducted in an atmosphere of old-fashioned calm. Many banks are habitually cautious, suspicious of innovations and reluctant to expose themselves to risk. Outsiders see the German banking scene as an exclusive club to which it is still very hard to be admitted.

Small specialist firms are one of German industry's strong points. In the mechanical engineering industry, for instance, which today is the country's biggest exporter, the vast majority are small firms which can supply equipment to exact, individual demands. The flagship of West German industry is motor manufacturing; it is so strong because it has made the most of Germany's reputation for sophisticated, high quality products. High tech is a key

Old and new Franconia come together as modern machinery harvests below the ancient ruins of Castle Neideck.

selling point. Daimler-Benz, which makes the Mercedes as well as trucks and buses, and Volkswagen (VW), producer of the famed "Beetle", are the giants among German car-makers; BMW has long been a leader in the technological race, while Porsche – founded by the man who designed the original "Beetle" in the 1940s – is still a favorite with yuppies of all ages, however few remain of them.

The highest job losses during the 1980s were in the traditional heavy industries. Because they still employ a large number of workers, the government has constantly intervened to keep these industries going, be it through subsidies or buying up shares. The giants of the heavy industry, firms like Thyssen, Krupps and Mannesmann, have found ways to survive and prosper by enlarging the technological input, transferring part of their production to low-wage countries and by diversifying, buying themselves into new businesses. As a result, for example, barely one-third of Thyssen's sales now come from steel.

Labor and Natural Resources

The relationship between management and unions has been stable. Central to the unions' power is their sheer size – the metal workers' union with two and a half million members was the largest non-Communist trade union – and the fact that they each represent an entire industry; if one union takes action, the whole industry is affected and thus has a drastic effect on the country as a whole.

Workers have a reputation for skill and conscientiousness, and thanks to a generous system of social benefits have working conditions which are among the best in the world. The German unions, ideological in words and gestures, but usually pragmatic in action, have won many privileges, including a shrinking working week and up to six

Owing to its unusual inheritance laws, farms are shrinking in size.

weeks annual holiday.

Of natural resources, Germany has very little – if one leaves out the character of its people. Although its results are impressive and put one in mind more of landscape gardening than of a basic industry, farming, in spite of all its outward picturesqueness, amounts to a very minor factor in Germany's economy.

The country's unusual inheritance laws, bequeathed by Napoleon, have left it a legacy of tiny farms. Well over one-third of all are less than four acres, and the average farm size is only about 40 acres. Most of these small plots are worked by people who have other jobs besides; less than 300,000 are fully employed in farming.

In spite of being heavily subsidized

A vineyard producing Moselle wines.

both from the EC and domestic coffers, annual farm incomes have steadily dropped since 1975. In the east, the establishment of agricultural cooperatives resulted in the amalgamation of private land into vast one-crop farming estates, which because of intensive use of chemical fertilizers have now become health hazards.

About one-third of the country's area is covered by woodlands, of which more than half is in state hands; it provides Germany with almost half its total timber needs, and also – and ever

Berlin has continued to attract many tourists.

more importantly – acts as a leisure and tourist resource. As regards other natural resources, domestic coal (both hard and lignite or brown) still supplies about 30 percent of all the energy needs, but is of diminishing importance; of the other main energy sources, 94 percent of its oil and 65 percent of its natural gas have to be imported. This growing dependence on imports of course has significant political implications.

Trade

In international trade, Germany is one of the world's giants; its visible exports are second to none, its imports only surpassed by those of the United States.

As exports account for roughly one-third of GNP (in Japan and the United States it is about 10 percent), some experts think Germany excessively dependent on exports and vulnerable to political pressure from purchaser countries. Key exports are finished goods like cars and machinery of all kinds, and consumer goods like electrical appliances, which benefit from the country's reputation for quality and sophistication.

Almost half of Germany's exports are sold within the EC, where its trading relationship with France is crucial. Lack of tariffs between EC countries, their proximity and community policy all foster strong trading links. Among imports the single largest sector is food and drinks.

Situated in the heart of Europe, the Federal Republic of Germany, with an area of about 137,200 sq miles (357,000 sq km) and a population of 77.75 million, embraces a great variety of landscapes, from the windswept seashores of the north via the vineclad hills and heavily wooded mountains of the central uplands to the majestic snowcapped peaks in the southeast.

Such beauty of the Black Forest.

The North German Plain is flat to the west of Berlin, but to the east it consists of hills running more or less parallel to the Baltic coast and usually less than 650 feet (200 meters) high, separated by wide, flat valleys often filled by shallow lakes.

Along the North Sea coast, the sea has broken up the ranges of dunes formed in bygone times, and divided them into separate islands, the mainland being protected by massive dikes while the Frisian islands are being gradually washed

Geography & Climate

View from the rock outcropping on the Walberia, over the Swiss Franconian landscape near Porchheim.

away by the waters. Only seven Frisian islands are now left, of which the best known is Norderney; of the East Frisian islands, Sylt is the most considerable. Extensive inundations throughout historic times have shaped the coastline. In 1276 the Gulf of the Dollart was thus created, and particularly in the 17th century several coastal villages and inhabited islands were devoured by the sea, catastrophes commemorated in folktales about spectral shipping lights and church bells ringing from the depth of the waters.

The Calm next to the Storm

While the North Sea coast is always beaten by the sea winds and threatened by storms, the Baltic coast presents a very different picture. There are few islands, no perceptible tides, and the great part of the coastline is covered by ice in winter, interrupting navigation for several months every year. The estuaries cut deep into the flat land, and the sea here laps a tranquil beach, a wood or an attractive fishing village.

The great inland plains sweep from the Dutch and Belgian borders in the west all through the breadth of the country right to the Oder and Neiße rivers and the Polish border in the east. The Lower Rhine Valley is dotted with farms and hamlets containing the comfortable type of houses seen in nearby Holland, while the Westphalian plain around Münster is a region which maintains its tradition of horse breeding and has many small, unpretentious castles and *Wasserburgen* (moated manor houses).

The area around Braunschweig with its fertile alluvial topsoil is renowned for its flourishing market gardens while further east the landscape is characterized by huge expanses of farmland and pastures, a method of cultivation inaugurated by Prussian landowners in the 18th century and intensified by the Socialist command economy. The marshy, watery lowlands east and southeast of Berlin were first drained and cultivated by Dutch agricultural engineers in the 17th and 18th centuries.

East of the Weser, the once predominant moorland is gradually disappearing as new methods of improving poor soils are discovered. The nature reserve of the Lüneburg Heath, however, has preserved for all time a typical stretch of the old time moorland. The

Die Bastei – towering rock formations near Bad Schandau.

once so bleak peat bogs and very wet pasturelands west of the Lower Weser and north of Bremen have been drained by Dutch methods and are largely under cultivation.

The Rhineland Schist Massif is an ancient mountain range cut by deep rifts which have been filled by the Rhine, Moselle and Lahn rivers. Between this range and the Thuringian Forest the land consists of various separate basins and heights, some volcanic such as the Vogelsberg and the Rhön. The Eifel plateau is known for its crater lakes, while

The German Forest

Like the beauties of the seaside, the attractions of the forest were first discovered by the Romantics in the 19th century: they rhapsodized it because it was dark and deep, mysterious and primordial, an ideal setting to commune with Nature. Forests play a prominent part in the fairy tales of the Brothers Grimm and Wilhelm Hauff, where they figure as the abode of dwarfs good and bad, of ugly witches and wise old men. Folklore inhabits the forest with dragons on the look-out for beautiful maidens, who are invariably rescued in the nick of time by knights in shining armor; and in many a romantic novel we read of coaches being waylaid by robbers and highwaymen, its passengers relieved of their valuables or abducted into captivity.

Times have changed, and the only danger forests pose for the modern traveler is losing his way. More than a quarter of Germany is still covered by woods, mainly of pine and beech and some oak; however, a pitiful "dying of the forest" during the last decade has resulted in a serious thinning-out. Among the most extensive and beautiful forested areas are the Odenwald with its associations with Charlemagne and the Nibelung, the coniferous Bavarian Forest area famous for its glass industry, and the Black Forest, home of the cuckoo clock and the eponymous gâteau. In the heart of the Black Forest lies Freiburg, full of half-timbered and gabled houses and among visitors very often the favorite of all German towns, even above Munich.

The best way to enjoy such woods is to take a day off and go on a walking tour, either on one's own or with an organized tour. Then you can forget the worries of the world for a time, listen to the wind sighing in the lofty treetops, pick mushrooms, feel the velvety carpet of pine-needles and leaves under your soles; and after scaling a summit or ridge to admire the spectacular view across a sea of undulating countryside, you should treat yourself to a plain, nourishing meal and a glass of beer at the nearest inn (often signposted) before turning back to rejoin the madding city crowd.

the thickly wooded Sauerland provides water for the Ruhr industrial region. The Thuringian Forest and the Erzgebirge (ore mountains) east of it are steep, craggy ranges, penetrated by few roads, an old mining region turned into a hiking and skiing paradise.

The border to southern Germany is marked by the Main which has its source at the meeting point of the Thuringian Forest, the Erzgebirge and the Franconian Jura, and flows westward to the Rhine. Franconia, which corresponds more or less to the Main basin and politically is part of Bavaria, consists of a vast, gently rolling and somewhat melancholic plateau and the Jura, a small limestone range where the best stone in Germany for facing buildings is found. It is an idyllic landscape with castles perched on mountain peaks, stalactite caverns, orchards and swiftly-moving little rivers. Its thickly wooded hills border Bohemia and Thuringia.

Going Westwards

Further west lies Swabia with a great variety of distinct landscapes, dotted with a heterogeneous collection of medium and small industries. The valley of the Neckar below Stuttgart is covered by vineyards and orchards while elsewhere low wooded hills darken the horizon. The southern skyline is barred by the

Vineyard near the enriching Moselle.

blue-tinged range of the Swabian Jura. West of the river Lech the hilly landscape of Upper Swabia evens out as it reaches the Bodensee (Lake Constance).

To the southeast the Bavarian Plateau tilts gently towards the Danube which is navigable from below Regensburg right to the Black Sea. Paths have been cut across the plateau by mountain torrents sweeping down infertile debris from the mountainsides, enabling crops to be grown and such towns like Augsburg and Munich to be established. The most attractive and fertile area lies between Landshut and Regensburg. East of Regensburg, the Bavarian Forest, the largest continuous forest in Europe, contains old glass-blowers' towns like Zwiesel, Frankenau and

Zugspitze, the highest peak in Germany.

Sunrise over softly rolling hills and farmland.

Bodenmais, the latter now a modern tourist center. This is a hiker's paradise (the highest peak, the Arber, at 4,750 feet [1,450 meters]), sheltered from wind, snow and avalanches.

To the west, between the Binger Gap and Basle, the Upper Rhine Plain widens out. As in the Alsace, its alluvial topsoil is very fertile and its climate of early springs and hot summers favors intensive farming as well as wine and fruit growing.

In the southeast the Bavarian and Allgäu Alps mark the borders with Switzerland and Austria. Although without glaciers, they have a beauty all their own, with some jewel-like mountain lakes and, farther down the northward valleys, long lakes fringed with forests and picturesque villages.

A Continental Climate

Germany's continental climate means that it can be really hot in summer and bitterly cold in winter. The north has milder winters and moderately warm summers; the further south one moves, the greater are the seasonal variations. July is both the hottest and the wettest month.

Spring comes rather late (April/May), but is a splendid season for forest walks. April often brings brilliant still days to the Rhine Valley and southern Germany, which is decked in blossoms. Early May, however, frequently sees the

Rich summer landscape in Bavaria.

return of icy weather. Summer means drowsy days along the rivers, dark blue skies along the coast, a certain easing of manners and a loss of inhibitions as everyone prepares himself for languid enjoyment.

On hot days, when the air is heavy and thundery, irritation mounts. Along the seashore vigorous and invigorating interaction between the sun and the iodic sea air tans bodies and burns noses. In August, mellow autumn starts, and October can bring bracing days which are tempered by the jolly times offered by Munich's *Oktoberfest* and countless wine and harvest festivals all over the country.

October and the first two weeks of November may bring an Indian Sum-mer or as the Germans say, an *Altweibersommer* (old women's summer) when the sun, particularly in the south, highlights the autumn tints.

At the first frost the Bavarian and Allgäu Alps, the Black Forest, the Sauerland and the Harz mountains, in spite of their modest altitudes, begin to get their winter covering of snow and to prepare for the winter sports season. Away from the mountain ski resorts, winter is often penetratingly cold and damp.

Many hotels outside major towns close for the whole winter season. Around Christmas time, life warms up, and then in February *Fasching* (carnival) provides a welcome break during the long slog towards spring.

Picture postcard view of the ski resort of Gamisch Partenkirchen near Zugspitze.

Flora & Fauna

The Germans are said to have some mythical ties with and almost religious feelings towards their forests, and perhaps this is one reason that roughly a third of the country is still covered by woods. The main forest regions are found in the center of the country. The Black Forest and the Bavarian Forest contain vast areas of spruce, while the western slopes of the Black Forest are especially abundant with silver fir. Native forests (i.e. unplanted ones) often contain juniper, bilberry, heather, mosses and lichens as well as mushrooms. Mushrooms are a great delicacy, frequently served in a rich sauce with game and dumplings. Collecting them yourself is advisable only if you know exactly which one are poisonous, so most people prefer to buy them at the market stall. The most highly regarded are the *Steinpilze* (edible boletus or cep) and *Pfifferlinge* (chanterelle).

The mountain forests tend to consist of silver fir and

Spring daffodils in a German park.

The rose, one of many of the cultivated German blossoms.

higher up, larch, which grows up to 8,500 feet (2,600 meters), mixed with spruce and stone pine. Above the timberline the mountain pine occurs as a prostrate shrub and beyond this you find rhododendrons and alpine plants. The vegetation of the plains is varied, but less exciting.

The northwest is characterized by heath land, with heather, gorse, grasses, mosses and lichens where it is dry, and club mosses, sundews and cotton grass in the wetter parts. Clumps of wind-blown trees accentuate the vastness of the open spaces which can look grand or melancholic according to your own frame of mind. In the wide coastal belt you also find large areas of bogs whose peat is often exploited for horticultural purposes, as fertilizer or as fuel for commercial hothouses.

Alder dominates the peaty fern woods and is the characteristic tree of river valleys, often with willow and poplar where it is very wet, or oak, ash, elm and hornbeam where it is drier. On the sandy soil of the Börde around Braunschweig and Magdeburg, dark pine forests provide an attractive contrast to the whitish bands of country lanes.

Call of the Wild

There are 54 *Naturparks* (protected wildlife parks) in Germany and some 900 *Naturschutzgebiete* (nature reserves), the latter less extensive and with access

Flowers and plants proliferate many gardens and window boxes in the summer.

sometimes strictly controlled because of their scientific role. The wildlife parks exist, particularly those in forests, for the enjoyment of walkers. Cars are often restricted to the main road, so that you can explore the area by bicycle or on foot. Scenic roads and *Wanderwege* (hiking tracks) are signposted or color-coded and are marked on small-scale maps as well as on tourist maps supplied by the local tourist office. If the weather is less than perfect, only the most dedicated of wanderers will venture forth; so if you are equipped with a rainproof greatcoat and sturdy boots, you will have the world all to yourself.

Franconian Jura

The largest of the nature reserves is in the Franconian Jura (1,150 sq miles

A nature reserve sign.

Müritzee et al

The Müritzsee in northern Brandenburg is a nature reserve with cranes, sea-eagles and ospreys and where bisons, Voronezh beavers and lugubrious mud turtles roam almost free. Much more common in all the larger forests are roe and red deer, hare and partridge. Wild boar, once hunted almost to extinction, has increased in population during the last decades and can be met with even in much-frequented woodlands and near villages.

The Vogelpark Walsrode, an ornithological park in the Lüneburg Heath, has some 900 species from all over the world, and the birds (flamingoes, ibis,

[3,000 sq km]) where you can go canoeing on the Altmühl or hike and cycle in the many valleys among wild dolomite rocks, mysterious caves and hillsides fragrant with juniper. Wildlife parks and nature reserves have been established in the most varied landscapes giving any visitor the intangible experience of nature – its diversity, vitality and spirituality.

Along the Baltic, for instance, north of Rostock, the peninsula of Fischland, Darß and Zingst is a huge conservation area mainly covered with a kind of jungle, a tangled wood of beech and pine that goes right to the water's edge, where the elements are in constant primordial combat and the seagull's metallic cry gains poignancy.

The horse, a much pampered animal today.

Birding in Germany

Germany is the place with probably the most wonderful network of 'autobahns' in the world - many travellers interested in nature think they are there so that you can quickly hurry through the country! On your way south to the gentle, sub-tropical environment of the Mediterranean or north to the harsh wilderness of the Nordic countries. And it is true that Germany is generally a heavily industrialized and densely populated part of Europe. But the landscape is actually quite varied and there are also large expanses of beautiful natural habitat for wildlife, even remote regions with endless marshlands and wild mountains and forests.

Germany is of course a federation of autonomous states and the local birders often list the birds as per state or 'landern' as these units are called. From the sandy beaches of Schleswig-Holstein across the large forests of Rhineland-Pfalz to the alpine terrain of southern Bavaria, the landscape and birdlife is rich and varied. Out of a total of just over 600 birds occuring in all of Europe, 421 species have been recorded from Germany.

Lately Germany has also made a name for itself in the European house as the green member of the international community. Through the 1970's and 80's a strong environmental movement became very influential and many Germans sincerely believe in and campaign for a healthier society. Birds have always played a key part in promoting nature awareness. They are important indicators of the state of the environment - if you find many birds some place, in diversity and in density, then chances are good that you are looking at an overall healthy piece of real estate. Birds are also the class of animals that are easiest to observe as they are large and conspicuous and mostly active by day. The common ones are easy to find and to identify yet there are thousands of different species to go and track down for the enthusiast.

The Coastal North

Sixty km off the German Atlantic coast lies what is possibly Europe's most famous bird observa-

House Sparrow.

Common cuckoo being fed by a Meadow Pipit.

tory, Heligoland. This tiny place has had an observatory and bird ringing station since 1910 when it was first discovered that a small section of woodland on the island acted as a sensational magnet for migrating birds. In fact the huge contraption built near the station took its name from there and today every bird ringing station in the world has a so-called Heligoland trap for catching birds so that they can be ringed and measured. In actual fact Heligoland is not one but two islands, the observatory is on the larger, Oberland while Dune Island is more touristy. Every year especially during autumn thousands of passerines like warblers, flycatchers, thrushes and buntings settle briefly on the island to rest before moving on, so every new day brings a fresh influx of birds and there are often many rarities found here. Amateur birders are welcome to visit the station or even help out with the work, but accommodation may not be available so write in advance: Voegelwarte Heligoland, Germany is address enough!

Heligoland is one of many places along this flat, sandy and picturesque part of the North Sea coastline which is great for birds. It is also great for people and one of Germany's prime vacation areas! The island of Sylt is packed with vacationers each summer but try to go to nearby Uthorn in spring or autumn and you will see equally massive congregations of birds. Little Terns, Ringed Plovers and Oystercatchers nest right in the open sand dunes and gravel banks. On nearby shallow shores and mudflats in sheltered sections of the coastline there is an abundance of shorebirds, gulls, ducks and geese.

Further south the Wangerooge Island close to the Dutch border offers a similar habitat. For birding avoid the German industrial vacation period in July and August. But anytime before and after that you will not find a better place anywhere for sandy beach and saline marshland birds.

On the mainland near Husum there are several good places, the Hamburger Halling is known for its large flocks of Barnacle Goose wintering every year, in spring you have Avocet, Ruff and Black-tailed Godwit breeding. The Elbe Estuary not too far from Hamburg has especially many ducks and different geese and also many sandpipers on the mudflats throughout most of the winter season.

Interior Lakes, Woodlands and Mountains

The lake Dummer is a natural oasis in an otherwise busy region of Germany near Osnabruck. It is regarded as one of the best birding spots in the interior of the country with a large water surface and surrounding reed beds providing habitat for an unusually large number of ducks, herons and shorebirds, including breeding populations of such specialities as Bittern, Black Tern, Marsh Harrier, Curlew and many ducks. Further south the Kuhkopf island in the river Rhine betwwen Mannheim and Mainz is a major German bird locality for breeding marsh and woodland birds especially. In fact it is so special that it has been declared a bird sanctuary under management by the DBV and access permit has to be obtained from the address listed below.

Also in central Germany one of the best spots for central European woodland birds is just north of Frankfurt near Marburg. Look out for Black kite, several woodpeckers, Serin, Black

Mallard ducks.

Marsch Harrier.

Redstart and Short-toed Creeper.

Further south in Bavaria at the northern foothills of the Alps Oberammergau near the Austrian border is the best jump-off place for montane birding. This river valley around the river Ammer is covered mainly in fir and pine forests and have resident specialists like Fieldfare, Crossbill, Siskin and all the woodpeckers found in central Europe including Middel Spotted and White-backed. Above the treeline which is here at around 2,000 meters elevation you have alpine birds like Alpine Accentor, Rock Thrush and Alpine Chough. It is a truly wonderful place - for birding or just for an outdoor holiday.

Exploring the East

Up until 1989 birding in East Germany was difficult and still today little information is available about many of the places there. It is an area full of opportunity because being less efficiently developed in many ways it has been left naturally richer. The farmland is less intensively cultivated compared to the west and there are large areas of wetlands and forests left untouched. The lakes and swamps at Niederspree are a genuinely remote and wild place with shy rarities like Crane and Black Stork confirmed breeding. Near Gorlitz there are resident Greylag

Greylag geese.

Stork roosting on a chimney top.

Goose, White-tailed Sea-Eagle and Goldeneye.
With reunification Germany suddenly ended up including parts of Eastern Europe which holds many eastern resident birds difficult or impossible to spot in the west. They include Great Bustard, Lesser Spotted Eagle, Ferruginous Duck, Bearded and Penduline Tit and many warblers like Greenish, Barred, Aquatic and River Warblers. It is going to be a challenge of the future to document the exact occurance and status of these and many other birds in the east.

More Information

Being in the center of Europe and the Western Palearctic region there are no birds in Germany which do not also occur many other places. Field guides covering Europe will include Germany as well; one of the most useful ones available on the market at the moment in the English language is Collins' *New Generation Guide to the Birds of Britain and Europe* by C. Perrins, 1987; although the classic *A Field Guide to the Birds of Britain and Europe* by R.T. Peterson et al is still preferred by some.

Information on where to go to find the birds is available from John Gooders' series on "Where to watch birds ... " titles on Andre Deutsch some of which also include the best locations in Germany. Each state in the federal republic will have its own ornithological centre co-ordinated by the "Deutsche Bund fur Vogelschutz" at Steinauer Strasse 33, 6 Frankfurt am Main-Fechenheim. For overall information on the status of nature conservation in the country the main contact is "Natur-schutz", Herbert-Rabius Strasse 26, 53225 Bonn.

cranes, emus, ostriches) are to be found very often wandering freely in natural surroundings. The tiny village of Rühstädt, southeast of Wittenberg in eastern Brandenburg, is said to be Germany's major stork-spotting center: every year more than twenty pairs nest there. In autumn, flocks of wild geese circle the darkening skies on their way to the south.

Environmental Concerns

Germany's wildlife and its whole ecological balance could be upset by the decline of the forests, and *Waldsterben* (death of the forest) has become one of the main concerns not only of the Greens and environmentalists, but of the population as a whole. Everywhere you see patches of forest where the trees have thinning crowns, yellowing needles and peeling bark. The threat had been going on for several decades before it was noticed about 1980. After a vast diversified research effort, its source was found: acid rain, which forms when sulfur dioxide from factories or power plants, or nitrogen oxide from vehicle exhaust, mixes with moisture and oxygen to form sulfuric or nitric acid in the atmosphere. Carried by westerly winds eastward, it hardly affects France, Great Britain or the Scandinavian countries, but works with deadly effect in Germany and the Czech and Slovak Republics.

When asked what their priority for increased spending was, 86 percent of Germans mentioned the environment, according to an opinion poll of 1991. Much opposition is directed against nuclear power plants (which supply 40 percent of the nation's electricity) both for safety reasons and because of problems with the disposal of nuclear waste.

Since reunification, pollution disaster by the antiquated technology and careless waste disposal of the former GDR's industries has become a target of environmentalist activities and government subsidies. While in the west the chemical industry after a number of scandals, is now subject to some of the world's strictest safety regulations, re-greening the industrial belt of the eastern region will need much more than tough legislation.

A chamois in the Hundshaupten Wildlife Preserve.

Who are "the Germans", what are they like? Are they an earnest and industrious people, well-mannered, given to tedious metaphysical speculation, honest but boring, subservient to authority, gregarious beer drinkers, sentimental yet insensitive, cautious bankers and thickheaded farmers, blond and blue-eyed, friendly and open-minded, crypto-fascists, full of *Angst* and constantly worrying, washing and polishing their cars for hours on end, good at sports but bad at games, indiscriminately producing geniuses and maniacs, obsessed with punctuality and order, decorating their gardens with ceramic dwarfs, nature lovers who find links with their mythical past in their deep, dark woods? With their economic power and historical ties both to the West and the East, are they Europe's great white hope, or a potentially dangerous nation which needs to be closely watched and reined in by its western partners?

Clichés are useful to differentiate, to formulate a first general idea about national and regional characteristics, to start looking more

People

67

A traditional suit worn by hunters and members of target-shooting clubs on special occasions.

German gesture and gusto outside a beer garden.

closely at the various amusing and infuriating solutions different people have found for the same problems. In shops and at bus-stops the individualistic English form orderly queues, while the orderly Germans shove and jostle. The most punky punks in London probably turn out to be high-school students from Germany. In chaotic Italy trains tend not to run on time, and the same sometimes happens in super-efficient Germany.

And what about regional stereotypes? The Bavarian wears *Lederhosen* and a tuft of chamois hair on his hat and empties steins of beer. The farmer from Lower Saxony breeds cattle and drinks small glasses of clear, potent schnapps. The good Swabian keeps his little cottage neat and tidy and in the evening goes to his local tavern to discuss politics with his cronies over many a glass of wine. The rugged Frisian fisherman is as talkative as a fish and does unspeakable things behind lace curtains.

In eastern Germany, clichés about regional behavior have hardly survived the repressive communist regime, but perhaps the wily Saxon, the backward Mecklenburgian and the straight-laced Brandenburgian will soon make a comeback.

Unhappy Childhood

For a long time, one of the most remark-

The German Language

Not only where the valleys are darkest and the forests thickest is it still possible to find Germans whose dialect is impenetrable even to their countrymen, and this despite the fact that school attendance has been compulsory for more than a hundred years. There is a certain exotic charm in feeling like a stranger in one's own country until you start asking directions.

Use of dialect is still quite strong. In western and central Germany variations may be slight from village to village, but the cumulative effect can be so great that dialects 50 miles apart are mutually incomprehensible. The reason is largely historical, and lies in the stability of the population and the long fragmentation of the country into a multitude of political entities with little intercommunication; on the other hand, Bavaria is relatively uniform linguistically because it has been politically unified for more than one thousand years.

In the south, nearly everyone grows up speaking the local dialect and continues to use it among family members, friends and neighbors. A taxi driver in Munich, for instance, is likely to speak with a heavy local accent – which on the lips of a pretty woman can soften into a mellifluous lilt – but will affect a standard High German pronunciation whenever he quotes some official scrap of information. In northern Germany you hear dialect much less often except along the coastal regions of Frisia, where people speak *Platt* (literally "flat"), which is very close to Dutch. In writing, High German is almost the only form used or at least attempted, and is the official form taught at school; the most prestigious pronunciation uses High German as spoken around Hanover.

Modern standard German developed after the mid-13th century from the dialects of the recently settled East Middle German areas, amalgamated into a form which gradually came to be used as the official language of the chancelleries of the area including Saxony, on which Martin Luther based the language of his Bible translation (1534). Like the King James version (1611) for English, so Luther's translation set new linguistic standards for German, and because of its wide circulation did very much to improve and unify the language, stabilizing a national medium of communication and quickening the demise of Latin as the language of scholarly discourse.

Unlike the French with their *Académie*, the Germans do not have an official body to regulate the language; the unofficial arbiter is the *Duden*, a dictionary published by the Bibliographisches Institut in Mannheim and bearing the name of the high-school teacher who in 1880 published his spelling guide to standardize the work of the printers.

able features of post-war Germany's mental make-up was the almost complete absence of nationalist feelings. If people identified with the nation at all, it tended to be defensively, awkwardly, as something blackened by historic deed and memory. It seemed that whatever national pride and patriotism – what Dr Johnson called "the last refuge of a scoundrel" – may once have existed, had been burnt out by past catastrophes. This virtual absence of a sense of national identity can be traced further back in history.

Although the Romantic movement during the first half on the 19th century glorified and idealized the German Middle Ages and the Holy Roman Empire of the German Nation, the moment the ideal was given substance under the impervious direction of Bismarck in 1871, many of the German principalities had to be dragged screaming to join the Kaiser's Second Reich. The empire disappeared 37 years later, which was not much time to forge a nation or

Children in traditional costumes of South Germany.

create a national identity.

With the empire, much of the prestige and authority of the established order, the nobility, army and church crumbled or vanished altogether. The unhappy episode of the Weimar Republic (1919–33) did little to inspire any sense of nationhood. Then Hitler propagated a common bond on dubious ethnic, racist grounds, invoking a supposedly German heritage.

In regard to nationalism, the Second World War and its disastrous end completed the process of disillusionment

careers under the Nazis or earlier, a decisive break was made with a past that was seen as continuous from the triumphs of 1871 to the glorification of Prussian virtues (and vices) under Hitler and the conflagration of half the world.

It would seem the first post-war German government under Adenauer, instead of trying to forge a national identity, turned to its erstwhile enemies and new allies in the belief that only by committing itself to a supranational, European structure could Germany become accepted and res-pected again.

This appears to have remained the guiding principle of Germany's political aspirations and the horizon for its definition of nationhood. The word is not taboo, and when the government under Brandt started a dialogue with the GDR, the relationship was explicitly between two states, acknowledging the non-existence of a common, overarching national ideal.

New Arrivals and Resettlers

In fact, Germany is a multi-cultural, multi-national society. Even before 1989, a quarter of the people living in West Germany were from outside. At the end of World War II and in its aftermath some 10 million refugees arrived from former German territory in the east. With the expansion of the economy and the need for cheap additional labor great numbers of foreigners came, some to

with the traditional ideology and structure personified by the self-proclaimed guardians of Germany's identity, its power, happiness and future. Although most of the people rebuilding the new Germany – not only the politicians and industrialists, but also the doctors and professors, the churchmen, judges, lawyers and journalists – had started their

A German housewife in festival costume.

of these groups of ethnic Germans have for generations been out of contact with Germany, do not speak the language and have only vestigial cultural affinities with their new home country and find adapting very hard. Problems and tensions also arise from the influx of East Germans since the end of 1989 both for economic and cultural reasons: jobs are difficult to find and human interaction patterns differ widely between the west and the east.

Post-reunification Blues

Since reunification, nationalist and racist slogans have appeared, prompting much soul-searching among West Ger-

open shops and restaurants and businesses, many to take on menial jobs as *Gastarbeiter* (guest workers). Italians, Greeks and Yugoslavs were the first to come and from the mid-1960s there was a great influx of workers from Turkey. Of the more than 4 million foreign workers in Germany today, roughly a third are Turks.

Since the 1980s the number of asylum-seekers from the Third World and Eastern Europe and of ethnic German resettlers from Poland, Romania and the Soviet Union has increased dramatically.

Between 1950 and 1988 some 1.6 million resettlers arrived from eastern countries, while in 1988 alone 190,000 came and in 1990 about 230,000. Some

A vintner samples his produce.

Student Fraternities

Among the few pre-war traditions still alive on German campuses are the student fraternities (*Verbindungen*), although their reputation has much declined. These are residential clubs, all male and also excluding conscientious objectors, whose members live and study together in mostly handsome old houses. Formerly, most upper-class students belonged to these bodies which were and still are supposed to inculcate a respect for tradition and hierarchy and a sense of honor.

Many trace their origins back to the anti-Napoleonic Wars of Liberation (1813–15), when a huge enthusiastic student movement proclaimed nationalist and democratic ideals. The movement was soon crushed by reactionary politicians, but memories of the heady months and fraternal sense of community lingered on and in time were much romanticized. Both the Nazis and, after the war, the Socialist government of East Germany outlawed student fraternities in favor of Party-controlled organizations.

Within a fraternity, members are grouped into *Füchse* (literally foxes, meaning the young-est members, like Boy Scout cubs), *Activitas* (fully active members) and *Alte Herren* (old boys), i.e. alumni, who keep a sharp eye on traditions being strictly upheld. At meetings, ritual is of the essence. Drinking and singing are done on command, the usual drink being beer, the songs old patriotic tunes from the Wars of Liberation. Quite a few fraternities still practise the anachronistic art of saber-duelling or fencing, and the disfiguring facial scars that often result, are regarded as a mark of honor and self-discipline. Uniforms and colors are worn, although rarely in public. There, members recognize each other by way of small emblems worn on the lapel.

Compared to Anglo-Saxon countries, there is little collegiate life in Germany, and the fraternities make up for this somewhat. They also constitute the closest German equivalent to the English "old boy network". Nevertheless, student fraternities are not widely popular; even at Tübingen, a highly traditional university town, a mere 2.5 percent of all students join (mainly from the law and medicine faculties).

mans. Perhaps born of frustration and boredom, of disillusion and posturing, the sometimes angry outpourings of the right-wing political fringe may be understood as a possible side-effect of the general disorientation, intellectual as well as emotional, that the majority of Germans might have felt since unification.

This reinforces a tendency that has been noticeable since the 1970s. In West Germany, following the anti-authoritarian revolt of the late 1960s, grassroots movements and self-help groups have become an integral part of the social structure. Subverting the established political and administrative channels, people have banded together in informal adhoc relationships; the Greens are the best-known

A typical young German boy.

organization that started this way.

The phenomenon not only includes movements protesting against industrial pollution, nuclear power plants, highways, and the destruction of historical buildings, but also applies to much smaller local, neighborly concerns.

Parents who are dissatisfied with traditional day-care centers found self-administered children's centers; an unemployed theater director stages plays at the local sports' center with amateur actors; students organize a helpline for drug addicts; clubs and restaurants are organized on a cooperative basis; day-care for the elderly and infirm is arranged through a network of friends and relatives.

Such initiatives, relying on independence, creativity and responsibility, show a fine disregard for the hoary cliché that in Germany everything has to be done by the book, through bureaucratic channels and with official seal and signature. It also means that people have lowered their political horizon, bypassing the regular institutions and regarding big politics as irrelevant as long as they do not impinge on their own local interests. This attachment to their home turf tends to give to their concerns a parochialism which foreigners are quick to associate with the concept of *Heimat*, a love for and idealization of one's native roots.

For East Germans, such attachment is much more precarious. The tremen-

An organ grinder in Nürnberg.

dous changes their country went through after 1949 – politically, physically, and more so emotionally and socially – were all directed by a tiny leadership group with next to no popular consultation or participation. Even when people felt the need to identify with some greater good, some higher ideal, they could only focus on the official "workers' and peasants' state" or the Party, never on the concept of a nation.

Now that the East Germans are suddenly forced to fend for themselves, to hold their own against well-off, confident and patronizing West Germans, they are somewhat at a great disadvantage which could cause them to be uncertain and strangely protective of their old habits and structures. All this will

change eventually; much indeed has already changed during the last two or three years, particularly in the cities. People with a natural ability for rough dealing survive splendidly, as do others who have an inbred sense of sophistication mixed with pride, a sound head for business coupled with determination and charm. Not by chance do these attributes have a feminine ring: in the east, both before and after '89, women have enjoyed a much more equal standing than in the west, where traditional middle-class values about women as housewives are only gradually disappearing.

So what are "the Germans" really like? Just forget all the clichés and generalizations and go see for yourself.

A radiant bride celebrates.

I t was in the beautiful Neckar Valley that the earliest human remains in Germany were discovered: *Homo heidelbergensis* is about half a million years old, while the better-known Neanderthal man lived in caves along the Rhine Valley only 50,000 years ago. Unfortunately he seems to have had no artistic ambitions and has left us no cave paintings. Sometime ago, excavations at Unteruhldingen on the Bodensee brought to light an early lake settlement, a village of wooden huts on stilts. A reconstruction has been made which testifies to the advanced building techniques used by New Stone Age man some 8,000 years ago. The huge megaliths found on the Lüneburg Heath date from the

Ancient castle architecture is a frequent legacy from Germany's imperial past.

Art & Architecture

same period; these tombstones are known as *Hünengräber* (graves of the giants).

As Julius Caesar notes in his book on the Gallic War, the Romans had a hard time subduing the various Germanic tribes or even keeping them at arm's length. Around the time of Christ's birth, the emperor Augustus made a serious attempt to expand his empire towards the north. After several defeats and much harassment, the Romans retired to southern Germany, planted vines and built heavily fortified settlements. Their major towns were built along the Roman pattern with theaters, public baths, cobbled roads, bridges, villas, basilicas and warehouses, to make life more bearable in remote and hostile Germania. Several emperors came primarily to take the waters. At Trier, the remains of the imperial baths of the early 4th century show them to have been one of the largest bathing complexes of the Roman Empire, while at the modern spa of Baden-Baden ruins of the 2nd-century baths built for Roman soldiers have been excavated. Above ground, few Roman buildings have survived apart from one remarkable exception: the Porta Nigra at Trier is the largest and best-preserved gateway of the ancient world. It was constructed with big limestone blocks (now blackened by age) held together with iron rods. The building is an impressive example of Roman skills in fortification: attackers could be trapped within its outer and inner gates.

Carolingian

Charlemagne, King of the Franks and later Emperor, wanted to build a Roman Empire under the sign of the cross. He and his immediate successors, the Carolingians, modeled their government and their architecture on classical ideals. To his court at Aachen, Charlemagne summoned scientists and artists from all parts of the known world. The finest and most characteristic example of Carolingian architecture is Aachen's Palatinate Chapel, which originally formed part of a large palace. It is an octagonal basilica with a two-storey arcaded gallery, which forms the heart of the present-day cathedral, with Italian columns and a plan after San Vitale in Ravenna. The gatehouse at Lorsch, east of Worms, is another of the few extant Carolingian monuments. The building illustrates the stylistic uncertainty of the period: classical forms are imitated, but no satisfactory integration has yet been achieved. As a result, the gatehouse is more like a Germanic wooden structure than a classical stone building.

Medieval kings and emperors of Germany had no single capital from which to govern their empire; they traveled from one center to another, setting up their court at each of them. Almost invariably these foundations derived initially from a religious colony, were usually laid out according to Benedictine rules – a church and cloister, cells, a refectory, chapter house, guesthouse, infirmary – but also including arrangements for the imperial retinue. Consequently, churches were frequently built with two chancels, the one at the west end, the *Westwerk*, reserved for the imperial retinue. Perhaps the finest Carolingian *Westwerk* is at Corvey near Höxter, south of Hanover, which was once the seat of an imperial throne.

Romanesque

Germany took to Romanesque art relatively late. The major influence throughout the Ottonian period (mid-10th to mid-11th century) were Byzantine and Roman models. Three great churches – St Pantaleon in Cologne, St Michael in Hildesheim and St Cyriakus in Gernrode – retain enough of their original form to exemplify this architecture. Ottonian artists included outstanding gold- and silversmiths as well as ivory carvers. A school of manuscript illustrators, patronized by the emperors and almost matched in skill by those of Regensburg, worked at Reichenau on the Bodensee. Superb pieces of craftsmanship from the 11th to 13th centuries are the portable altar of Paderborn; the prophet panels of Augsburg, the oldest surviving stained-glass windows in Germany (c.1140); and the tomb of Henry the Lion in Braunschweig Cathedral.

Romanesque architecture and art spread all over Europe from about the year 1000, with its greatest flowering before 1150. It is characterized by the rounded arch, the pillar, column, vaulted construction and a sense of monumentality and space. It had its origins in France, and French masons from Reims decorated Bamberg Cathedral (c.1230), one of the finest examples of late Romanesque architectural sculpture. In general, the buildings were plainer, more austere and less perfect than those of the classical age. Churches and abbeys were built of massive stone with little space for windows, and crowned by defiant towers.

Gothic

While in France early Gothic followed, Germany continued to build in Romanesque style until about 1250. The new style, a mixture of Norman and Bur-

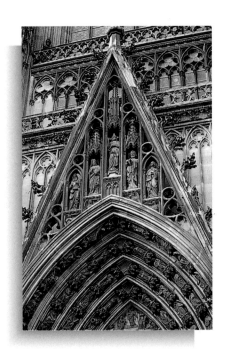

Entrance to Cologne's cathedral.

Sculptural figures in Gothic style at the Cologne cathedral.

gundy architecture, was propagated by Cistercians from Burgundy who were among the most active monastic orders of the Middle Ages. Cologne's cathedral, begun in 1248 and consecrated in 1332, is Germany's most famous Gothic church building, but the cathedrals at Freiburg and Regensburg are also of the highest order. The Gothic cathedral, soaring heavenward, became the most potent symbol of a town's prosperity, and its rich tracery and sculpture were a proud indication of the skills of the local artisans. Pointed arches, exterior buttresses and vaulting not only enabled buildings to reach ever-increasing heights, but also allowed walls to be broken by grandiose stained-glass windows. A typical type of German Gothic

architecture is the *Hallenkirche* (church hall) which originated in Westphalia. It is characterized by aisles constructed at the same height as the nave and separated from the nave by tall columns. Many dating from the late Gothic period (14th/15th century) are still to be seen in Westphalia and further south: Munich's Frauenkirche and St Lorenz in Nürnberg both date from the second half of the 15th century.

As the 14th century saw the development of a new urban middle class, so these secular patrons began to build impressive town walls as well as fine public buildings and private mansions. Münster offers beautiful examples in both its town hall (1355) and its cathedral (1225–65). In north Germany, brick

Gothic became increasingly fashionable, with splendid examples in Lübeck, Schleswig and Stralsund.

Renaissance

A renaissance in its true sense never existed in Germany. A prerequisite was missing: that of a classical past to which such a movement could relate. Both religious and secular buildings were still based on Gothic concepts, and Renaissance elements are most conspicuous only in the façades and ornamental work. Only in the south are there some buildings truly in the mold of Italian Renaissance architecture. The Fugger memorial chapel in Augsburg (begun

The ornate fountain tower and facade of the 14th century Church of Our Lady in Nürnberg.

Old German families take pride in the coat of arms often sculpted on the walls.

in 1509) shows clear Venetian inspiration, and Augsburg's town hall, completed in 1620 by Elias Holl, is the only one among a great many North European civil structures that could claim to belong to Renaissance architecture in the Italian sense. The clear lines and restrained decoration of the Residence at Landshut found little favor and remained the exception.

There was a decline in church-building after the Reformation. The Protestants were content with the old buildings, after stripping them of their ornaments and pictures; their aim was austerity and sparseness. The conservative attitude of the Catholic Church may have been responsible for the fact that the adaptation of Italian Renaissance

German homes of 15th century architecture.

concepts was not encouraged. An interesting regional version, however, the distinctive Weser Renaissance style, flourished briefly in the Hameln area.

Before the 1400s no names of individual artists stood out. The first truly great German painters emerged in the 15th century with the Cologne school, led by Stephan Lochner (died 1451), whose altarpiece is one of the outstanding artistic treasures of Cologne's cathedral. Tilman Riemenschneider (c.1460–1531), "the Master of Würzburg", carved magnificent altarpieces for churches in

A quaint house in Rothenburg.

Würzburg, Bamberg, Rothenburg, Creglingen and elsewhere, and used subtle gradations of light and shadow to heighten the plastic effect.

The sculptor and painter Veit Stoß (c.1445–1533) hailed from Nürnberg, where some of his greatest works are still to be seen at the churches of St Sebaldus and St Lorenz. Among late Gothic sculptors, his work is remarkable for the expressiveness of the faces and dramatic use of drapery. Painter Mathias Grünewald (1460–1528) showed a healthy respect for the Middle Ages,

A carving in the Black Forest Museum in Triberg.

although he was born at the end of the period. He was a master colorer, and his greatest creation is the Isenheimer Altar at Colmar in Alsace.

With the Renaissance and the return of classical notions of art and science, a new realism in art emerged, liberated from traditional scholarship and dogma. Albrecht Dürer (1471–1528) from Nürnberg, the greatest German artist of the 16th century, had acquired during his travels in France and the Netherlands, the ability and expertise to create works of art that were a bridge between the late Gothic and the modern trend.

He was familiar with anatomy and the techniques of drawing in perspective, a master of gold-

smithery, painting and graphic art. His portraits are especially remarkable; vividly human, the faces are mirrors of the soul and of great character. His travel diary, which survives, draws a vivid picture of the artist and his times, of costume and culture and even mentions the quality and price of food and lodging.

Lucas Cranach the Elder (1472–1553) is best known as a painter of the Reformation because he was on friendly terms with Luther and his circle, and painted their portraits. Strikingly graceful realistic works were the hallmark of Hans Holbein the Younger (1497–1543). He later became court painter to Henry

A marble tomb carving by Tilman Riemenschneider in Bamberg's cathedral.

A Renaissance Artist Abroad

In 1520–21, the great Nürnberg artist Albrecht Dürer went on an extended tour of the Netherlands, accompanied by his wife and a servant. The following glimpses from his diary show the dangers of travel and how the artist was honored and entertained by friends and patrons.

But it was while landing at Arnemuidn that a great misfortune happened to me. As we got near the quay and flung the hawser out, a big ship forced its way alongside, just as I was getting off, having let the crowds of passengers disembark first. The only people left on board besides me were Georg Közler, two old women and the captain with a small boy. While the other ship continued to push and I together with those others mentioned above were still on board and unable to make way, the strong hawser broke; at that very moment a strong stormy wind seized our boat and carried it off. So we all started crying for help, but nobody dared.

Again the wind blew us further out to sea. The captain tore his hair and cried, for all the mates had gone ashore and the boat was carrying no ballast. Fear and desperation gripped us, for the wind was strong and there were only six people on board. So I told the captain to calm down and put his trust in God and consider what could be done. He replied that if he managed to set the small sail he might be able to put the boat back on course. So we worked with all our strength and finally got the sail halfway up and the boat under control. And when the people on shore, who had already given up all hope, saw us successfully grappling, they came to our assistance and we made the shore…

When I arrived at Bruges, Jan Prevost put me up at his house and the very same evening arranged for a delicious meal and invited many people for me to meet. Next day I was invited by Marc de Glasere, the goldsmith, to a delicious meal with many guests invited on my behalf. Then they took me to the House of the Emperor [the Prinsenhoft], which is big and splendid. There I saw Rogier's painted chapel and paintings by a great old master; I gave four *Stüber* to the lad who unlocked the doors. Then I bought three coombs of ivory for 30 *Stüber*. Then they drove me to St Jakob and let me see the beautiful paintings by Rogier van der Weyden and Hugo van der Goës, who both were great masters. Then I saw the alabaster Virgin at Our Ladies Church, made by Michelangelo of Rome. Then they took me to many churches and showed me all the beautiful paintings, of which there are a great many. And after I had seen the paintings by Jan van Eyck and Dirk Bouts and Hans Memling, we at last arrived at the painters' chapel, which has good things inside. Then they served a banquet for me. From there I accompanied them to their chambers [the guildhall]. There many good people had foregathered, goldsmiths, painters and merchants; I had to have supper with them, and they presented me with gifts, gave me all the news and treated me with great honor. And the brothers Jakob and Peter Mostaert, the city councillors, presented me with 12 jugs of wine, and then everybody accompanied me back home, more than 60 people, with great torches.

Before he left Bruges, Dürer did a charcoal drawing of Jean Prevost and gave 10 Stüber to his wife, presumably as payment for his lodging.

VIII of England and created celebrated portraits of the English nobility before dying of the plague in London. Hans Baldung Grien (1485–1545) was a precursor of Mannerism: by deliberately distorting the proportions of his figures, he sought to involve the viewer more closely in the work.

Baroque

The 17th century was marred by the devastation and impoverishment of the Thirty Years' War and a dearth of German creativity, but the latter half of the century saw splendid achievements in

Moritzburg Castle, near Meißen.

A statue in the Moritzburg grounds.

the Baroque and Rococo styles. The Baroque was characterized by irregularity of form and great variety, its aim being to suggest movement, an upsurge in visual and spiritual terms. When pushed to its extremes, it became the Rococo, whose fantastically swirling lines were employed mostly in decoration. The exuberant new style seemed particularly appropriate to Catholic southern Germany, an answer to the Counter-Reformation's vigorous exaltation of the cult of the Virgin and the saints. It flourished especially in Swabia and Bavaria, where the Asam brothers perfected an unsurpassed blend of architecture, stuccowork and painting in their churches, and the Dientzenhofer brothers created the stunning pilgrimage church of Wies.

In Franconia the Baroque movement was patronized by the prince-bishops of the Schönborn family with residences in Bamberg, Würzburg and Mainz. Balthasar Neumann (1687–1753) worked for them, and with his supreme achievement, the Residence at Würz-burg, he enriched South German Baroque through what he had learned from French, Viennese and Italian masters.

By the 18th century Germany consisted of over 300 separate principalities, many of which were vying with each other to build the most splendid palaces and employ the most fashionable artists and musicians. After the Napoleonic Wars (1803–15) and with Prussia's rise to supremacy, these small states, much reduced in number and almost completely shorn of their political and military influence, continued to compete against each other in patronizing the fine arts; very few were inclined to spend money on the improvement of the cultural and social situation of the population. This courtly self-indulgence, while strengthening regionalism and parochialism and slowing the marching pace of progress, turns out to be our gain. It fostered such musical geniuses as that of Bach, Haydn, Händel, Mozart, Beethoven and Wagner, and resulted in buildings whose splendors and delights

Rococo decorations in the Schönborn residence in Würzburg.

are now open to the public for admiration and enjoyment: the palaces and parks of Charlottenburg (Berlin) and Sanssouci (Potsdam), Nymphenburg (Munich) and Wörlitz, Moritzburg, Brühl, and the churches at Ettal, Vierzehnheiligen and Ottobeuren, to name just a few.

Neo-Classicism

In the late 18th century a reaction set in against much of the Baroque and Rococo exuberance. Excavations of Roman and Greek sites and the writings of the German archeologist and aesthete J.J. Winckelmann (1717–68) brought new orientations and inspirations for a

The more recent section of the Schloss Ermitage
built in the mid-18th century at Bayreuth.

neo-Classical movement in art and architecture. It seemed the appropriate
style for Prussia's imperial aspirations

and can be seen at its most impressive in
Berlin in the works of Schinkel and
Langhans, and in Munich, where von

Klenze and Gärtner were the foremost exponents. Although to our eyes these buildings may sometimes look ponderous, heavy and menacing, yet at their best they caught the spirit of what

Winckelmann called the "noble simplicity and tranquil greatness" of Greek art. Occasionally classical models determined the replanning of whole towns like Karlsruhe, which was transformed

Nymphenburg statuary in Munich.

Fürstenzug frescoes in Dresden.

into a neo-Classical city between 1800 and 1826, and Mannheim, laid out in a strict grid pattern (1720–78).

Romanticism

Neo-Classicism became sterile around 1830 and gave way to the Romantic movement in literature and painting (C.D. Friedrich, J.F. Overbeck, C. Spitzweg, M. von Schwind) and neo-Gothic in architecture, of which the castle of Neuschwanstein is the most remarkable and fantastic monument. Many of the castle ruins along the Rhine were likewise renovated and remodeled, just like the Baroque had remodeled many authentic Gothic buildings. In

interior designs and furnishings, the Biedermeier style (1815–50), a development without a counterpart in any other European country, was characterized by comfortable, lightweight furniture, full of grace and simplicity, often utilizing cherry wood elegantly set off against black detailing.

By the middle of the century, industrialization had spawned a wealthy clientele enamored of highly ornamented reproductions of medieval and Renaissance furniture. In architecture this period, the *Gründerjahre* (founders' period) was highly eclectic, making use of Classical, Romanesque, Gothic, Renaissance and Baroque elements at will. Handled tactfully, this inherently chaotic mix could produce handsome villas like those

Biedermeier

From roughly 1800 to the mid-19th century, bourgeois interiors in Germany, Austria and North Italy tended to be decorated in the Biedermeier style; its simple and restrained furniture is very fashionable today and commands high prices. It derived partly from the forms of French Empire decoration, but its characteristics were evolved by German craftsmen. On the one hand, its emphasis on comfort was characteristic of the first half of the 19th century throughout Europe and America, but on the other its practicality looked forward to the modern period. Jugendstil, the German version of Art Nouveau, was much influenced by it, and even the Bauhaus, that pioneer of modern design, found inspiration in its forms and craftsmanship.

The term derives from "Papa Biedermeier", a comic figure of middle-class comfort, solid, humdrum, pleased with himself, who finds his greatest happiness in the bosom of his family. This is reflected in the countless watercolors which record middle-class homes of the period: an atmosphere of simplicity, relaxation and domesticity pervades these interiors.

Even in the tallest rooms, furniture and furnishings rarely rose higher than eye-level. Walls were painted in clear, bright colors and ceilings in white or gray. As a background for the smaller scale of Biedermeier furniture, some rooms had their walls covered with wallpaper or fabric in fine stripes or small flowered patterns. Despite comfortable chairs and no lack of other small pieces of furniture, Biedermeier rooms had an austere look, which was accentuated by simple parquet flooring or even bare boards covered with a few rugs.

Biedermeier furniture at its best is of remarkable sophistication and functionality. Light and bright woods predominate, like cherrywood, pearwood, maplewood, ashwood and walnut. Lines are simple and elegant, and ornamentation is restrained and understated. Chairs have graceful straight or slightly curved tapering legs and invitingly slanted backs, while tables and cupboards chiefly glory in unadorned fields of polished wood with decorative grain.

As a reaction against Biedermeier and a symbol of the new wealth created by industrialization, by the mid-century, German interiors were getting ever more cluttered and the furniture heavier and highly decorated. This trend culminated in the extravaganzas of neo-Gothic designs.

The beauty of Biedermeier was rediscovered in the 1960s, and it has remained a favorite among connoisseurs and interior designers since then. One of the most impressive early Biedermeier interiors can be seen at Goethe's house in Weimar.

lining the Alster in Hamburg, but more often resulted in the pretentious hulks of public buildings like the Reichstag in Berlin and inner-city apartment blocks everywhere. At the turn of the century Jugendstil or Art Nouveau with its sinuous lines based on plant motifs, enjoyed widespread popularity. In Germany it was mainly used for decorative purposes (interiors, furniture, jewelry, clothes), but occasionally also for factory buildings (by the architects P. Behrens and J.M. Olbrich) and resplendent mansions like Munich's Stuckvilla.

Modern Art

The first third of the 20th century saw an extraordinary flowering of German art and architecture. Inspired by the French, artists like M. Liebermann and M. Slevogt created a German version of Impressionism, while before World War I, two groups of painters and sculptors developed a new style classified as Expres-

Classic German architecture.

satirical vein; Kurt Schwitters (1887–1948) was a playful abstractionist, and Max Ernst (1891–1976) provided a link between Dadaism and Surrealism. German theater was revolutionized by the great director Max Reinhardt (1873–1943) and his Wagnerian ideas of drama as a *Gesamtkunstwerk* (a production encompassing all branches of the creative arts). Fritz Lang (1890–1976) made highly Expressionist films, and the Austrian Arnold Schoenberg (1874–1951) broke with classical notions of music by composing on a dodecaphonic scale. A most remarkable group of artists and artisans came together at the Bauhaus, founded by Henry van de Velde in Weimar in 1906, under whose successor

sionism. The *Blaue Reiter* (blue rider) with W. Kandinsky, F. Marc, A. Macke, P. Klee and others, staged its first exhibition in Munich in 1911, while in Dresden the *Brücke* group with E.L. Kirchner, E. Heckel and K. Schmidt-Rottluff had organized in 1905.

The tragic futility of the war and the great social, political and economic upheavals in its aftermath, had much impact on the artistic imagination and creativity, and all the arts saw much innovation, including theater, film and music. Max Beckmann (1884–1950) painted forceful, highly symbolic scenes of middle-class culture, while George Grosz (1893–1959) and Raoul Hausmann (1886–1971) worked in a

Doorway details of the Classic style.

The modern Chamber Music Hall in Berlin.

Walter Gropius (1883–1969) it gained international recognition. It was conceived as an academy, where many of Germany's most innovative and gifted painters, architects and designers taught classes to a select group of students. Many of its ideas and creations exerted a powerful influence, were rediscovered after World War II and continue to inspire architects and industrial designers

to this day.

Art and architecture under the Nazis were state-controlled, and the bland monumentalism of Hitler's favorite architect Albert Speer, the kitschy eroticism of painter Adolf Ziegler and the posturing symbolism of sculptor Arno Breker effectively severed the creative links with German and European artistic traditions, creating a hiatus which modern German art has been strenuously attempting to bridge or to ignore. Museums almost never exhibit Nazi art, although their storerooms are full of it.

The German art scene, including theater, film, literature and music, is greatly diverse and highly subsidized. Part of the explanation for this lies in the absence of a true national capital or focus in the same league as London, Paris or Rome, in a strong tradition of public patronage and in the fact that there is no federal ministry responsible for cultural affairs. The strong yet unfocused patronage of the arts dates back to the 18th century, when each royal court, dukedom or free city would maintain its own opera house, theater and perhaps even a museum. This multiplicity of cultural centers is being continued in the Federal Republic, where the individual region

Performing & Literary Arts

99

The musicians of Oberammergau.

Ruins of the theater built in the early 1700's in the Rock Gardens of Sanspariel.

have responsibility over the arts, and they feel a sense of duty and local pride in keeping up the tradition. In western Germany today (the situation in the east is still much in flux quickly outdating all data), some 50 opera houses, 70 orchestras, over 100 theaters and nearly 1,500 museums receive subsidies; all the opera houses and almost all the main German theaters are publicly owned either by the region or city or by both in partnership. The average public theater expects to need only 15 to 20 percent of its income from box office sales. In literature and the fine arts, a great number of grants and prizes are offered, sponsored by federal, regional and municipal authorities, by big companies or local businessmen. The prolif-

eration of literary prizes has been criticized as lowering aspirations and the general standard of output, but whether there exists a direct relationship between the amount of financial input and the quality of artistic creations is highly debatable.

Public spending on the arts in Germany is the most lavish in the free world – per capita it is roughly four times the British level. In typical middle-class fashion, culture is seen as not just entertainment but also a means of permanent education, both moral and spiritual. The diversified structure of patronage has the advantage that it provides a fairly even spread of activity around the country. Every medium-sized town maintains a good opera house, several

Traditional and folk music ring popular with most Germans.

Richard Wagner (1818–83)

But for one man, Bayreuth with its fine Baroque and Rococo buildings would be just another pretty town, a typical example of a capital city of one of the smaller former German principalities. But here, as soon as you enter a souvenir shop – always a good indicator of a town's own estimate of its cultural interest and worth – you will be engulfed by trinkets featuring Richard Wagner, his bust in plaster or chocolate, his portrait on book-covers and pencils.

Since 1876, when the first complete cycle of "*Der Ring des Nibelungen*" (The Ring of the Nibelung) was performed here, Bayreuth has become a famous and fashionable mecca for opera-lovers from all corners of the earth. Wagner spent the last years of his life up at his Villa Wahnfried ("peace from madness"), now a museum, before he died in Venice at the height of his fame.

For someone who was to revolutionize western music almost single-handedly, Wagner had a good start. His stepfather was a painter and actor-singer, and this artistic and theatrical background was a formative influence. Wagner was self-taught on the piano and always wrote his own libretti, which was very unusual in those days. A wayward student, his main interest lay in studying the scores of old masters like Beethoven, Mozart and Weber.

With grandiose conceptions culminating in the idea of a *Gesamtkunstwerk* (an all-encompassing work of art combining poetry, music, dance and the visual arts), a strong and self-centered ego and an addiction to a lavish lifestyle, Wagner found it difficult to go through the accepted motions of building up a career. Well into middle age, he had to struggle to keep off starvation, flee creditors and find acceptance for his compositions. Most of his works – if performed at all – were disastrously received. Apart from the early "*Rienzi*" and "*The Flying Dutchman*", his operas are all based on Nordic-

The Festspielhaus was built in the 1870's specifically for the production of operas from Richard Wagner.

German legends. With their complex interrelation of dramatic, verbal and musical symbolism, they are not exactly light fare.

In 1864 Wagner had to flee Vienna to avoid imprisonment for debt. He went to Stuttgart and there found himself, at the age of 51, at the end of his tether. Then something like a miracle happened. In the same year the 18-year-old Ludwig II (better known as "Mad King Ludwig") ascended the throne of Bavaria; already a fanatic admirer of Wagner, he immediately invited the composer to Munich to continue work on the *Ring*. The rest is history. The relationship, as it tends to be when two kings reign together, was at times tempestuous.

Wagner is still a controversial figure. After the First World War, he was much abused because he was identified with the nationalism and triumph of the Wilhelmine era (1888–1918). Today, the mythical Germanic background still makes many people uneasy, as does Wagner's anti-Semitism, and feelings about his work and personality often run high (with his detractors seldom listening to his music).

The annual Bayreuth Festival is an elegant and stylish affair, eagerly awaited not only by the glitterati, but also by serious music lovers (although few of the latter can afford the ticket prices).

theaters as well as various museums of fine arts, crafts and local history. Big cities like Frankfurt and Hamburg will offer much better quality and range of artistic performance than its British or French equivalents, say Manchester or Marseille.

It is of course the established classics that draw the biggest and most regular audiences. Shakespeare, Schiller and Brecht are the most widely performed playwrights, followed closely by Goethe, Lessing and Kleist; among foreign dramatists, Chekhov, Shaw and Ibsen are the most popular with the middle-of-the-road audiences. Cities are in constant competition with each other, to see which of them can lure the biggest names among conductors, theater directors and choreographers, and frequently foreigners are taken under contract to revive a flagging reputation. While most mainstream theaters are heavily subsidized, relatively little money is given to smaller companies, experimental groups performing on the fringe. In this area, private and company sponsorship is only gradually establishing an interest.

Breaking into Big-time Art

In painting, one of the centers of 20th-century German art is the highly industrialized Ruhr area, where wealthy private collectors donate lavishly to their local museums or found new ones. Düsseldorf has the best 20th-century art collection in Germany, followed by Stuttgart, and in Cologne the chocolate tycoon Ludwig has filled a whole new building with his very diverse and provocative collection. Until very recently the art market tended to be almost a closed shop to outsiders, with the big dealers concentrating their efforts on big private collectors and museums. There was little encouragement for people who were willing to spend some money on contemporary or traditional art, but found the elegantly appointed

The Opera House in Dresden.

showrooms of big galleries intimidating, the atmosphere mysterious, the staff snobbish. Times are changing, and especially in Berlin and Munich you can find smaller galleries with friendly dealers who offer affordable art. The old structure of the art market tended to prefer artists with an established reputation who were both a safe investment and a status symbol. For several decades, German art production was not adventurous, following conventional taste or latching on to new movements originating abroad. One of the most distinctive German art groups, the *Neue Wilde* (new wild ones), formed around a small innovative Berlin gallery in the mid-1970s, but only became accepted in Germany after successful exhibitions in New York and Paris had supplied them with an international seal of approval. Artists like Lüpertz, Baselitz,

A Berlin theater.

Penck and Polke, with their ironic, colorful and clever works halfway between Expressionism and Realism, are now regarded as modern classics. Best-known is probably the late Joseph Beuys of a slightly earlier generation, a conceptual artist, professor at the Düsseldorf Academy and talented showman, who always wore a felt hat and mostly worked with felt, fat and wood. His poetic imagination found a practical outlet in the environmental movement, where he became a founder member of the Greens.

Experimental music is, for some strange reason, flourishing in Germany, where composers like Stockhausen, Kagel, Henze, Ligeti and Cage have found a tiny but very receptive audience among the public and the official dispensers of patronage. Jazz and rock music by bands of all shades and persuasions fill huge open-air theaters;

The Museum of Modern Art in Bonn.

some of it sounds derivative, with a home-spun quality, the lyrics much in tune with the current anti-consumerist, small-is-beautiful trends. In Munich, Germany's filmmaking capital, such well-known film directors as Wenders, Herzog and Reitz started their careers which have now taken them to Hollywood and into the international circuit.

Of German Literature

In the 1960s, German literature moved

known exponents of this trend, both fine writers with strong political and social commitments. More traditionalist literature was produced by Siegfried Lenz and Martin Walser with their novels of closely observed social relationships and conventions. The Austrian novelist and playwright Thomas Bernhard was a class of his own; his vehement attacks against the brutality and stupidity of mankind in general and of Austrians in particular are as desperate and powerful as they are witty. Since the late 1970s writers have been retreating again from public and social themes into their private worlds of individual feeling and inwardness, mirroring a general trend in Western literature exemplified by the historical or pseudo-historical novel. A list of fine German and Austrian writers of the last 20 years would include Arno Schmidt, Peter Weiss, Adolf Muschg, Uwe Johnson, Elizabeth Plessen, Gert Hofmann, Hans Magnus Enzensberger, Sten Nadolny and the poets Ingeborg Bachmann and Paul Celan, all of whom have been translated into English.

Post-war architecture

Much of post-war architectural effort was directed to the heroic and sometimes brilliant restoration of damaged buildings. In Berlin, the Hansa Quarter was a new and imaginative project, gathering together such internationally renowned architects as Niemeyer, Le

away from its painfully struggling post-war concerns of coming to terms with Nazism, the war, moral and social devastation and the debasement of language. For more than a decade angry young writers expressed their disenchantment with Germany's materialism and conformist new society. Heinrich Böll and Günter Grass are the best-

Corbusier and Gropius. This for a long time remained an exception. Usually public housing was undistinguished, and the suburban tower-blocks of satellite towns no less drab. Some modern churches are strikingly bold and handsome with beautiful stained glass, and there are several superb new museums by Mies van der Rohe (in Berlin), James Stirling (Stuttgart), Hans Hollein (Münchengladbach), Alexander von Branca (Munich) and in Frankfurt along the Schaumainkai.

The last decade has seen a revived and more broadly-based interest in public and private architecture, both for new buildings and for the restoration of historic monuments. Here again lavishly subsidized pre-'89 Berlin has taken the lead. Commissioning German and foreign architects like Hollein, Puttfarken, Moore, Porthogesi, Stirling and Isozaki to design residential, industrial and public buildings, the city has acquired a fine cross-section of late Modernist architecture.

The fashion of razing old buildings and whole town quarters has been superseded by effort to save and restore, often initiated and organized on a local or even a street level. Fine examples can be seen in Bremen, Mainz, Nürnberg and many other places, while in eastern Germany, where neglect and decay were much worse, some town centers these days seem to have completely disappeared behind scaffolding, as renovation and rebuilding goes ahead at great speed.

A contemporary work of art in the Museum of Modern Art.

The German fondness for festivals and keeping up old customs and rituals can be enjoyed at any time of the year if you are in the right spot at the right moment. **Carnival**, celebrated mainly in Catholic areas between mid-February and mid-March, and Munich's **Oktoberfest**, the world's greatest beer festival, are the best-known occasions for jollity and drinking. If you look closely at the regional or local *Veranstaltungskalender* (calendar of events), you would realize that almost every town throughout the length and breadth of the country has its own fairs and festivals, celebrating some historical event like an imperial visit, deliverance from the plague or the successful defense against beleaguering armies. Many festivals date

Young girl wearing a traditional costume complete with a flowery crown participates in a village parade.

The Oktoberfest in Munich.

from the late Middle Ages or the Renaissance, others are of more recent origin. Carnival in its present form, for instance, started as a semi-political demonstration against repressive authorities in the early 19th century, and the Oktoberfest traces itself back to a royal marriage celebration in 1810.

In former times, festivals often coincided with trade fairs, linking economics and entertainment in a thoroughly satisfying way. With the advent of industrialization and free trade in the 19th century, traditional trade fairs began to disappear because of improved communications and changes in business organization. The festivals in many places, however, remained, and the former trade fair was turned into a fun-

fair. The farmer's calendar supplied further occasions for merrymaking. Harvesting, the driving down of cattle from the summer pastures, the slaughtering of fattened pigs and fowl, sowing and planting the new year's crop – the important markers of the natural rhythm of growth and decay were reasons for big feasts complete with competitive games, music and dancing, often preceded by a solemn church service.

The farming population is decreasing at a rapid rate, and farming methods have changed enormously; with two or even three harvests a year, the annual harvest festival of former times loses something of its importance and specialness. In spite of great changes or more probably because of them, a re-

Beer tents are an integral part of every volkesfest celebration.

vival of old traditions and customs is noticeable, especially in rural areas where the loss of communal activities geared to the agricultural cycle is more keenly felt. People in the countryside show renewed interest in the way things were done in the old days and consult elderly neighbors who are knowledgeable in local history, genealogy and folklore.

For Old Times' Sake

Participation at a **country wedding** can feel a bit like entering a time-warp, where older rituals are performed with much ceremony and attention to details. A *Polterabend* precedes the wedding day, a noisy, boisterous affair with much speech-making, drinking, telling of bawdy jokes. Next morning the wedding ceremony takes place. The bride is "abducted" by friends from her youth and has to be "ransomed" by the groom. On the way from the church or the registrar's office to the place of the wedding party, the car or carriage with the newly-weds is hijacked and has to be ransomed again with ample schnapps and banknotes discreetly tucked in envelopes. The wedding lunch usually is a family affair where the in-laws pay each other compliments and look brightly into the future. The big celebration in the evening, sometimes held in a specially erected marquee, brings together most of the village population. Gifts are

A volksfest parade with participants
in traditional Bavarian costumes.

tendered, invocations pronounced, a
band strikes up and food is served at
long trestle tables; then the floor is
cleared for dancing, and reveling often
continues until dawn. There are countless local variations of wedding customs
and rituals. In Bremen, for instance,
there is a custom whereby a man still
unwed on his 30th birthday must sweep
rubbish from the cathedral steps, attired
in top hat and tails, then marry the first
pretty girl who kisses him.

In Germany it is more common to
rent a house or flat than to buy one.
Building one's own house is rarer still
(although the trend is changing), so
much so that the hardworking Swabians
are singled out as a people whose main
ambition in life and work is to build a

house of their own. The completion of a
new house is preceded by the **Richtfes**
(roof-topping ceremony), when a fir tree
(in northern Germany) or a wreath o
crown (in the south) is planted on top o
the roof timbers. This is accompanied
by a speech by the foreman who ask:
God's blessings on the house and it:
inhabitants.

Honorary town guards parading in traditional uniform.

Most children start school when they are six. The first day is prepared with great excitement. An indispensable prop of the celebration is the *Schultüte*, a paper cone or cornet made of cardboard and decorated with all kinds of transfers showing scenes from fairy tales, animals and flowers. Sold at stationers, they are often as big as the child carrying them. The mother stuffs them with sweets, biscuits, rubbers, rulers and pens and secures the top with crêpe paper tied with a ribbon. The child then sets off for school, usually accompanied by its mother or father and carrying this huge paper cone and a brand-new satchel.

Small is Beautiful

Traditional customs like these were for a long time rather neglected. Particularly during the 1960s and 1970s, they tended to be regarded as quaint and old-fashioned, symbols of outmoded patriarchic and authoritarian relationships. But recently the pendulum has swung back a bit. Like the careful restoration of old buildings, the concern about nature less for mythical than environmental reasons, and a tendency towards *Innerlichkeit* (inwardness) in literature, the renewed interest in historical festivals and old customs is part of the small-is-beautiful trend, a movement away from the big issues towards smaller ones which can be managed at a lower level of societal organization, by parts of the community, street committees and self-help groups. Such a movement partly and very selectively recreates conditions prevalent before industrialization and the great leveling of national politics under Prussian hegemony, and as such exhibits some of the features of Romanticism which act as a counterbalance to the anonymity of the political machinery and government bureaucracy.

The most numerous and well-advertised of festivals take place at the end of the wine harvest (late August/early September), although the organizers are not too particular about dates: the red

wine festival at Aßmannshausen on the Rhine is held in May, while another Rhine resort, Eltville, puts on its wine harvest celebrations at the end of October. Wine-growers set up stalls in the marketplace or along the main street within the pedestrianized area, some supply chairs and tables as well. Sausages with mustard and a roll are sold,

Haflinger horses, favorite work horses in the mountainous regions of central Europe, exhibit their spirit in a festival.

the streets are hung with garlands of lights and greenery, and at the height of the festival a wine queen or princess is proclaimed and escorted through the streets by a long procession. The largest and best-known of German wine festivals is the **Dürkheimer Wurstmarkt** (Dürkheim sausage fair). Its history goes back almost 600 years to a fair that came about as a result of the annual pilgrimages that were made to a hillside chapel in order to obtain indulgences. The unique attraction is a giant barrel said to be the world's biggest, which

Children riding a swing carousel at a city festival held every September.

instead of containing its potential 1.7 million liters of wine now operates as a restaurant accommodating up to a thousand guests. Around it typical vintners' booths are set up, roofed but open at the sides and fitted with narrow tables and benches.

The **Landshuter Fürstenhochzeit** (Landshut royal wedding) every three years celebrates with a sumptuous pageant the marriage of the son of Duke Ludwig the Rich of Bavaria to Princess Jadwiga (Hedwig) of Poland in 1475. The Duke invited all of Europe's royalty

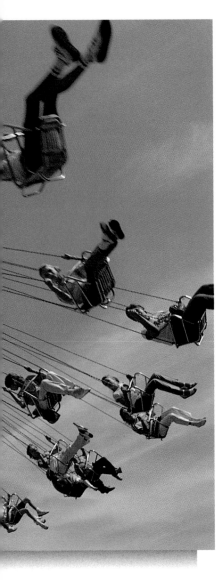

pageantry has also kept alive the **Tänzelfest** (dance festival) at Kaufbeuren, a very old historical children's costume festival held in mid-July. Some try to trace its origin back to a pre-Christian cult, but the general view is that it was instituted by Emperor Maximilian in 1497 after he had been favorably impressed by a boys' shooting competition; the emperor still plays a central role in the festival. The main event is a procession illustrating various scenes from Kaufbeuren's history, from its foundation in Frankish times to the 19th century. On both days of the festival children perform delightful demonstrations of historical dances and roundelays in period costume. Firework displays and an evening tattoo by torchlight conclude the show.

The tragic story of Agnes Bernauer, well-known to German schoolchildren through Hebbel's drama, is reenacted each year in the Bavarian town of Straubing. It tells how Albrecht, the son of Duke Ernst of Munich and later to become Albrecht III of Bavaria, secretly married Agnes, a barber-surgeon's daughter. The Duke was dead set against the marriage and tried to persuade the couple to change their minds. When this failed, he decided Agnes would have to die; so during the husband's absence, the Duke had her drowned in the Danube in 1435. With dozens of festivals as substantial and popular as these the Germans seem to feel little need for contrived theme parks and highly commercialized entertainment.

and nobility, and during a week-long orgy guests and townsfolk consumed 33 roast oxen, 490 calves, 1,133 sheep, 1,537 lambs, 684 pigs, 11,500 geese, 40,000 chickens and oceans of beer and wine. It is now staged in June for the benefit of summer visitors, although the wedding took place in November.

The Bavarians' love of tradition and

Berlin, new capital of a new Germany, has a nervous, febrile atmosphere, a potent tenseness and a sense of urgency, which is perfectly balanced by the sly, wry humor of the Berliners. Add to this the fact that it lies in the heart of a newly open and liberalized Central Europe, and you have two strong connecting links with its situation during the 1920s and early '30s, its almost mythical heyday. Even after the fall of the Wall in 1989 and the end of its 40-year long division, it remains a city in limbo. But then again it seems to thrive on times of insecurity and improvisation, become particularly lively, glamorous, inventive and stimulating when things are out of kelter, when the sobriety of the real world is suspended.

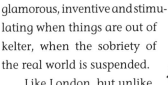

The Victory column seems an appropriate comment on Germany's reunification.

Like London, but unlike, say, Paris and Rome, Berlin has no true city center. The famous Alexanderplatz, described as a "seething human jungle...the quivering heart of the city" by Alfred Döblin in his definitive novel about Berlin at the end of the 1920s, was

Berlin & Brandenburg

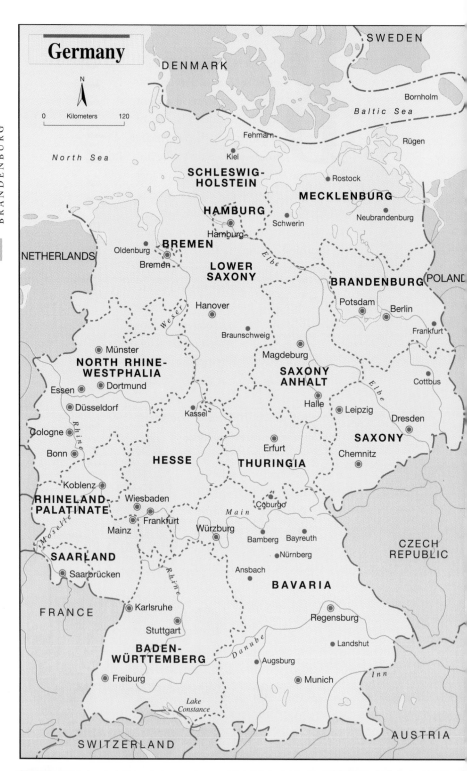

Germany

N

0   Kilometers   120

SWEDEN

DENMARK

Baltic Sea

Bornholm

North Sea

Fehmarn

Rügen

Kiel

**SCHLESWIG-
HOLSTEIN**

Rostock

MECKLENBURG

HAMBURG

Schwerin

Neubrandenburg

Hamburg

Oldenburg

BREMEN

Elbe

Bremen

**LOWER
SAXONY**

NETHERLANDS

BRANDENBURG POLAND

Potsdam

Berlin

Hanover

Weser

Braunschweig

Frankfurt

Münster

**NORTH RHINE-
WESTPHALIA**

Magdeburg

Elbe

Cottbus

Essen

Dortmund

**SAXONY
ANHALT**

Düsseldorf

Kassel

Halle

Leipzig

Cologne

Rhine

Dresden

Bonn

Erfurt

SAXONY

HESSE

THURINGIA

Chemnitz

Koblenz

**RHINELAND-
PALATINATE**

Wiesbaden

Coburg

Main

Moselle

Frankfurt

Würzburg

Mainz

Bamberg

Bayreuth

CZECH
REPUBLIC

SAARLAND

Nürnberg

Saarbrücken

Ansbach

Rhine

BAVARIA

FRANCE

Karlsruhe

Regensburg

Stuttgart

Landshut

**BADEN-
WÜRTTEMBERG**

Danube

Augsburg

Inn

Freiburg

Munich

*Lake
Constance*

AUSTRIA

SWITZERLAND

Berlin tourist bus.

practically obliterated by wartime bombing. The historic center, the avenue Unter den Linden, with its monumental 18–19th-century government buildings, is too grand for the jumble and joy of everyday life, and glitzy Kurfürstendamm too commercialized to admit the flow of cultural cross-currents.

This absence of a true center has strengthened the individualism of Berlin's patchwork of districts and suburbs, proletarian Wedding, anarchic Kreuzberg, factory-clustered Siemensstadt, tranquil Tiergarten, Bohemian Prenzlauer Berg, leafy Charlottenburg, posh Steglitz or rural Heiligensee. When tired of sightseeing, take advantage of the well laid-out public transport to visit less frequented places and get a feel for the size, variety and atmosphere of this huge conglomeration with a hinterland of lakes, rivers, canals, forests and pastures, its 1,604 bridges and viaducts, 38,000 heads of cattle and even some vineyards within city limits, in a corner of the Viktoriapark.

Berlin is quite a young city. It grew from two parishes on the river Spree founded c.1230, and in 1470 became the main residence of the Hohenzollern rulers. Wrecked during the Thirty Years' War, it was built into a city proper by Frederick William (r.1640–88), the *Großer Kurfürst* (Great Elector), who welcomed thousands of French and Dutch Protestant refugees and used their agricultural and artistic knowledge to cultivate the lands and beautify the towns of his

A regular scene at the Berlin.

dukedom. His son, the vain Frederick III (r.1688–1713), erected Schloß Charlottenbeurg and crowned himself King in Prussia (becoming Frederick I of Prussia), amazing and infuriating the Holy Roman Emperor. Under his grandson Frederick II, called "the Great" (r.1740–86), stately monuments were erected along **Unter den Linden** (under the limetrees), and Berlin was built up as a manufacturing town and leading center of culture.

Industrial growth began in the mid-19th century, which among other things

Siemens, founder of one of the world's greatest engineering firms. German unification in 1871 gave the new capital a big boost to development. The city was filled with representative government offices, museums, churches, and around the factories grew slums like the proletarian districts of Wedding and Neukölln.

During the First World War, demonstrations against the war and for a democratic republic gathered force until a wave of strikes and street protests forced the emperor to abdicate in November 1918. On 9 November 1918, Germany was declared a republic in the Berlin Reichstag, the seat of parliament, while at the same time the radical Spartacists declared communist revolution from a balcony of the Kaiser's palace. Political chaos ensued, aggravated by economic depression.

In the 1920s, Berlin had some 4 million inhabitants and was larger than Paris. The Golden Twenties were a time of often violent unrest, high inflation and mass unemployment. It was also culturally exciting, with artists, filmmakers, theater directors, playwrights, novelists and musicians coming together in a stimulating mix.

Foreigners flocked to the city and celebrated its inebriating, liberal atmosphere. Hitler put an end to this; he ruled from Berlin, had his nefarious schemes worked out in the same government buildings that imperial, defeated Prussia had used. In the early months of 1945, 363 Allied bombing raids reduced large

meant an influx of thousands of peasants to work in the factories and, to house them, the construction of the infamous Berlin tenement buildings, arranged in military formation with one main gateway leading onto huge housing blocks separated by dank courtyards. Among the pioneer industrialists were Borsig, who built locomotives, and

The new perspective to the Berlin Wall.

parts of the city to rubble.

After the war, when Germany was partitioned into four occupation zones, Berlin found itself deep inside the Soviet zone. Because of its historic, cultural and symbolic importance, it received special treatment, and from 1945 until 1990 was officially administered by representatives of the four war-time Allies, although as time went on a German civilian government took over most municipal affairs.

When in June 1948, the occupying powers in western Germany introduced a currency reform to ease economic recovery, the Soviets retaliated with a blockade of the city. This was overcome, after 11 months, by massive Allied airlifts and the courage and resilience of the Berliners. A few months after Bonn was declared the capital of the Federal Republic of Germany in mid-1949, East Berlin became the capital of the German Democratic Republic, the "workers' and peasants' state". In June 1953, a demonstration by disaffected and dissatisfied workers turned into a street battle, stones were hurled against Soviet tanks, and some people were killed and many wounded.

After this tragic event, bitterness against the brutal Socialist regime grew in both Germanies, firing the flames of the Cold War. The two sectors of the city grew apart, as did the two countries. To stem the flood of refugees to the west – mostly young people and members of the professions – in August 1961 the border was fortified by a 60-mile-long (100 km) wall, effectively severing all contact between the two sectors.

Both governments poured huge subsidies into their parts of the city to boost economic activity and present a cultural showcase to the world. This had the effect of a mirror-like proliferation of cultural institutions, so that today the reunited city boasts three opera houses, a staggering seven symphony orchestras, two examples of various kinds of museums and twice as many theaters as any other city its size. But while the Wall was still standing, Berlin needed much morale-boosting, such as President Kennedy's rousing words on his visit in 1963: "All free men…are citizens of Berlin, and therefore, as a free man, I take pride in the words *Ich bin ein Berliner*."

Subsidies for industry and art, for social services and community-based activities flowed ever more freely, amounting to DM23 billion in the last years and making Berlin Germany's leading industrial city in terms of jobs. Optimism returned in the early 1970s under Brandt's courageous *Ostpolitik*, aimed at easing tensions between the two Germanies and with the eastern bloc as a whole.

Both parts of the city used the occasion of the 750th anniversary in 1987 to renovate many historic buildings and monuments and to brighten up the streets and squares with greenery and modern sculpture.

Finally the sea-change in world politics initiated by President Gorbachev directly affected the strange, surreal situation of Berlin. In the autumn of 1989, East Berliners took their cue from Poland and Hungary and nearby Leipzig and began to rebel. On 9 November, the GDR government lifted all travel restrictions, and East Berliners and East Germans swept through the Wall to the West to sightsee, to shop or just to have an ice-cream, amid scenes of joy and excitement unequaled in Europe since 1945. Soon after, the Wall began to be torn down, and in July 1990 currency union removed one of the last important barriers.

Although the concrete slabs of the Wall have been removed, a broad gash of wasteland remains. It was formerly mined and studded with watchtowers, now it has been turned into a bicycle track or has been reseeded and replanted. Walking or driving across it still arouses a chilly, numbing tremor. The two parts of the city are as yet very different in appearance and living standards, in lifestyle and psychology. Paradoxically, at the moment the eastern section seems to be the more stimulating, lively and innovative of

The Kudamm, the glitzy showcase of west Berlin.

the two and to attract the less commercialized, more unconventional and adventurous spirits among artists, craftsmen, entrepreneurs and activists.

The Modern Center

The **Kurfürstendamm** (avenue of the electors) – usually shortened to "Kudamm" – is the glitzy showcase of western Berlin, with elegant hotels like the posh "Kempinski" and shops, famous coffeehouses like the **Café Kranzler**, a paradise of cream cakes where you can also have a freshly baked *Berliner* (jam-filled bun), and slightly down-market department stores. Shoppers crowd the sidewalks, jostling with

street performers, lottery ticket sellers and tourists.

Here more concentrated than anywhere else in Berlin do you feel to be in the heart of Central Europe, with all the languages and physiognomies of Eastern European countries strongly represented. The avenue was the brainchild of Chancellor Bismarck, who after the Franco-Prussian war of 1870–71 fell in love with the Champs-Elysées and resolved to build a street like it at home. Its heyday was in the 1920s and '30s, when the American novelist Thomas Wolfe described it as the "largest coffeehouse in Europe". Although heavily bombed in 1945, it is again an exciting and colorful meeting-point of many cultures. A good idea is to take the bus that runs

A mime artist applying make-up.

the whole length of the $1^1/_2$-mile-long (3-km) street.

Near the start of the Kudamm are two villa-lined sidestreets. The elegant Fasanenstraße has many beautiful Jugendstil houses, several modern art galleries and a museum devoted to the great Berlin artist, socialist and feminist Käthe Kollwitz (1867–1945), who did highly expressive graphics and wood-cuts. The **Literaturhaus Berlin** (house of literature) in the Uhlandstraße is a bookworm's paradise with a café in the winter garden upstairs, good for a rest between shopping and sightseeing.

The famous Berlin landmark, the jagged **Kaiser-Wilhelm Gedächtnis–kirche** (memorial church to Emperor William I), stands right at the begin-ning of the Kudamm. Built in 1895, it was bombed during the last war and has been left a ruin as a memorial to the war's ravages. Strikingly powerful, it has rightly been called one of the few buildings to be improved by the fall of bombs.

The modern church tower next to it has bright-blue stained-glass windows made in Chartres. Inside the nearby **Europa Center** is a computer-control-led waterfall of purple, green, blue and yellow neon lights quite in character with the tacky shopping arcade. The whole area is decorated with modern sculptures and fountains, making it a charming open-air gallery.

Turn into the **Tauentzienstraße** for a visit to what claims to be the largest

The Kaiser Wilhelm Memorial Church said to look better
after the ravages of war.

shop in continental Europe. The **KaDeWe** – short for Kaufhaus des Westens (department store of the West) – is an object of near-reverence, the pinnacle of consumer culture. The food hall on the top floor is the highlight, with a bar serving oysters and champagne to revive fatigued shoppers.

Just around the corner from the Kudamm stands the city's main train station. If every self-respecting metropolis needs a teeming, seedy core, then this is Berlin's version. **Bahnhof Zoo** has been a black-market center for much of this century, and still today pimps, beggars, con men, street vendors and drug pushers all peddle their living here, their victims mainly poor East Europeans who had expected gold-paved streets. Al-though definitely not glamorous, it is a major connecting point in northern Europe and a welcome stopover for railway travelers between Paris and Peking.

Opposite the station you find the Berlin Zoo, a disappointing spectacle, the animals looking sad and unhealthy. Pass through the bizarre, exotic *Elefantentor* (elephant gate) on the south side and emerge at the western tip of Berlin's "green lung".

In 1846, the poet Victor von Scheffel wrote that the **Tiergarten** (animal garden) "is the only place where the Berliner can convince himself that the world contains nature, green trees and the darkness of woods at night". Right at the beginning of the grand avenue that cuts through this huge woodland is one of

Berlin Zoo.

Germany's best-known porcelain factories. It was founded in 1751 and bought a decade later by Frederick the Great, since when it has been known as the **Königliche Porzellanmanufaktur** (royal porcelain manufactory), abbreviated KPM.

The Tiergarten began as a private hunting park and was turned into a public garden in 1742. Its layout with paths and artificial lakes is the work of Peter Josef Lenné (1789–1866), Berlin's prime landscape architect of the 19th century. It is a favorite summer venue

Panel detail from the base of the winged column of Victory.

for picnicking and sunbathing in the buff. The park was also the setting for many of the scenes in Wim Wenders' haunting film about his home city, *Wings of Desire* (1986).

Halfway along the grand Straße des 17 Juni which runs through the heart of the Tiergarten, stands the impressive **Siegessäule**, a 220-foot-high (67-meter) column crowned by the golden goddess of victory. Climb to the top for a bird's-eye view of the park. The street, formerly called the East-West Axis and used by Hitler for military parades, now sports a colorful weekend market for antiques and secondhand goods, which starts very early in the morning.

The **Hansaviertel** north of the Siegessäule is an exemplary collection of diverse architectural styles from the 1950s. Close by, the elegant neo-Classical **Schloß Bellevue** set by the banks of the Spree, was built in 1785 as a royal summer house and is now the official Berlin residence of Germany's president. Further along the Spree banks you come upon the futuristic **Kongreßhalle**, its cantilevered front meant to imitate the stretched awnings of tents which provided entertainment for Berliners in this part of the town in the 18th century. Built in 1957, it is popularly dubbed the "pregnant oyster".

A walk right to the opposite southern side of the Tiergarten brings you to a little culture-cluster east of the Potsdamer Platz.The **Kunstgewerb–emuseum** houses arts and crafts from the Middle Ages to the present day, from Flemish tapestries to Jugendstil furniture designed for an Indian maharajah. The nearby **Neue Nationalgalerie** is devoted to paintings of the late 19th and 20th centuries. Adolph von Menzel's (1815–1905) realistic depictions of factory work and of grand society balls are vivid, moving images of his age; there are some exquisite Impressionists and many oddly unmoving modern works by Beuys and Stella.

Opposite the museum lies the big yet unobtrusive **Staatsbibliothek** (state library), and north of it the Philharmonie, a Bauhaus-inspired design by Hans Scharoun (1893–1972), famous for its revolutionary layout and near-perfect acoustics. Its legendary post-war conductor, Herbert von Karajan, headed it for several decades almost until the moment of his death in 1989. Just north of the Potsdamer Platz, a discreet mound marks the site of the bunker where Hitler and Eva Braun committed suicide on 30 April 1945.

The east end of the Tiergarten is marked by the **Brandenburger Tor**, a 12-column gate erected in 1791 as a symbol of peace, a clean break with the warmongering of Frederick the Great, who had died five years earlier. It is topped by a quadriga, a grand copper sculpture of Nike, the goddess of victory, on her chariot. In its time, it has seen many of the great entrances and exits of German history. Napoleon marched through to take Berlin in 1806, and William I rode past on a white horse to celebrate German unification in 1871. William II made an ignominious exit in his Daimler after abdicating in 1918, and Hitler used it for great torchlight processions. In 1961 it was caught in no-man's-land behind the Berlin Wall, but was formally reopened in December 1989 for Berliners to celebrate New Year's Eve with the party of their lifetime.

Beyond the gate stands the massive hulk of the neo-Classical **Reichstag**, opened in 1894 to house the German parliament, which seldom lived up to the dedication on its façade: "*Dem deutschen Volke*" (to the German people). Restored after wartime damage, it is used for ceremonial meetings and may again become the seat of the German parliament. At present, it holds an exhibition devoted to "questions on German history", which is disappointingly bland.

Unter den Linden

The majestic avenue "under the limetrees", lined by grand neo-Classical

Brandenburger Tor by night.

The imposing Reichstag may resume its position as Parliament House.

government buildings, stretches from the Brandenburg Gate east towards the pre-war city center. It was begun by Frederick William, the Great Elector, who in 1648 planted the first walnuts and limes to flank a riding path towards the hunting grounds of Tiergarten and Grunewald; he ordered that anyone damaging them would have his hand chopped off. Its present appearance dates from the mid-19th century, when the master architect Karl Friedrich Schinkel (1781–1841) made the avenue the centerpiece of his new design for

after passing the giant statue of Frederick the Great on horseback.

The **Humboldt University** was founded in 1806 by the writer and diplomat Wilhelm von Humboldt, brother of the explorer and naturalist Alexander, during the Napoleonic occupation of Berlin. It has a fine tradition of liberal thinking, its eminent alumni including both Grimms, Marx, Engels and Einstein. Embossed in the marble on the front of the staircase is a famous Marx quote put there by the Communists: "The philosophers have only interpreted the world differently; the point is, however, to change it." Since reunification, its 19,000 students have had a miserable time, with closures and cuts in all departments, and have staged sit-ins and demonstrations.

Designed like a Roman temple, the **Neue Wache** (1818) served, as the name implies, as a new guardhouse for the imperial palace opposite, now destroyed. It is basically a very grand stone sentry-box. Every age re-dedicated it according to its own priorities. After First World War it was a monument to the Unknown Soldier, Hitler used it in praise of militarism; and for the Communists, it was a memorial to the victims of Stalinism. It has now reverted to its pre-1933 use.

The last building in this row is the former **Zeughaus** (arsenal), fronting the Spree. Begun in 1695, it took 35 years to complete and became Berlin's first Baroque palace. In the 19th century it was a weapons museum and today hosts

Berlin, with palaces, museums, embassies and office buildings along its entire one-mile length.

After wartime bombing, long stretches have been rebuilt as offices and apartment blocks with the ground floor given over to shops and cafés. Halfway along, the north side is taken up by three imposing buildings in a row,

The Französischer Dom.

special exhibitions on historical themes. The most distinctive feature of the gloomy building are the sculptures of dying warriors in the back courtyard. They were designed full of sorrow and compassion, by the great Berlin architect Andreas Schlüter (c.1664–1714), all of whose buildings, incidentally, were destroyed for one reason or another, so that only architectural ornaments by his hand survive.

Before crossing the broad Schloßbrücke and moving from Prussian to modern Berlin again, three build-

The Dom Cathedral.

ings to the south of Unter den Linden deserve mention. The **Deutscher Dom** with a broad, polished bronze cupola, and the **Französischer Dom** with a Huguenot museum and viewing tower, were both vanity pieces of the 1780s commissioned by Frederick the Great and modeled on two churches in Rome. They have no religious function today. The nearby **St Hedwigskirche** was modeled (unsuccessfully) on the vast dome of Rome's Pantheon. The story goes that Frederick the Great, asked how he wanted the church to look, turned over

The Old National Gallery.

a coffee-cup and said: "Like this."

Beyond the Schloßbrücke lies the wide **Marx-Engels-Platz**. Here stood Schlüter's masterpiece, the royal palace, bombed during the war and blown up in 1950 as a "symbol of imperialism". The glowing glass-house on the site is the **Palast der Republik**, where the parliament of the former GDR used to meet. In its construction asbestos was used, which was declared a cancer risk shortly before reunification, and it is now closed, with an uncertain future.

Slightly to the north lies the **Museumsinsel**, where five museums await the intrepid visitor. One of them, however, the **Neues Museum**, was very heavily damaged and is not due to exhibit again till year 2000. The **Nationalgalerie**, replete with grand colonnades and heavy triumphal stairways, gives a flavor of late 19/early-

20th-century art.

There are some graphic portrayals of factory life by Menzel and Liebermann, a few French Impressionists, a rapid overview of German artists from the turn of the century, and on the top floor scores of vapid historical and landscape paintings and stodgy portraits of the monarchs of the period.

The **Altes Museum**, built in 1830 and the earliest of the five, with its 285-foot-wide (87-meter) façade propped up by 18 Ionic pillars, is a neo-Classical extravaganza on a grand scale. Formerly the royal Egyptian collection was stored here; now it houses temporary exhibitions. The huge granite basin in the courtyard is 23 feet (7 meters) wide and was hewn from a single piece of rock; like the museum itself, it was designed by Schinkel.

By far the most stunning exhibits are kept in the **Pergamon Museum**, where large ensembles of whole cities have been reconstructed and mythical names from the ancient world – Babylon, Assyria, Mesopotamia – spring to life. Its dazzling wealth is due largely to the Egyptologist Richard Lepsius (1810–84), who set out in 1842 and – to make a long story short – for just a few fine pieces of Prussian porcelain obtained permission from the pasha Mohammed Ali to take home every treasure he could find. Eight years later he returned to Berlin in triumph, giving the city the richest Egyptian collection in the world.

The Pergamon Altar itself consists of a broad staircase that sweeps up to a

Pergamon Museum.

line of columns. Around the base, a frieze depicts the ferocious battle that Zeus fought against the giants to gain control of Mount Olympus. It was built between c.180 and 160 BC, as a temple to Athene, took eight years to excavate and 20 to reconstruct.

Pergamon was a city state in the eastern Aegean, at what is today the town of Bergama in Turkey. Among the other treasures are the almost complete market gate from Miletus in Asia Minor, a giant two-tiered edifice of Corinthian marble columns built by the Romans in AD 120; the huge crenellated Ishtar Gate (6th century BC) from Babylon, made of flaming blue glazed tiles and decorated with horses and mythical creatures; and part of the wall of the palace

Nikolaiviertel, the old quarter.

of Mshatta, a desert fortification of the 8th century in what is now Jordan, 148 feet (45 meters) long and with intricate early Islamic patterned reliefs in its weathered rock.

The fifth museum is the **Bode-Museum** with very fine objects of Egyptian, early Christian, Byzantine and Western European art. This includes a 6th-century Ravenna mosaic, several outstanding pieces of sculpture by Italian and German Renaissance masters (Luca della Robbia, Riemenschneider) and paintings by Cranach, Elsheimer and Dutch and French artists of the 16/17th century.

To leave the island of museums you cross the Spree once again. To the south, beyond a tiny park, you find the charming **Nikolaiviertel**, a restored quarter old Berlin burghers' houses clusterin around the city's oldest parish churc the eponymous twin-steepled Gotl Nikolaikirche, erected in 1230 and co secrated as Berlin's first Protestant chur in 1559. It now houses part of the cit historical museum. Among the notal buildings is the stately **Palais Ephrain**

The Botanical Garden.

the Rococo mansion of Frederick the Great's Jewish banker and now also a museum of local history.

The **Gaststätte Zum Nußbaum** (tavern at the walnut tree), a typical Berlin building of the turn of the century, was the favorite watering hole of the famed local cartoonist Heinrich Zille (1858–1929). This remodeled area, in spite of its slightly artificial character, provides a soothing counterpoint to the busy, bustling streets around and has nice shops, restaurants and pubs.

By now you will have noticed the

Schloß Charlottenburg.

dominating **TV tower** (1,200 feet [365 meters]), a needle-like design with a revolving café and observation deck. It stands at the famed **Alexanderplatz**, bombed during the war and rebuilt in bland, modernistic fashion with huge box-like steel-and-glass buildings. Two houses on the south side survive from the 1920s: the Berolinahaus, housing municipal offices, and the Alexanderhaus, a department store. Both were designed by Peter Behrens, whose students included Le Corbusier, Gropius and Mies van der Rohe.

in the run-down Kreuzberg district. Since the fall of the Wall, the action has shifted to the eastern part of town, where rents are still much lower.

West of the Marx-Engels-Platz, the **Oranienburger Straße**, by night one of Berlin's seedier red-light districts, has become a lively, slightly chaotic center of the alternative culture scene. Its focus is the art-house collective "*Tacheles*", housed in a large abandoned cinema. It is the home and workplace of an international set of artists and kindred spirits. Besides original works of art, you find here theatrical and musical performances and a crowded, smoky café and bar with lots of atmosphere.

Northeast of the Alexanderplatz lies the area of **Prenzlauer Berg**, a run-down workers' district which already under the Socialist regime was a mecca for the sub-culture of the whole country. Some 70 percent of the people live in flats built before 1919, but the houses look worse from the outside than inside. Around the Kollwitzplatz and Schönhauser Allee you find many fringe theaters and cozy authentic Berlin *Kneipen* (pubs). The nearby water tower (1875) is the area's emblem. Opposite stands the red-brick synagogue built in 1904. It was heavily damaged by the Nazis but not demolished, and between 1976 and 1978 has been carefully restored.

To the north, the **Husemannstraße** is a shopping street, rebuilt 1987 in late 19th-century style. There is a fascinating Friseurmuseum (hairdressing mu-

The Berlin alternative scene, **die Szene**, has always been rather small and relatively inaccessible to the casual visitor. Before 1989, a mixed crowd of artists, writers, superannuated hippies, foreign workers, drug addicts, punks, pimps, skinheads, craftsmen, musicians and others concentrated in the cheap housing area around the Oranienstraße

The Egyptian Museum.

seum), and in one of the numerous pubs and bistros you should try two Berlin specialities: *Kartoffelpuffer mit Apfelmus* is a kind of potato pancake served with applesauce, and *Buletten* is a sort of hamburger made of minced meat, bread, egg and spices.

Charlottenburg and the West

Charlottenburg, a residential district west of the Tiergarten, has as its main attraction the big and beautiful **Schloß**

Charlottenburg with its lovely park and a few small museums nearby. The palace, Berlin's first building of artistic merit, was built by Frederick William III in 1695 for his wife Sophie Charlotte, a woman of taste, wit and compassion. The inner courtyard is graced by a superb equestrian statue of the portly Great Elector, designed by Schlüter (1703). Begun as a summer house, the Schloß was later much expanded.

On the central tower, note the charming conceit of the gilded statue of the goddess of fortune turning like a weather vane. Inside, the state rooms are rather gloomy, but the Queen's chambers, sumptuously furnished with mirrors and Baroque scrollwork, are more cheerful. The west wing, the former orangery, houses temporary exhibitions. The east or Knobelsdorff wing has a splendid collection of 18/19th-century paintings, notably stunning landscapes by C.D. Friedrich, Watteau's *Voyage à Cynthère* (1720) and David's impassioned painting of Napoleon crossing the Alps (1800). The gardens, part formal French, part natural English, are one of the city's most enchanting spots, with fountains, long pebbled walks, statuary, pavilions and a trout pond at the far end.

Opposite the main entrance of the Schloß, three buildings by Schinkel, originally used as mess halls for officers of the royal bodyguard, now house notable museums. The star of the **Ägyptisches Museum** is the one-eyed beauty called Nefertiti – discovered on the Upper Nile in 1912 – her high cheekbones and warm gaze hauntingly expressive; note also the grand Kalabsha Gate (c.20 B.C.), which shows the Roman emperor Augustus as a pharaoh. The **Antikenmuseum** has a well-preserved collection of ancient Greek and Roman artifacts, beautifully presented in light, spacious rooms. A few steps along the tree-lined avenue you find the Bröhan-Museum, mainly showing Jugendstil interiors of the first two decades of this century.

To the south, the spindly Eiffel-like **Funkturm** (radio tower; 425 feet [130 meters]), a Berlin landmark built in 1928, offers a fine view of the city from its upper platform. Below it are exhibition grounds and a vast silvery congress center, while to the west stands the huge Olympic stadium, built for the 1936 Games which Hitler used as a propaganda piece for his new order.

In the quiet, leafy suburb of **Dahlem** you find several distinguished museums with superb art treasures elegantly displayed. Until the Second World War the objects were dispensed in museums, palaces and private collections. In 1943 the best pieces were stored away in saltmines in Thuringia, where US forces found them in 1945. They were sent to the National Gallery in Washington, D.C., and returned in the 1950s after the Americans and Russians each agreed to return wartime art loot to "their" Germans. So some treasures went to East Berlin, while the majority eventually found a home here in Dahlem.

Berlin illuminated.

Lake Wannsee.

Schloß Babelsberg in Potsdam.

Of the several museums, the most important is the **Gemäldegalerie** (painting gallery), a vast array with some of the greatest works of European art. The layout is arranged chronologically and by nation. The German Old Masters give a splendid performance: Multscher,

Schongauer, Dürer, Altdorfer and Grien, Holbein the Younger with portraits and Cranach with a delightful *Fountain of Youth*.

The Italian section includes several Botticellis and Filippo Lippis as well as a glorious set of Canalettos. Among the

um's bright modern café looking out onto the gardens.

The **Kupferstichkabinett** (department of prints and drawings) holds wonderful, delicate works by Dürer, Brueghel, Rembrandt, Botticelli and scores of others, as well as lithographs and artists' sketchbooks. The Skulpturengalerie is mainly devoted to German sculpture; it is best on medieval and Renaissance works (Riemenschneider, Multscher, Donatello). The ethnological **Museum für Völkerkunde** is almost as noteworthy for its beautiful displays as for its wondrous objects. It is one of the greatest and most complete of its kind in Europe.

There are enthralling, mysterious statues and ornaments from Central and South America, delicate golden jewelry and cult objects and a dazzling group of sailing boats from the South Seas, dramatically lit and eminently touchable.

The **Museum für Indische, Islamische und Ostasiatische Kunst** – in plain language: for Oriental Art – has something of everything, from minutely executed illuminated Islamic manuscripts and voluptuous Indian sculpture to Zen paintings, Chinese wooden and ceramic sculpture and Japanese lacquer.

Dutch and Flemish painters there are Brueghel the Elder's vivid, funny canvas of *Dutch Proverbs*, several self-portraits and portraits of his wife Saskia by Rembrandt as well as his *Man with a Golden Helmet* (now attributed to his School), serene interiors by Vermeer and boisterous scenes by Frans Hals. Before moving on, take a break at the muse-

Havel and Spree

To the west of the city lies the vast **Grunewald**, bordering on the river Havel, where on weekends joggers and

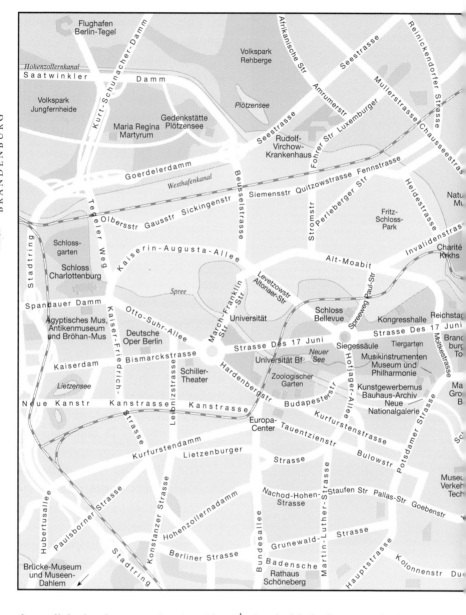

dogs off the leash race each other. The forest was established in the Middle Ages to help drain the disease-ridden swamps of the Havel and has been almost completely replanted with pines and other deciduous trees after the Second World War. The charming 16th-century Jagdschloß (hunting lodge), partly remodeled in Baroque style, holds a good collection of Dutch and German painting of the 15/19th century. Further south along the riverbank you come to the **Wannsee**, not in fact a lake but a large bay and huge bathing area in

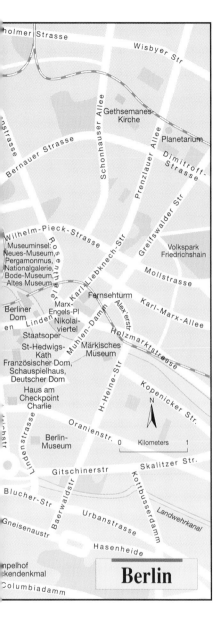

Spreewald, where there is a network of 300 canals.

forest and splendid informal garden laid out by Lenné and Count Pückler-Muskau. **Schloß Kleinglienicke** is a graceful ensemble of manicured lawns and eccentric garden ornaments, mock ruins, temples and gilded unicorns. The squat sandstone palace by Schinkel now houses a sanatorium.

The Havel is traversed at this point by the Glienicker Brücke, where in February 1962 the pilot of a US spy plane was exchanged for the Soviet master spy Rudolf Abel; it was later used for several more such swaps. The road continues to Potsdam and its assorted pleasures and treasures (see Brandenburg chapter).

From Wannsee, cruise boats leave for tours of the beautiful, dreamy Havel lakes, where among the deep woods the

summer.

The long Königsstraße leads to two enchanting palaces close to the water. **Schloß Babelsberg**, a neo-Gothic folly with turrets and crenellated parapets, dates from the 1830s. Nature is the main attraction here, with the surrounding

Raunchy Berlin.

main street, where a few original one-story 18th-century houses and the odd mulberry tree remain. Down at the pier, excursion boats touring the **Großer Müggelsee**, which is fed by the Spree, stop frequently next to little restaurants and woodlands. The area is popular in summer for sun and sailing, and in winter for ice-skating.

Brandenburg

The *Land* Brandenburg still does justice to its old nickname of "pounce-box of the Holy Roman Empire": it is a region of sand and moor, of lakes, pine trees and army barracks. Mostly flattish and sparsely populated, its quiet charm can be very captivating; endless fields and pastures interspersed with sizable forests under an immense sky invite the cyclist and the leisurely driver. The country lanes are narrow and often cobblestoned and lined with trees which touch crowns in the middle. Its people are industrious and content with little, have a dry sense of humor and a fierce sense of duty.

There is some light industry in the east, but its main business is agriculture, supplying fruit, vegetables, meat and flowers to Berlin, the "stomach of Brandenburg". Its most famous sons are the novelists Theodor Fontane (1819–89) – whose massive *Wanderungen durch die Mark Brandenburg* is a wonderfully evocative guidebook – and Heinrich von Kleist (1777–1811), the architect and

top brass of the Communist regime had its secluded villas. A short excursion takes you to the **Pfaueninsel** (peacock island), a nature reserve for all manner of beasts, trees and plants. The mock-Gothic "ruined" castle with brilliant white turrets and a gate with portcullis, the work of a local carpenter, was built by Frederick William II as a hideaway for his mistress, the daughter of a trumpeter. Picnicking is allowed only in a specially designated area.

For another pleasant excursion to the countryside, take the S-Bahn to the small town of **Friedrichshagen**. It was founded in 1753 as a settlement for Bohemian cotton spinners who were required to plant mulberry trees for the rearing of silkworms. Walk down the

The Sun King motif in Schloß Sanssouci.

painter K.F. Schinkel (1781–1841) and the agricultural pioneer A.D. Thaer (1752–1828), who was born in Celle but built his model farm near Wriezen in eastern Brandenburg.

Before the rise of the town of Potsdam and the kingdom of Prussia in the 17th century, the history of Brandenburg was marked by the subjugation and christianization of the Slav population and the laborious process of colonization and cultivation.

To turn the sandy soil and vast tracts of marshy land into fields and grazing land required much work and expertise. As natural conditions were quite similar to those in the Low Countries, the rulers and large landowners of Brandenburg since early times encouraged immigration on a large scale; they were especially keen on settlers from the western seaboard. Already in the 12th century we hear of Flemish colonists in western Brandenburg. Later, Dutchmen and Huguenots, fleeing religious persecution, arrived in great numbers.

The Dutch drapers who were called to Lübbenau in the mid-16th century started the tradition of pickling small cucumbers in brine, for which the town is well-known even today. Other Dutch exiles taught Brandenburgians the art of distillation to produce schnapps. A kind of cross-fertilization occurred around 1700, when Huguenots on their way from France passed through Baden on the right bank of the Rhine, where they learned to grow tobacco and when they arrived in Schwedt in east Brandenburg, they immediately planted tobacco fields. To this day, these two regions are the only tobacco-growing areas in Germany.

Frederick the Great with his ambitious plans to make Prussia a European power, needed all the experts he could get; he "imported" Dutch tailors and shoemakers, gardeners and master-builders, gunsmiths and dike-builders by the hundreds to build barracks and housing for his troops and their families, and to equip the soldiers with clothes and weaponry.

Perhaps equally important for the prosperity of the region was August Thaer, the pioneering landowner, who set up Germany's first agricultural college at his estate in Möglin near Wriezen, and was a scientific breeder of cattle. One of Brandenburg's better-known dishes, leg of lamb with broad beans, owes much to his improvements in sheep-farming. Another favorite dish is carp, which is served cooked or fried; it is reared in huge ponds at Peitz near

Sanssouci Palace.

Cottbus. Beer has been produced in Brandenburg since the 13th century; hops were grown around Berlin as early as 1291.

Against all the odds, for a long time people tried to grow wine in Brandenburg; the earliest vineyards seem to have been planted at Werder, south of Berlin, around the year 1400. People complained that it was as rough as swallowing a saw and sweetened it with honey, until the whole unhappy experiment came to an end in 1700, and Werder concentrated on growing fruit trees instead, with tremendous success.

After the electors of Brandenburg decided to establish their second residence at Potsdam in 1660, the reclamation and cultivation of land speeded up, and the growth of Berlin, building of railways and industrialization in the mid-19th century made Brandenburg a strong backbone of Prussia during its imperial quest.

Potsdam: Power and Might

Apart from the capital Potsdam, no other city offers outstanding architectural or historical importance in the entire region. But Potsdam alone with its interesting buildings and other cultural attractions make a visit worthwhile.

In fact, it is only after a visit to **Potsdam**, symbol of Prussia's will to power and mirror of its astonishing success, can one put Berlin, its progeny, into a historical framework. Founded in 993, the town remained of little importance before Frederick William I established it as his summer residence and garrison headquarters.

In 1713 it was a village of 1,500 souls living in 220 reed-roofed houses, while 25 years later it contained 8,000 people as well as 3,500 soldiers and officers. Expert craftsmen from Holland, France and Bohemia were working in their own quarters in different parts of the town. It was Frederick William's son, Frederick the Great, who with his successors endowed Potsdam with many beautiful and imposing buildings, Frederician under the architect G.W. von Knobelsdorff (1699–1753) and neo-Classical under Schinkel.

Heavy bombing in April 1945 destroyed much of the historic building mass, and later the GDR government had the famous Stadtschloß (royal-palace) razed, regarding it as a symbol of Prussian militarism. A hotel now stands on the site. In August 1945 Truman, Stalin and Churchill met here to sign the Potsdam Agreement on the future of post-war Germany.

The Baroque palace and gardens of **Sanssouci** (French for "without worry") are among the loveliest in Germany. The Schloß (1745–7) is not grand but great, a long one-storey Rococo building with a succession of richly decorated rooms, including a marble room, a concert room, the room where the French philosopher Voltaire used to stay, as

well as Frederick's study and bedroom. It stands on top of a series of broad south-facing terraces where Frederick planted vines with the aim of producing wine as good as French; the old vines look very decorative. After having been moved around several times during the last two centuries, Frederick's corpse was finally laid to rest only recently in the

The gardens of Schloß Sanssouci.

vault on the terrace he himself designed, between his favorite greyhounds according to his last wish.

The extensive gardens, designed by Lenné and completed by the amateur garden architect, Prince Pückler-Muskau – best-known as the inventor of a half-

frozen type of ice-cream – are sprinkled with various buildings. The orangery, originally a storehouse for tropical plants, contains a number of guest-rooms and copies of Italian masters. The biggest building is the Neues Palais (1763–69), its façade graced with 428

The Orangerie in Potsdam.

grimy gods and demigods, its 200 rooms designed for royal guests and including a grotto, a once fashionable piece of artificial rusticity. The Schloßtheater is among the most beautiful German Rococo theaters and is used for performances of opera and drama.

Modeled on a Roman villa, Schloß **Charlottenhof** (1826–29) is surrounded by a spacious terrace with a fountain. The Roman Baths, a neo-Classical and Romantic group of buildings, today serves as an exhibition center. The most charming building is the circular Chinese teahouse with life-sized gilded oriental figures on the outside and a splendidly displayed collection of European and Chinese porcelain inside. Potsdam itself is definitely worth a walking tour, too, with several rebuilt historical monuments grouped around the busy modern – but not ugly – pedestrian mall. At the start of the mall rises a smaller version of Berlin's Brandenburg Gate, while to the right you see a strange mosque-like building in two-tone brick, the pumping station for Sanssouci's fountains.

Follow the street along the banks of a Havel bay and arrive at the neo-Classical **square Nikolaikirche**, designed again by Schinkel, next to the former town hall (now an arts center). The film museum, which first served as an orangery and then as the royal studs, is a reminder that the Potsdam suburb of Babelsberg before the war was Germany's Hollywood, producing many great films, and later the GDR's main production center.

Head straight north, past the Peter-Pauls-Kirche inspired by Istanbul's Hagia Sophia and with a tower modeled after the campanile of S. Zeno in Verona, to enjoy the tiny **Holländisches Viertel** (Dutch quarter), an ensemble of Dutch-style brick houses built c.1740 for immigrants from Holland. Further north is the Russian quarter of Alexandrowka (1826), built for the descendants of the Russian singers Czar Alexander had sent as a present to Frederick the Great.

South of the city center stands the **Einstein Tower** (1920–24, by Erich Mendelsohn), an icon of modern architecture. The tower-like building, which rests on a long base, was built to verify Einstein's theory about a red shift of the solar spectrum. Einstein himself had a house in nearby Caputh, an artists' colony on the banks of the Tampliner See south of Potsdam.

With time to spare, do not miss the

Public transport in Frankfurt an der Oder.

Cecilienhof (1913–17), a residence built for Crown Prince (later Emperor) William II, a nephew of Queen Victoria (they did not get on very well). The house is mock-Tudor, of ample proportions, and has recently been converted into a luxury hotel. The room where the Potsdam Agreement was signed has been kept in its original state and can be visited.

South Brandenburg

Another popular excursion point for Berliners is the village of **Werder** situated on a peninsula, with half-timbered houses, a friendly café run by an artist, and a few fishermen. Every bit of ground is planted with fruit trees (cherry, apple, pear), and in late spring the annual tree blossom festival attracts thousands of visitors.

On the drive from Potsdam south to Jüterbog you come through rolling, wooded country, sparsely populated, the domain of charcoal burners and candle-makers, with vast blazing yellow fields of rape, the source of much honey. **Jüterbog** is only gradually waking up to the 20th century. Its strong medieval walls are almost completely intact. At the late Gothic church of St Nikolai, one of Luther's most intransigent opponents preached and sold indulgences; his strongbox is on view.

North of the town stands the mighty **Zinna** monastery with a 13th-century basilica and remarkable wall paintings

The Spree Forest.

of the 15th century, discovered in the abbot's chapel only in the 1950s. The stained-glass windows depict the founding fathers of the Cistercian order, Sts Benedict of Nursia and Bernard of Clairvaux.

East of Jüterbog, the town of **Lübbenau** lies in the heart of the region inhabited by Sorbs, and is the starting point for boat tours through the **Spree Forest**. The Sorbs, also called Wends, are a Slav group descended from the many tribes which lived in eastern Germany before the colonization of the 12th and 13th centuries. They were the only recognized ethnic minority in the former GDR, number about 100,000 members and have their own language, newspaper and pressure group.

Every five years they stage a huge festival when traditional dress is worn, old songs are played and dances performed. In this area town names are given in both German and Sorbian.

The river Spree here forms a network of some 300 canals, and many of the Sorbian villages and hamlets can only be reached by boat, the solid ground often being flooded in winter. At Lübbenau you can embark on a tour along the canals in traditional flat-bottomed boats, which are propelled not by rowing but – like in Cambridge and Venice – by punting.

The frontier town of **Frankfurt an der Oder** was much damaged by bombing and has a strange, slightly desolate beauty. It is the birthplace of the novelist and playwright Heinrich von Kleist, whose clear and simple style has a subdued power not unlike Kafka's. The Altstadt with its well-built modern blocks of flats is remarkable for its three imposing historical brick buildings: the handsome Rathaus with highly attractive Gothic gables; the grandiose ruins of the Marienkirche (begun after 1253), one of the largest hall churches in Brandenburg; and the former Franziskanerkirche, now a concert hall, with intricate net and star vaulting.

The charming neo-Classical Kleist museum is built on the banks of the Oder; beyond lies Poland. Crossing the border is easy for EC members, and Frankfurters tend to do their shopping in Slubice (a Frankfurt suburb before 1945), where everything is much cheaper.

On the road from Frankfurt to Berlin you pass the village of Buckow, where the writer and dramatist Bertolt Brecht (1898–1956) lived after the war, directing modern plays at his Berlin theater. The lake is haunted by a huge rooster said to appear in times of crisis.

North Brandenburg

North of Berlin lies the city of **Oranienburg** on the site of a castle built around the year 1200 to protect the colonization drive. The exact area is now occupied by a Schloß with a fine Porcelain Room and a landscaped garden planted for the Dutch Princess Louise

Henrietta of Nassau-Orange, first wife of Frederick William, the Great Elector. She was the most exalted member of that large, enterprising band of Dutch men and women who did so much to improve Brandenburg's agriculture and fortunes. In 1650 she ordered the building of a model farm with sheep-pens, a brewery and a dairy to give courage and instruction to the region devastated by the Thirty Years' War.

One of the most beautiful, quaint and well-preserved old towns of Brandenburg is **Wittstock**, called the "Rothenburg of the east", with a brick Gothic church, a 13th-century castle, picturesque rows of half-timbered houses and almost complete medieval fortifications with watch-towers and a city gate.

Narrow cobblestoned country lanes make for a bumpy ride eastward to the jewel-like **Schloß Rheinsberg**, where Frederick the Great wrote a book expounding the ideals of the pacifist and enlightened ruler which was published by Voltaire in 1740; the young author himself, however, later turned out to be anything but pacifist.

The Schloß, much enlarged in the 1730s, has several rooms with fine wall and ceiling paintings, a library, mirror hall and much original furniture. The enchanting grounds are laid out in formal French style and afford striking vistas of the Schloß and the surrounding lake. Among Berliners, it has a long-standing reputation as a trysting-place for lovers.

Saxony-Anhalt

169

This area in the southwest of the former GDR is a region full of contrasts; some aspects are very pleasant – like the dark wooded slopes of the eastern Harz mountains or the vineyard-covered banks of the rivers Saale and Unstrut – while others can be quite worrying, especially the environmental hazards caused by negligent handling of chemical waste. There are architectural jewels like the half-timbered town of Quedlinburg, and there are the ugly slag heaps around Halle and Bitterfeld. The wise traveler will adopt a selective vision.

Dutch-style houses at the harbor in Greetsiel.

While the Saxon part of this composite region was only created 130 years ago, the more southerly Anhalt has had a historical identity for several hundred years. The region was partly colonized under Charlemagne in the 9th century. Halle and Magdeburg became very prosperous as members of

Windmills and pedalos blend with the landscape.

the Hanseatic League (and built universities) in the 13th to 15th centuries; and under Frederick the Wise (r.1486–1525) the town of Wittenberg became a center of artistic activity, when Albrecht Dürer and Lucas Cranach were patronized by him, and of the Reformation, when he made both Martin Luther and Phillip Melanchthon professors at the university. In 1603 the House of Anhalt was split into several lines, thus slipping easily into a not very enlightened parochialism, and the ravages of the Thirty Years' War plunged the whole region into a long slumber. The Harz was a center of silver mining, Mansfeld the chief town of the copper mining area, an industry that began here in 1199 and was discontinued only in 1990. The rail-

road – with the first passenger service opened between Magdeburg and Leipzig in 1839-40 – was instrumental in bringing industry and its blessings to the whole region. The big chemical factories of Buna and Leuna were constructed at the turn of the century, while in the 1920s Dessau with the Bauhaus became for a short time a focus of modern German art and crafts.

Like neighboring Thuringia, Saxony-Anhalt's cuisine is known chiefly for its meats and spiced sausages and for its locally produced wine. In Salzwedel, beer has been produced since 1300, the best-known brand being *Taubentanz* (dance of the pigeons). The same town is credited with having invented a strange-looking kind of pastry

German cherry kirsch.

called *Baumkuchen*, now quite common in all parts of Germany. Among the few festivals still celebrated is the cherry festival of Naumburg on 26 June, commemorating the abortive siege of the city by Imperial troops in 1432.

Wising Up at Wittenberg

To tour Saxony-Anhalt, you could start at once-famous **Wittenberg**, now something of a cultural backwater. Of all the places associated with Luther and the Reformation, this was perhaps the most important in terms of political and intellectual support. It belonged to the domain of Frederick the Wise, whose patronage attracted many bright young scholars; the town at that time consisted of some 400 houses with about 2,500 inhabitants. Humanism, whether in scholarship or art, symbolized the new approach, a spiritual re-awakening to the glories of Greek antiquity and the Greek language, and it originated in Toscana, the area around Florence. Several of the Wittenberg professors had spent their student days in Italy, and the doctrine glorifying the individualist thinking together with the rediscovered original, authentic teachings of the Church Fathers had a strong impact on Luther's concepts of making the Bible accessible to everybody. He believed it was the Word, the text as written, from which the believers should draw their faith, and not through the interpreta-

Wittenberg Castle Church.

tions and explanations of intermediaries like priests, bishops or popes. His close friend Phillip Melanchthon (who adopted a Greek form for his German name Schwarzerdt, "black earth") became professor of Greek at Wittenberg at age 21. At that time, Luther himself was still a highly respected member of the established Catholic Church, prior of some ten monasteries, professor of theology and official city preacher. It was only after he fastened his 95 "theses" to the door of All Saints Church on 31 October 1517, criticizing some prin-

enlarged later, only two late Gothic winding staircases and the solid corner towers remain of the original building. The adjacent **Schloßkirche** contains realistic sculptures of Frederick the Wise and John the Constant as well as the plain tombs and statues of Luther and Melanchthon. The church where Luther used to preach, the **Marienkirche**, has impressive 15th-century portals opening to the aisles, and a bronze font with reliefs by Hermann Vischer the Elder (1457). Its greatest glory is Cranach's painting of the crucified Christ together with Luther and Frederick the Wise (1547).

The much-renovated **Lutherhaus**, where the Reformer lived from 1524 onwards, is now a museum and includes Luther's study and the pulpit from the Marienkirche. The nearby Lutherhalle houses the world's largest museum devoted entirely to the Reformation; there are several fine Cranachs as well as a great many documents and graphics giving a vivid picture of the revolutionary upheaval that started in this small town. The market square with its fountain of 1617 is surrounded by graceful Renaissance burghers' houses. The most splendid one is the impressive **Cranach-Haus** with adjoining courtyards, bought by Lucas Cranach the Elder in 1514 and at that time containing 84 rooms and 16 kitchens. It was here that Cranach together with his sons set up his highly successful painting workshop, employing some 30 assistants. In 1520 he joined the apoth-

ciples of the church in general and the practice of indulgences in particular, that the Reformation and the establishment of Protestantism started.

In honor of this famous event, the town today calls itself "Lutherstadt Wittenberg". Among its attractions is the impressive **Schloß** built for Frederick the Wise between 1490 and 1525; much

ecaries' guild and opened a pharmacy which is still in business today.

Decorative Dessau

For almost 400 years, from 1474 to 1863, **Dessau** was the residence of the dukes of Anhalt-Dessau and a pearl of neo-Classical architecture. Wartime bombing destroyed 95 percent of the town center, but some of the historic buildings have been reconstructed and present a charming ensemble surrounded by a sea of undistinguished modern houses. The Baroque **Schloß Georgium**, enveloped by beautiful formal gardens, houses an impressive art collection of German, Flemish and French masters. The **Bauhaus**, that revolutionary center of art and design, moved from Weimar to Dessau in 1925, and the building itself as well as several villas for the professors and instructors and the **Bauhaussiedlung** in Dessau-Törten can be visited. The permanent exhibition in the main building displays objects, drawings and photographs and shows clearly how the architects and designers responded to the mechanized needs of the 20th-century office, factory and home.

Two graceful palaces lie close to Dessau. At the Rococo **Schloß Mosigkau**, the collection of Dutch paintings is hung in the 18th-century manner, the canvases close together and the smaller ones at the bottom, the big ones quite high up. The spacious park includes a Baroque garden (1750), a maze,

two orangeries and a Japanese garden with a teahouse, an enchanting piece of Japonoiserie.

East of Dessau, **Schloß Wörlitz** (1769–73) stands in beautiful grounds; the palace, modeled on the neo-Palladian Claremont mansion in Surrey and designed by F.W. von Erdmannsdorf (1736–1800), was the first

Worlitz Park, the first continental "English garden".

neo-Classical building erected in Germany. A showpiece of the former GDR government, it is in immaculate condition and contains important sculptures and paintings of the 16th and 17th centuries. The park, laid out in 1765, was the first of many "English gardens" on the continent, marking the break with the formal French style in favor of a more natural – although still totally artificial – design. Besides a lake which offers rides in a gondola, there are many bridges, statues and grottoes and several fanciful examples of garden architecture, including a Gothic house and temples to Flora and Venus. The whole project was designed as the summer residence of Duke Leopold Friedrich Franz von Anhalt-Dessau. He was an interesting and likable character and a philanthropist who lowered taxes and in 1773 opened his grounds to the public because he regarded them as a "pedagogic institution to enlighten and instruct".

The city of **Halle**, south of Wörlitz, lies right in the middle of the industrial heartland of the former GDR; about half of the GDR's chemical output was produced around the city, with few environmental safeguards. The most pleasant area is the partly reconstructed quarter around the Pauluskirche, where some cheerful cafés and *gemütliche* restaurants can be found among the stately mid-19th-century villas. The city's original source of wealth was salt, one of the most precious commodities of the Middle Ages, which was extracted from Halle's rich mineral springs. For more than two hundred years it was a member of the Hanseatic League, and in the 18th century its university became a bastion of the German Enlightenment, while at the same time French Protestant refugees did much to revitalize its trade. Halle's Protestantism was of the Quietist variety, peaceful, contemplative and often involved in charitable work. A.H. Francke (1663–1727), Germany's best-known Quietist, taught theology at Halle University and established a foundation which included an orphanage, school for the poor, pharmacy and printing and publishing house; the foundation was highly influential on account of its educational philosophy which insisted that enthusiasm, joy and play should be an indispensable part in the upbringing of children.

The city is heavily industrialized and for the most part rather ugly. Its sights include the **Rote Turm** (red tower, 15th century), the late Gothic **cathedral** and on the old market square a fountain of a boy and a donkey, Halle's historic symbol. The composer G.F. Händel was born here in 1685 and for a while served as cathedral organist; his family home is now a museum with a large collection of musical instruments. In the area around the **Pauluskirche** with its well-preserved 19th-century town houses you will find several lively coffee houses, some with a literary flavor, others hung with modern paintings and playing jazz music.

Between 1775 and 1810, **Bad Lauchstädt**, southwest of Halle, was a fashionable spa and counted much nobility as well as Schiller and Goethe among its guests. Goethe himself decided to built his own theater here (1802), for performances which were meant to put the audience into a state of serene contemplation, something he obviously thought other theaters did not provide. The charming neo-Classical building where he himself directed, has been beautifully renovated and is again being used for performances of Goethe plays and Mozart operas.

The town of **Merseburg**, halfway between the huge chemical works of Buna and Leuna, has suffered much from wartime bombing and industrial pollution. It is chiefly known for its place in the annals of German literature: two magic spells of the 8th century kept in the cathedral library, the one to cure horses from leg injuries, the other to untie shackles, are rare documents of a pre-Christian, Germanic culture. The cathedral high above the river Saale, is partly Romanesque, its richly furnished interior including several old tomb slabs and the sumptuous sarcophagus of a 15th-century bishop.

Passion, full of realistic details of medieval life, while the west choir is graced by twelve figures of benefactors, the Naumburg Rider – the idealized image of a medieval knight – and Queen Uta with her beatific smile. Both these stunning ensembles were executed by the same anonymous Naumburg masters who also worked at Hildesheim and Mainz and in France. Note also three brilliantly painted 13th-century windows.

The much-restored late 13th-century **Wenzelskirche** has a finely crafted bronze font of 1441, two paintings by Cranach and a grand organ (1746), which after its installation was tested by J.S. Bach and found satisfactory. From the bell tower (202 steps) you have a splendid view straight into narrow backyards of fruit trees and kitchen gardens. The **Marktplatz** is graced by a handsome gabled late Gothic town hall (1528) with a monumental spiral staircase, and nicely restored 16th-century patrician houses. In January, a famous pigeon market is held here.

Naumburg Nobility

Beautifully situated at the confluence of the Unstrut and Saale, the silhouette of the old town of **Naumburg** is defined not by factory chimneys but by church spires, reminders that it was a bishopric from 1028 to 1564 and an important medieval trading center. The cathedral of **Sts Peter and Paul** (begun 1210, southwest tower completed in 1884) with its four noble towers houses some world-famous works of sculpture. The west rood screen has vivid reliefs of Christ's

Among the foothills of the Harz mountains, right in the Bode Valley where witches used to dance around the sheer cliffs, lies quaint **Quedlinburg**. With its more than 1,600 half-timbered houses lining narrow streets and crooked alleys, it is an architectural gem; many of the façades are inventively decorated with carved figural and abstract ornaments. In 1962, some 300 houses were included in the UNESCO list of World Heritage treasures and put under conservation order. To walk down the winding lanes is a picture-book experience, especially as the town is much less commercialized than comparable places in western Germany like Goslar and Rothenburg.

Towering above the town is the hilltop Renaissance castle first built by the Saxon duke and first German king, Henry I (875–936), as a defence against attacks by invaders from Hungary. Next to the castle courtyard is a small medieval garden, a charming reconstruction of horticultural history complete with herbal and medicinal plants and ornamental flowers like lilies and acanthus. The adjacent Romanesque church contains reliquaries of Henry I and Otto the Great (10th century) as well as the tombs of the royal couple Henry and Mathilda in the crypt beneath the Gothic choir. Henry was a driving force in the conquest and colonizing of the eastern lands; his campaigns took him as far as Bohemia, Schleswig and what is now Poland. His wife founded a religious institution for ladies of rank, and its abbesses and prioresses, mostly of noble rank, frequently became a real power in the land. Their morals may have slipped a bit over the centuries: Abbess Anna Amalia, sister of Frederick the Great,

was the lover of the flamboyant, notorious guardsman von Trenck; while the prioress Aurora von Königsmarck, mother of a famous general, was a mistress of the King of Saxony, August the Strong. Near the old castle is a museum devoted to the poet F.G. Klopstock, born here in 1724, whose father was secretary to the current abbess; Klopstock wrote the epic *Der Messias*, whose dynamic thrust broke the ground for a great creative period of German poetry.

Nearby **Wernigerode** is another very pretty town with enchanting *Fachwerk* houses and a quaint gabled town hall (16th/17th century); its beams full of intricate ornamental carving. The massive hilltop Schloß (1881) includes among its 250 rooms a historical museum with displays of early textiles, weapons, instruments of torture, furniture and numerous objects and documents pertaining to peasants' wars and witch trials. In the Bürde, a rich agricultural region continuing westward as far as Braunschweig, lies the large industrial town of **Magdeburg**, again a place whose past is more interesting than its present. Already in the time of Charlemagne it was a busy trading center, and in 937 Otto I founded the monastery of **St Mauritius**, for several centuries an intellectual and artistic focal point in eastern Germany. During the Reformation, the town became an early and zealous promoter of the Protestant cause, and the residing archbishop in due haste moved his seat to Halle. Protestant refugees from France and the Palatinate ontributed much to its cultural and commercial prominence. In January 945, bombing destroyed about 80 percent of the town center, most of which has been gracelessly rebuilt.

Among the few survivors is the cathedral, Germany's oldest Gothic church 1209). There is a delicate 13th-century group of the Wise and Foolish Virgins as well as the tomb of Otto I and statues of his great German emperor and his wife Editha. The intimate cloister, which has also remained unscathed, has splendid examples of medieval sculpture, sometimes playful, sometimes solemn and didactic. The fine Romanesque church of **Unser Lieben Frauen** is today used for concerts and other cultural activities. At St Magdalen's chapel the beautifully proportioned tracery windows bear witness to the superb craftsmanship of Magdeburg's Gothic stonemasons.

The **Alter Markt** and the Baroque **Rathaus** have been neatly restored; the large equestrian statue in front of the town hall is a copy of the famous Magdeburg Rider of 1240. To enjoy a glass of wine and a snack in medieval surroundings, there is the cellar tavern **Buttergasse** housed in a late Romanesque hall inside the Rathaus; because the hall was filled with rubble during the Thirty Years' War, it has survived the last 350 years almost intact. The **Kulturhistorisches Museum** (museum of cultural history) contains not only the original Rider but also medieval sculpture, models and objects pertain-

ing to the history of technology (a steam locomotive of 1862) as well as much painting and sculpture of the 19th and 20th centuries, including works by Barlach and Rodin.

The small, dreamy town of **Stendal** north of Magdeburg, fortified with a city wall in about 1300, once enjoyed great prosperity through the weaving and trading of cloth, and belonged to the Hanseatic League (1359–1518). Some monuments from its great past remain. The richly decorated **Rathaus** was built c.1480, and in front of it stands a 16th-century **Roland column**, symbol of municipal independence; the present statue is a copy made after the original was blown down by a hurricane in 1972. The **Marienkirche** has much interesting statuary and an astronomical clock of the late 16th century. South of the old town, the **Nikolaidom** is worth a visit for its portal (c.1390) crowded with beautifully carved Biblical figures and scenes, ornate stepped gable and luminous 15th-century stained-glass windows.

The town's famous native son was **J.J. Winckelmann** (1717–68), an art historian and pioneer of scientific archaeology, whose championship of the genius of Greek culture and art guided the growth of neo-Classicism; his family house has been turned into a small museum. Winckelmann was highly esteemed by Goethe and many others, and the French novelist Henri Beyle (1782–1842), author of *The Charterhouse of Parma*, out of admiration took the pseudonym "Stendhal".

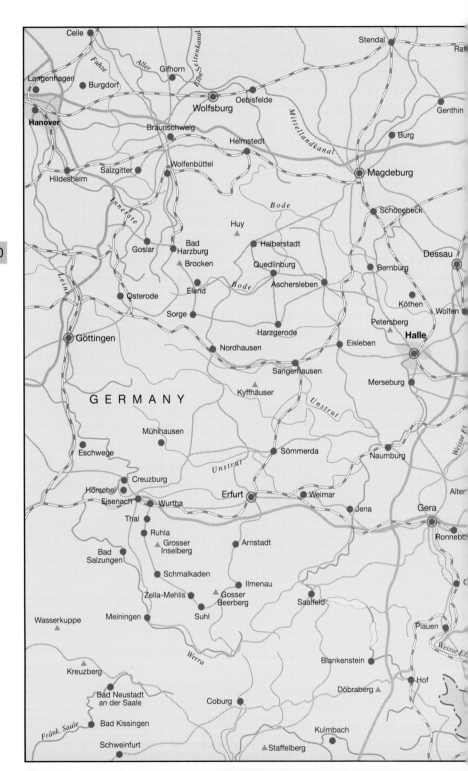

Celle

Langenhagen
Burgdorf

Hanover

Fuhse

Aller

Gifhorn

Elbe-Seitenkanal

Wolfsburg
Oebisfelde

Braunschweig

Helmstedt

Salzgitter
Wolfenbüttel

Hildesheim

Mittellandkanal

Stendal

Ra

Genthin

Burg

Magdeburg

Innerste

Bode

Huy

Goslar
Bad
Harzburg
Halberstadt

Brocken
Quedlinburg

Schönebeck

Dessau

Bernburg

Leine

Elend
Bode
Aschersleben

Osterode

Sorge

Göttingen

GERMANY

Harzgerode

Nordhausen

Köthen
Wolfen

Petersberg
Halle

Eisleben

Kyffhäuser

Sangerhausen

Unstrut

Merseburg

Weisse El

Mühlhausen

Eschwege

Unstrut

Sömmerda

Naumburg

Alter

Creuzburg

Hörschel
Eisenach
Wurtha

Thal

Erfurt

Weimar

Jena

Gera

Ronnebi

Ruhla
Grosser
Inselberg

Arnstadt

Bad
Salzungen

Schmalkaden

Ilmenau

Zella-Mehlis
Gosser
Beerberg

Saalfeld

Wasserkuppe

Meiningen

Suhl

Plauen

Werra

Weisse El

Kreuzberg

Bad Neustadt
an der Saale

Coburg

Blankenstein

Döbraberg

Hof

Fränk. Saale
Bad Kissingen

Schweinfurt

Kulmbach

Staffelberg

Central Eastern Germany

Henningsdorf
Werneuchen
Kostrzyn (Küstrin)
Falkensee
Havel
Berlin
Potsdam
ourg
Frankfurt
Slubice
Rzepin
(Reppen)
Fürstenwalde
Oder-Spree-Kanal
Ludwigsfelde
Königs
Wusterhausen
Spree
Oder
Eisenhüttenstadt
Luckenwalde
Treuenbrietzen
Guben
Wittenberg
Neisse
P O L A N D
Schwarze Elster
Lübbenau
Cottbus
Forst
Herzberg
Finsterwalde
Sorau
Elbe
Torgau
Lauchhammer
Senftenberg
Bad
Muskau
Hoyerswerda
Spree
Riesa
Grossenhain
Oschatz
Grosse Röder
Beissenbg.
Zgórzelec
Zwickauer Mulde
Meissen
Radebeul
Bautzen
Döbeln
Dresden
Zschopau
Freital
Pirna
Zittau
Freiberg
Chemnitz
Liberec
(Reichenberg)
Jablonec
(Gablonz)
au
Aue
Annaberg-
Buchholz
C Z E C H
R E P U B L I C
Teplitz
(Teplice)
Fichtelberg
Most
(Brüx)
Terezin
(Theresienstadt)
Mladá Boleslav
(Jungbunzlau)
Keilberg
Chomutov
(Komotau)
Elbe
Labe
Iser (Jizera)
Karlovy
Vary
Eger (Ohře)
Moldau (Vltava)
Praha
(Prague)
Kladno
Rakovnik
N

0   Kilometers   40

The region in the southeast of the former GDR bordering on Poland and the Czech Republic, for centuries was one of the cultural and commercial powerhouses of Germany. Even under the Socialist regime, writers and artists in Leipzig and Dresden retained some of the old witty, pugnacious, slightly surreal spirit which now after reunification seems bound to play an increasingly important role in the country's cultural life. The region is varied in its beauty and attractions; there are splendid Baroque and neo-Classical buildings, great art collections, wide expanses of fields and forests and – once you have crossed the heavily industrialized belt running from Plauen to Chemnitz – the southern part with the dark woods and snow-covered peaks of the Erzgebirge and the craggy, picturesque sandstone outcrops of

The King's Tower and Crown in the Zwinger.

Leipzig & Saxony

the Elbsandsteingebirge. The Saxons are a quick-witted, gregarious, self-confident and crafty people who like to take things easy most of the time; occasionally, however, they get into a fighting mood, and in recent history stood in the forefront of the demonstrations which led to the demise of the Communist government. Saxon women have great charm and vivacity, and pretty girls are so plentiful they are said to grow on trees.

From early days Saxony profited from its position along the major east-west trade routes. It acquired strategic importance after Henry the Lion built a castle at Meißen in 929 during his campaign against the Slav Sorbs, and its political identity was forged under the long reign of the royal house of Wettin which ruled from 1089 until 1918. In the 12th century, silver mining started at Freiberg (near Chemnitz) which before 1618 was the most important town in Saxony. Around 1500, Emperor Maximilian I granted wide-ranging trade privileges to Leipzig, whose trade fairs from that day to this have had great commercial impact. After the Thirty Years' War, which brought little loss and some territorial gain, Saxony's fortunes were given a boost under Augustus the Strong (r. 1694–1733), who endowed Dresden with its greatest Baroque buildings and attracted a host of artists, musicians and craftsmen to his residence. In the early 18th century, Leipzig became the major publishing and printing center of the German-speaking world. Industrialization started

in the early 19th century and greedily fed on the rich natural resources of the region, with Chemnitz becoming the "Manchester of Saxony"; at the same time, a strong trade union movement gained Saxony a reputation for being "red". In 1918 the last Wettin king abdicated, muttering: "Now you try clearing up the mess." Then the Nazis first won the elections and later lost the war. In 1945 the territory was occupied by the Red Army and so eventually became part of the GDR. The Leipzig "Monday demonstrations" in autumn 1989 became a symbol for all of eastern Germany of the waning power of the Socialist regime, giving encouragement and inspiration to the surge for liberty and reunification.

Time Out at Dresden

A sensible way to explore Saxony is to make **Dresden** one's base from which to make trips to Leipzig, Meißen and other places. The regional capital, Dresden used to be known as the "Florence on the Elbe" because of its magnificent architecture and cosmopolitan atmosphere. Sadly, it has never really recovered from the ferocious British fire-bombing on the night of 13/14 February 1945. However, most of its art treasures were stored in remote sites during the war and thus survived, and some of its most beautiful buildings have meanwhile been reconstructed; renovation work is continuing at great speed. The lively city center gets

Dresden the state capital of Saxony, across the Elbe River.

even more attractive after dark, with throngs of people promenading along the elegant boulevard for some window-shopping or an ice-cream or snack at a sidewalk café, and pavement artists perform music or entertain with a variety show. Together with the mild weather, Dresden's atmosphere has a definite southern charm.

It was already an important town by the 13th century, and in the 15th century became the residence of the Saxon princes (later kings). Within one generation, the German Elector and King of Poland, Frederick Augustus I, filled it with some of the most marvelous Baroque buildings in Germany, relying mainly on architect M.D. Pöppelmann (1662–1736). Some of the buildings he

had erected to please his countless mistresses – not for nothing is he called Augustus the Strong and is said to have had 365 children, almost all illegitimate. Building upon the old royal cabinet of curiosities, Augustus eventually put together one of the greatest collections of paintings and works of art in Europe. Today these treasures are housed in various museums and palaces in and near Dresden.

A good start for a tour of the city center is the **Prager Straße**, a broad boulevard lined with fashionable shops, restaurants, hotels and coffee houses and graced with fountains and trees (saplings as yet). At the **Altmarkt** the Baroque **Kreuzkirche**, internationally famous for its boys' choir, stands next to

The Zwinger is a treasure house of Renaissance art.

the rebuilt new town hall (1906–12) with a viewing platform of 260 feet (80 meters) and the neo-Classical Gewandhaus (cloth hall).

Beyond the trolley tracks you find Dresden's most famous building, the **Zwinger** (keep), built in 1711–28 by Pöppelmann. It consists of seven linked buildings around a wide courtyard; the staircases and parapets are adorned by a great many putti and allegorical sculptures. Tucked into a corner, there is an elegant recessed nymphaeum with a small pool watched over by several el-

Sculpture detail from the Zwinger.

egant nude figures. The gilded roofs of the gate towers and grand exhibition rooms look splendidly sumptuous. Besides museums of science and zoology, the great collection of Old Masters has recently been rehoused in the Zwinger, its original home. There you find Raphael's "Sistine Madonna", portraits and self-portraits by Rembrandt and superb works by German painters (Dürer, Holbein the Younger, Cranach) as well as by Dutch and Flemish artists (Rubens, Hals, Van Dyck), Italians (Titian, Giorgione, Veronese) and masters from the 17th and 18th centuries (Poussin, Lorrain, Watteau, La Tour). The Venetian painter Canaletto is especially well represented, partly because Augustus commissioned him to produce a painting a month over several years. The famous porcelain collection, one of the largest in the world, which includes not only superb pieces from Meißen but also an astounding array of Chinese and Japanese porcelains, after many years can once again be found in its original setting, the Grünes Gewölbe (green vault).

Dresden city panorama with the Semper Opera House.

Most of Dresden's historic buildings stand close together near the sluggish Elbe, and from the Zwinger it is just a few steps to the **Theaterplatz** with the well-restored Italiante **Semper-Oper**, the opera house built after designs by G. Semper (1871–78) to replace the previous opera house where Wagner had been chief conductor and where several operas by Wagner and Richard Strauß had their world première. Across the square, the huge Catholic **Hofkirche** (court church) has a fine Silbermann organ and on its parapet 78 statues of saints. Nearby lies the vast palace of the Saxon rulers, an accumulation of buildings erected between 1530 and 1701, much of it still in ruins after the last war. At the back of the Schloß, the **Langer Gang** (long passage), built in 1586, consists of an elegant white pillared arcade and a forecourt used for jousting, with the original markers still in place; the outside façade shows a huge ceramic frieze of the Saxon rulers (1874–1908).

The Arty Albertinum

Passing the Academy of Arts with its ribbed dome and statue of Nike, the goddess of victory, you come to the squat **Albertinum**, a museum with two excellent collections. The Modern Masters supplies a grand overview of 19th/20th century German artists (Friedrich, Spitzweg, Menzel, Böcklin, Liebermann, Corinth, Nolde, Kollwitz, Dix), French

The Elbe River from Die Bastei near Bad Schandau.

Impressionists and Post-Impressionists (Manet, Monet, Renoir, Degas, Toulouse-Lautrec) and contemporary eastern German painters, including Werner Tübke. The other collection comes from the royal treasury: roomfuls of precious objects, some beautiful and many outrageous, crafted in silver and gold, ivory and glass; pride of place goes to the toy-like "Court of Delhi on the Birthday of the Great Mogul Aureng-zeb", a tour de force produced by the Brothers Dinglinger in 1708 of 137 gilded and enameled figurines studded with 3,000 diamonds, rubies, emeralds and pearls.

In front of the museum stand the evocative ruins of the **Frauenkirche**, an empty shell rising from weed-covered rubble, while in its back a broad promenade runs along the bank of the Elbe affording fine views of the tame river, steam ferries, sweet meadows and the northern suburbs. This is the long **Brühlsche Terrasse**, a fashionable meeting place in earlier days. It derives its name from Count von Brühl, prime minister to Augustus the Strong. His wardrobe included 1,500 wigs, prompting Frederick the Great to quip: "Too many wigs for an empty head."

Cross the river on the Augustusbrücke and take a look at the impressive copper-gilt equestrian statue of Augustus the Strong (1736). The nearby Baroque **Japanisches Palais** (Japanese palace) with a prehistoric and ethnographic museum, began life in 1715 as a "Dutch palace" and only received its present incarnation 20 years later – so swiftly did the fashion for "exotics" change. A pleasant way of reaching the natural and man-made beauties in the vicinity of Dresden is to take the ferry maintained by the Weiße Flotte (white flotilla) company. Boats dock at the Brühlsche Terrasse and go upriver via Pillnitz (beautiful palace) and Bad Schandau (great scenery) to the Czech border, and downriver stop at Meißen (porcelain factory).

Southeast of Dresden lies the delightful **Schloß Pillnitz**, built over a period of a hundred years. The earliest buildings are the Wasserpalais and Bergpalais (water and mountain pal-

aces) by the court architect Pöppelmann (1720–23), airy constructions with pillared porticos and arcades. The splendidly varied park, laid out in 1778–80, contains smaller Dutch, Chinese and English gardens, an orangery, a mall – to play "pall mall", an early version of croquet – and a famous 30-foot-high (9-meter) Japanese camelia, planted some 250 years ago and said to be the oldest example of this species of tree in Europe.

The small resort of **Bad Schandau**, popular with serious hikers, lies in the heart of the **Elbsandsteingebirge**, where the tranquil Elbe has cut deeply through soft sandstone. Before the last war, this beautiful region with dramatic scenery known as "the Switzerland of Saxony", was Germany's second most popular tourist destination, after the Rhine Valley. The spa makes a good base for exploring the densely wooded hills and hamlets and to go on paddleboat cruises on the Elbe. There are several fine half-timbered houses and an interesting Heimatmuseum documenting the river traffic through the ages. A breathtaking view along the winding Elbe Valley can be had from the summit of the highly romantic **Bastei**

A porcelain goat outside the factory in Meißen where most of the porcelain is made.

pinnacle (1,010 feet [310 meters]).

Nearby lies the fascinating **Königstein**, once the country's mightiest fortress, on a table mountain towering more than 820 feet (250 meters) above the river. It was built for the kings of Bohemia c.1200 and in 1591 became Saxony's state prison. Many whom posterity has judged less harshly were imprisoned here, including the Russian anarchist Mikhail Bakunin (1849-50), the socialist August Bebel (1874), the caricaturist Th. Th. Heine (1899) and the dramatist Frank Wedekind (1899-1900). J.F. Böttger, too, spent an uncomfortable year here (1706-7), vainly trying to produce gold from inferior substances on order by Augustus the Strong. To everybody's surprise and much to his relief, he succeeded in creating the first true porcelain in Europe the following year.

The castle occupies a magnificent site, and with its many interesting and well-preserved buildings and fortifications is a castle-buff's dream come true. There are 15th-century cannons and hidden staircases, a 500-foot-deep (153-meter) well, gloomy cellars and dungeons and the casemates where Dresden art treasures were stored during the war.

Meißen Porcelain

Since 1710 Germany's most famous porcelain has come from **Meißen**, north-

A potter at work in Meißen.

west of Dresden. Because Henry the Lion built a castle here in 929, the town is regarded as the "cradle of Saxony". It stopped rocking many centuries ago, and although not damaged during the war, the Altstadt with its many half-timbered houses, of which only those around the market square have been restored, is in a sorry state. The **Marktplatz**, however, presents a lovely sight: the **Rathaus** with transom gables and steep gable roof (1472); several handsome Renaissance mansions; and the **Frauenkirche** (1460), a hall church with three naves, a fine late Gothic altarpiece and in the tower a set of porcelain bells of 1929, the earliest porcelain carillon ever made. Next to it stands the picturesque, vine-covered

tavern Vincenz Richter (1520), formerly the clothiers' guildhall. Dominating the town are two grand hilltop buildings. The twin-towered **cathedral** (begun 1270) has monuments to early Saxon rulers, an altarpiece by Cranach and magnificent 13th-century statues and a rood screen by the Naumburg masters. The **Albrechtsburg** was long a seat of the Saxon princes and is full of their souvenirs. The distinctive feature of the west façade is the spiral staircase cut from one solid stone block. The late Gothic castle, much rebuilt in the 17th century, from 1710 to 1864 housed the Meißen porcelain factory.

The modern factory in the northern outskirts, still produces Germany's most prestigious porcelain, the best-known motif being the blue-and-white *Zwiebelmuster* (onion pattern) based on a Chinese pattern of pomegranates and peaches. The factory's distinctive mark, showing crossed swords, was first used in 1723. There is a guided tour to watch craftsmen demonstrating the time-honored manufacturing processes, a museum and a shop with a splendid selection of china tableware of traditional form and design as well as delicate copies of figurines by the most famous Meißen porcelain sculptors, J.G. Höroldt (1696-1775) and J.J. Kändler (1706-75); the smaller pieces make lovely souvenirs, much appreciated by the connoisseur. Meißen is the center of Saxony's wine-producing area in the Elbe Valley; the region covers about 750 acres of good, mainly white wines. Bishop

Burghers' houses along Katharinenstraße in Leipzig.

Benno is traditionally credited with introducing the first vines here c.1060. Records go back to 1460; in the 1880s the vineyards were completely destroyed by the ferocious insect phylloxera – which wrought havoc all over Europe – and replanting only began early this century under the guidance of an experienced grower from Oppenheim in Rhinehesse.

East of Meißen, the ocher-colored

Schloß Moritzburg, surrounded by a lake with swans, was built as a hunting lodge for the Saxon princes in the 16th century and later much enlarged. Several rooms are hung with family portraits; reading the name-tags, one realizes the intricate and wide-spun network connecting the aristocratic houses of Europe. Other rooms are decorated with hunting trophies, stags' antlers preserved and displayed with the same loving care as the family portraits. The park includes a tiny Rococo pheasantry, now an ornithological museum, with a pool nearby complete with miniature harbor and lighthouse.

The old industrial city of **Chemnitz**, called Karl-Marx-Stadt from 1953 to 1990, contains few sights after wartime bombing of the city center. The **Schloßkirche St Maria** has a majestic, beautifully decorated north portal (1505–25), recently moved to the interior to stop further deterioration. Among the noteworthy buildings in the city center are the Rote Turm (12/15th century), formerly the municipal prison, and the **Neues Rathaus**, its interior a rare example of pure Jugendstil (1907–11). Katarina Witt, the beautiful Olympic ice-skater, was born in Chemnitz.

The **Erzgebirge** (ore mountains) with its silver and copper deposits was once a major source of Saxony's prosperity. Today it is a hiker's paradise, a popular skiing region and the supplier of the distinctive wooden figurines which form part of the traditional German Christmas decoration. The main resort is the twin town of **Annaberg-Buchholz**, founded at the height of the "silverrush" in the 15th century. When those deposits were exhausted, mining went on, first for cobalt and then until very recently for uranium.

Today the town's main cottage industries are lace-making and the production of wooden toys and decorative trimmings. The **St Annenkirche** (1499–1525), the largest church hall in Saxony,

has an interesting altarpiece showing miners working the local silver mines. In winter, the whole area becomes a skiing resort. **Oberwiesenthal** has a large number of ski runs, lifts and a toboggan run as well as a cable car to the **Fichtelberg**. The latter, at almost 4,000 feet (1214 meters), offers a great panoramic view.

The old town hall in Leipzig.

Leipzig: Fair City

Saxony's largest city, **Leipzig**, famous for its trade fairs and connections with Bach and Goethe, is architecturally much less spectacular than Dresden, but outpaces its old rival in intellectual and artistic affairs. By the 13th century it was already an important trading center at the crossroads of transcontinental highways and around the year 1500 was granted extensive privileges for its fairs. From the end of the 18th century until the partition of the country, it was Germany's prime publishing and printing city; now Frankfurt and Munich have taken its place. In the 19th century engineering and chemical industries supplanted the old trading emphasis. It was heavily bombed during the war, and rebuilding has been mainly modern. The city suffers from some pollution but it does have some charming features and the center retains a surprisingly cosmopolitan touch.

The broad Markt lies on the north side of the Altstadt with the gabled Alte Waage (old weigh-house; 1555). The Saxons have long been known as a nation of coffee-drinkers, and Leipzig is their mecca. There is no more appropriate a place, to have a cup and try the equally delicious pastry than the nearby **Kaffeebaum** (coffee tree), Saxony's oldest coffeehouse in a building of c.1500, with Goethe, Schumann, Lessing and Liszt for spiritual companions.

Close by is the charming **Naschmarkt** (*naschen* means to nibble, implying a sweet tooth) with a statue of the young Goethe, who studied law here (1765–68) and bestowed the epithet "Little Paris" upon the city, set in front of the Baroque Alte Börse (old bourse). Down a covered arcade, the Mädlerpassage, one of the city's characteristic galleries, you come to the historic restaurant **Auerbachs Keller**, where Goethe set a diabolical scene from *Faust* and which is enlivened by big carved figures of Faust and Mephistopheles on a mermaid. East of the Naschmarkt is the **Nikolaikirche**

(begun in the 12th century) with a spacious white neo-Classical interior, pillared and galleried. The clandestine "Monday meetings" started here in 1982 and culminated in the "Monday demonstrations" of 1989, so embarrassing to the Communist rulers of the GDR. West of the Naschmarkt lies the 15th-century Gothic **Thomaskirche**, fronting a quiet, intimate square. Its most famous organist and choirmaster was J.S. Bach, whose *St Matthew Passion* was first performed here in 1729. The Thomaner Choir still enjoys a worldwide reputation, and motet recitals are held here each weekend.

The eastern part of the city center is taken up by the rebuilt opera house, the **Neues Gewandhaus**, with its acclaimed orchestra whose greatest conductor was probably the composer Felix Mendelssohn-Bartholdy (1809–47). Next to it are the modern university buildings (fine view from the café near the top). North of the Altstadt you find the Baroque **Gohliser Schlößchen**, once a literary center and now housing the world's largest archive on Bach and his times; in summer, concerts are performed here. A few steps further down stands the old farmhouse of c.1700 where Schiller in summer 1785 wrote part of *Don Carlos* and a first version of the *Ode of Joy*. Huge and ponderous, the Völkers-schlachtdenkmal (memorial to the battle of nations) north of the city commemorates the victory of the allied forces of Prussia, Russia and others against the French under Napoleon in 1813.

J. F. Böttger, father of German porcelain.

Thuringia, the "green heart of Germany", offers the visitor a wonderful mix of superb cultural and historical monuments, and landscapes from the serene to the dramatic with an extensive mountain range that looks like a petrified, wooded sea which provides excellent hiking and skiing opportunities. J.W. Goethe and J.C. Schiller, Martin Luther, Lucas Cranach and J.S. Bach are just the most famous contributors to the region's great past.

The *area* originally was part of the dukedom of Saxony, which in the Middle Ages covered a huge area between Bavaria, Brandenburg and Bohemia. The House of Wettin, the Saxon royal family, had a strange fascination for miniaturization, or so it seems: whereas other principalities tried to acquire new territories by means fair or foul, the Wettins constantly partitioned and subdivided their lands whenever an old count died or a young girl married her uncle. On historical maps Thuringia provides

J. S. Bach, pride and son of Thuringia.

Thuringia

199

the most colorful patchwork of tiny principalities of any German region. Even in 1918, shortly before Germany became a republic and all crowned heads were stripped of their titles and privileges, it still consisted of eight nominally sovereign states.

The rulers of these small entities, too weak and poor to engage in military or political affairs, usually turned their weakness to good account in so far as they concentrated on making their life as agreeable as possible by collecting works of art, patronizing musicians and writers and setting up theaters for the pleasure and amusement of their noble friends and favored commoners. Prime example of this kind of provincial patronage was Anna Amalia (1739–1807), Duchess of Saxe-Weimar and friend of literary luminaries like Goethe, Herder, Wieland and Charlotte von Stein.

When Time Stood Still

Little seems to have changed in Thuringia in the last 70 years apart from the building of a few more roads and houses. There are no industries worth mentioning, and driving along the smaller roads lined by linden and plane trees, their crowns forming a canopy, you experience a landscape which is not spectacular, but peaceful and eminently pleasing.

The cool, moist pine woods of the **Thuringian Forest** are traversed by the famous hiking trail, the **Rennsteig**, first documented in 1330 but probably much older. It runs from Hörschel near Eisenach in the northwest to Blankenstein on the Bavarian border at an average height of 2,300–2,600 feet (700–800 meters); the 100-mile-long (168-km) footpath, well-marked and only occasionally intersected by a motor road, will take good walkers five days to cover.

Skiing in this region began in the 1870s, and in 1893 one of its pioneers conquered Thuringia's highest mountain, the **Großer Inselsberg** (3,000 feet [916 meters]), on 9-foot-long Lappian skies. The skiing season lasts from October to April, and the main resort is the village of **Oberhof**. It has superb facilities formerly reserved for the GDR's sporting elite and now open to everybody, and also offers spectacular tracks for cross-country skiing. For more leisurely walks, try the 30-acre Rennsteiggarten with pretty mountain parkland and a splendid collection of alpine plants from all over the world.

The city of **Eisenach** started out as

Domestic scene at Wartburg.

three separate market squares on the medieval trading route, the *via regia lusatiae*; of its ancient walls, only the Nikolaitor (c.1200) remains, one of the oldest city gates in the *region*. It already was a prosperous town in the 13th century, when quarrels among the ruling family led to prolonged economic and political decline.

From 1572 to 1757, Eisenach was the ducal residence of a branch of the House of Wettin and enjoyed a cultural heyday. A meeting of Germany's student societies on the Wartburg in 1817 became the occasion for a huge demonstration against the reactionary politics of the Austrian Chancellor Metternich and provoked countermeasures which effectively put the whole of Germany into a political slumber for 30 years. The Wartburg has also given its name to a series of saloon cars that had been manufactured at Eisenach since 1898, production of which has only now been discontinued.

In the old town quarter you can find several well-restored picturesque houses. The late Gothic town hall, remodeled in the Renaissance, has a charming tower with a splendid black shingle roof; its curious slanting position is due to postwar renovation. The building is prettily decorated with flower boxes and houses a cheerful Ratskeller.

The house in which Johann Sebastian Bach was born in 1685 fronts an intimate tree-shaded square. It is now a museum of the life and music of Bach

Medieval Wartburg Castle has as many stories to recount as its history is long.

and his family. One of the oldest and finest half-timbered mansions, dating from the 15th century and gracefully restored after the war, is the house where Luther stayed as a student (1498–1501); it is also a museum with exhibits including details of his translation of the Bible.

Even if you know the **Wartburg** from pictures, the real thing still comes as a surprise: an imposing stronghold built on the top of a steep hill, with high walls and an intricate series of buildings peeking out from behind. The splendid medieval castle, the former seat of the

Statue of Roland in the Fischmarket, Erfurt.

landgraves of Thuringia, dates from 1067 and was a major cultural center in the 12–13th century. Building work continued into the 16th century, and the whole complex was much restored during the 19th century, at the height of the Romantic period.

The atmosphere is not awesomely feudal but invitingly informal, with half-timbered buildings grouped around two courtyards. The tour starts at the Ro-

manesque "Palas", a kind of hall which has recently been stripped of all later additions, so that you stand on the same rough stone floor that the minstrel Walther von der Vogelweide, Luther and Goethe trod on.

The rooms, some of which are used for exhibitions, are decorated with furniture assembled from various localities, and the ceilings have impressive beams still unwarped after 400 years.

Cranach-Haus in Weimar.

The chapel has 14th-century frescoes and there is a gallery reconstructed in the 19th century in medieval style, with wall paintings (1854/55) by Moritz von Schwind illustrating episodes from Wartburg history. This chamber is named after St Elizabeth, wife of the Thuringian landgrave and a great lady known for her charity, who spent her married life in the castle before moving to Marburg in 1227.

In 1207 the famous *Sängerkrieg* (Minnesinger war) is said to have taken place on the Wartburg, a contest between the most famous German minstrels, which ended in a draw between Walther and Heinrich von Ofterdingen. In the hall where this is supposed to have happened you are shown the ex-

act window through which Heinrich came flying in from Italy, aided by the magician Klingsor. Richard Wagner, who stayed at the castle in 1842, took the story as a subject for his opera *Tannhäuser*.

Visitors are also shown the tiny room where Luther took refuge after his excommunication in 1521 and in 10 months translated the New Testament from Greek into German. The cell is furnished with a chair and table and a footrest made of whale bone, while a black spot on the wall marks the impact of an inkwell that Luther had flung at the devil. The castle's windows and turrets afford splendid views across Eisenach's leafy suburbs to the gently rolling hills of the Thuringian Forest.

Going Eastwards

The pleasant, sleepy town of **Gotha**, east of Eisenach, is perhaps best-known for the *Almanach de Gotha*, an annual guide to Europe's nobility, which was published here. The city center is very attractive and well-restored, with a free-standing Renaissance town hall and town houses of the 17th and 18th centuries, brightly colored and often decorated with a family coat-of-arms. On a hilltop beyond the Rathaus lies **Schloß Friedenstein** (1643–55), the first Baroque palace in Thuringia. The ducal apartments and reception rooms have been converted into a museum. The west tower houses the court theater (1683), where in 1774 for the first time in Germany actors received fixed seasonal engagements; the charming interior has largely been preserved in its original state.

Erfurt's Color

The capital **Erfurt** is one of the oldest towns in eastern Germany. It was first mentioned in 742, when the English monk St Boniface on his mission to convert the heathen Germanic tribes, founded a bishopric here at a ford over the Gera. Situated on the main medieval highway running from the Rhine to Russia, the town grew prosperous and was endowed with a university as early as 1392. The university, however, was closed in 1816 due to lack of demand – at the time its 18 professors were teaching a mere 14 students.

Erfurt's traditional trading commodity was woad, a blue dye, which in the 17th century was supplanted by cheap supplies of indigo; at the same time Leipzig became the more powerful trading center. Between 1664 and 1802 the town belonged to the Electorate of Mainz, and it is for this reason that its main church is a cathedral, although the region is by tradition predominantly Protestant.

Since the 18th century it is a center for agricultural and horticultural produce. In 1970 it made the headlines, when Willy Brandt and Willi Stoph, the leaders of the former FRG and GDR, met here for the first time and broke new ground in east-west relations.

A good start for a tour of the city is the **Fischmarkt** with fine Renaissance houses; note especially the one called **Zum roten Ochsen** (To the Red Ox), the mansion of a rich woad merchant dating from 1562 and now housing an art gallery. Close by you find the remarkable **Krämerbrücke**, the only medieval bridge of houses north of the Alps. It is lined with 33 picturesque half-timbered houses now occupied by artists' studios and antique shops.

The nearby Renaissance **Dacherödensche Haus** with a richly ornamented doorway (1557) and idyllic courtyard saw Goethe and Schiller as visitors after the philologist Wilhelm von Humboldt (1767–1835) had married the owner's daughter and taken over part of the house. It fronts the **Anger** (village green where washing was dried), now the main shopping mall and formerly the quarter where woad was traded.

The museum here, housed in a splendid Baroque building, displays a fine selection of medieval religious art and 19/20th-century German painting (Friedrich, Spitzweg, Liebermann, Corinth, Feininger), especially strong on "*Brücke*" artists. The triple-spired cathedral on high ground was begun in 1154 as a late Romanesque church, but is now mainly late Gothic. It contains a stucco altarpiece (c.1160), fine Gothic oakwood choir stalls and huge stained-glass windows (1370–1420), which depict the complete iconographic program of medieval Christian art. Next to it, the handsome church of St Severus (14th century) has an ornate sarcophagus of the saint.

Weimar's Inspiration

A short drive eastward from Erfurt lies **Weimar**, one of the most pleasing towns in east Germany, both in terms of aesthetic appeal and cultural interest. It is intimately associated with Goethe (who was born in Frankfurt) and Schiller (who came from Marburg), and is full of skilfully restored Renaissance and Baroque mansions and burghers' houses, tree-lined streets and leafy squares, simple stalls selling wine and honey, souvenirs and *Bratwurst* – and of tourists from all

corners of the world, with some 4 million visitors in 1991.

Then continue the pilgrimage to the altar of German neo-Classicism and Romanticism which started almost as soon as Goethe – by then already famous for his bestselling *The Sorrows of Young Werther* – arrived in town (1775) to take up a ministerial position at the

Statue of Goethe and Schiller in front of the Nationaltheater.

court of Duke Carl August. By then, the rulers of the duchy of Saxony-Weimar had already established their residential capital as a center of the arts: in 1696, Germany's first opera house was opened here and Bach was a resident from 1708 to 1717. In 1772 the writer

Wieland became a tutor to the duchess Anna Amalia's sons.

Literary Giants

It is best to start a walking tour at the

Deutsches Nationaltheater (German national theater), where many of Goethe's and Schiller's plays were first performed (Goethe was its manager from 1791 to 1817), and where in 1919 the constitution for a new and democratic Germany was adopted by parliament. In front is a famous double statue (1857) of Goethe and Schiller clasping hands. The two literary giants, although quite different in temperament and outlook, were close friends and collaborated on a number of literary magazines; they disapproved, however, of daily newspapers as being too shallow and committed to sensationalism. In their youth both were enthusiastic iconoclasts, but Schiller later embraced liberal ideals, while Goethe assumed the mantle of lofty conservatism and became a champion of established power.

Nearby stands the elegant **Wittumspalais** (widows' palace), where Anna Amalia lived and kept a literary and artistic salon; it is now a museum devoted to the poet and dramatist C.M. Wieland (1733–1813). Among the duchess's regular guests was the influential philosopher J.G. von Herder (1749–1803), who advised German writers to stop aping the French and to find inspiration in their own national history and traditions. He served as court preacher at the city church, now called **Herderkirche** which contains a famous painting by Lucas Cranach the Younger (1555) of the Crucifixion, with Luther and Cranach the Elder, both well-fed and sumptuously dressed, standing next to the Cross. Just around the corner is the charming 16th-century **Kirms Krackow house** with a picturesque inner courtyard, now a museum devoted to Herder and documenting his influence on German thought.

A few steps south you find the Baroque **Schillerhaus**, furnished with period – but not the writer's – pieces. In the attic is the room where in six weeks, barely communicating with his family downstairs, he wrote *Wilhelm Tell*. Nearby stands the **Goethehaus**, its plain façade hiding a fascinating and beautiful array of rooms, highly evocative of Goethe's daily life and highly intellectual pursuits.

He lived here for 50 years, from 1782 until his death in 1832. The rooms, small by modern standards, are well-designed according to function and needs and contain much of the original decoration and furniture, with the warm colors of polished wood glowing softly in the muted light. Goethe believed that colors affect one's frame of mind, so the dining room is a sunny yellow, the study a soothing green, the reception room light blue. There is a tranquil garden at the back with rose bushes and a tiny arbor. Everywhere around the house you feel the presence of a mind eminently curious and disciplined, of somebody who knew his own worth, enjoyed the good life and felt at ease on his Olympian heights.

Further south, on the banks of the Ilm, stands the cottage to which Goethe retired for longish spells while he worked on *Wilhelm Meister, Iphigenie* and *Torquato Tasso*, wrote nature poetry and drew very accomplished sketches of the park. Weimar's most beautiful Renaissance building, the elegantly gabled **Cranach-Haus** (1549), gaily decorated with mermaids, the family emblem, fronts the **Marktplatz**. Here you also find the town hall, completely reconstructed in the style of c.1500. Nearby is the house, now a museum, where the Hungarian composer Franz Liszt lived from 1869 to 1886, surrounded by younger composers and acolytes.

In the red-carpeted salon stand one of his pianos and the portable clavichord he used to keep his fingers in training when he was traveling. The building opposite was occupied from 1919 to 1925 by the Bauhaus, the innovative and influential school of art and design.

For a rest between sights, there are many cafés in the pedestrianized area as well as two famous hotels, both rather plain from the outside but with long lists of distinguished guests. The **Elephant** lays claim to Cranach, Bach, Liszt, Wagner, Tolstoi and the father of quantum physics, Werner Heisenberg, and was immortalized in Thomas Mann's historical novel *Lotte in Weimar*, whose main character is Charlotte Buff, one of Goethe's sweethearts.

The **Russischer Hof** (formerly the Hôtel de Russie) was a favorite of writers and composers like Schumann, Berlioz and Turgenev and the singer Eleonora Duse; the building has recently been refurbished and put under conservation order, so the rooms are sparkling with old glamor.

At the **Alter Friedhof** (old cemetery) south of the Altstadt, there are the funerary chapel of the Weimar dukes and the tombs of Goethe and Schiller; Schiller's remains have an obscure history – like Mozart's – and are possibly buried not under the official slab but in the unmarked tomb nearby, but nobody knows for certain. Also buried on the grounds are Johann Peter Eckermann (1792–1854), whose illuminating *Gespräche mit Goethe* makes him the German Boswell, and Charlotte von Stein (1742-1827), Goethe's confidante during his first years in town.

Northwest of Weimar is the site of the notorious concentration camp of **Buchenwald**, where in the years between 1937 and 1945 some 240,000 prisoners from 35 nations were held and 56,000 of them died – a chilling memorial place.

The countryside around Weimar is ideal for short excursions. The quiet cobbled country lanes lead across softly rolling hills decorated with clusters of trees to villages and hamlets with a single inn which usually serves local beer and a hearty meal. Popular places are the Rococo **Schloß Belvedere** with an "English" park designed by Goethe, Pückler-Muskau and others, and the village of **Buchfart** with a covered wooden bridge (18th-century) over the Ilm and a church with a fine carved triptych by J. Linde (1492).

Most centrally situated in Germany, Hesse is also one of the richest; its wealth comes from Frankfurt, Germany's banking and commercial capital, and the heavy industry of the Frankfurt area and around Kassel, further north. It lacks distinctive character, perhaps because its historical identity is so sketchy. Its present area was long split between various local rulers, such as the dukes of Hesse-Nassau, who reigned in Wiesbaden, and another branch with its residence in Darmstadt. The major part of Hesse became a Prussian province in 1866, and the region was created in 1945.

Hesse embraces a stretch of the Rhine's east bank, around Rüdesheim, where the Rheingau, as well as being the country's highest-yielding wine growing region, produces some of Germany's best wines. To the north are the attractive wooded heights of the Taunus and

Frankfurt & Hesse

211

The old Opera House in Frankfurt.

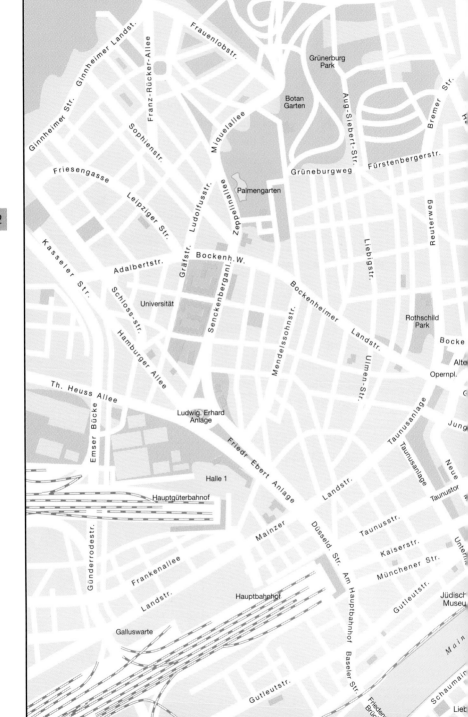

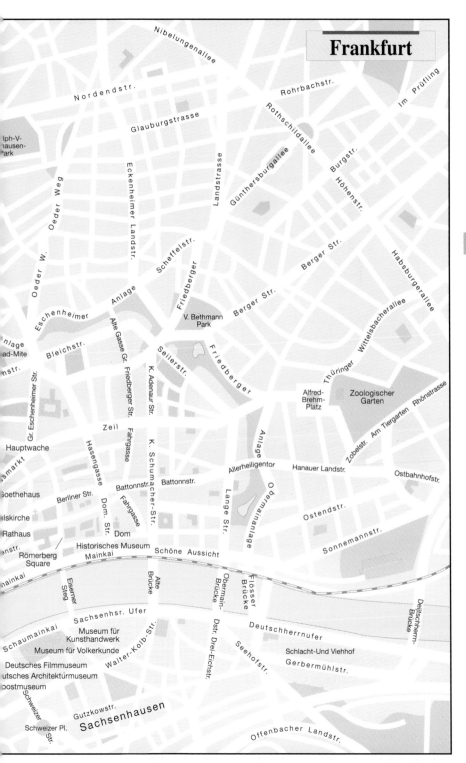

The financial landscape in Frankfurt.

Westerwald, and the scenic Lahn valley; this river flows past several interesting towns including Limburg (with hilltop castle) and Marburg (famous old university). Other noteworthy Hesse towns include Fulda, an ancient episcopal seat, and Kassel, with its exuberant Wilhelmshöhe park.

The name derives from the Chatti, a powerful Germanic tribe and the most dangerous German opponents of the Romans during the AD 1st century, against whom a *limes*, a defensive frontier line, was constructed up the Lahn

Römerberg Square, a site of Renaissance architecture.

river and across to the Main. In the 12th century the region fell to the landgraves of Thuringia, and after 1567 it was divided between two ruling houses.

Among its culinary specialities, mention should be made of *Frankfurter Würstchen*, the original hot dog, which are always served in pairs; the *Äppelwoi* (cider, 10 percent to 12 percent proof) of Frankfurt; wild boar in the Kassel region; and wine derivatives like *Sekt* (sparkling wine) and *Weinbrand* (brandy), of which the best-known brands are produced in the Rheingau.

Germany's Golden Egg

Frankfurt's impressive skyline of glit-tering steel and glass towers has earned it the nickname of "Mainhattan" or "Bankfurt"; it is the heart of Germany's banking and financial world, a bustling, pushy city, admired but unloved. The inner city, however, has several interesting patches, and at the foot of the skyscrapers more often than not you will find quiet, leafy streets lined with solid bourgeois villas, cozy cafés and elegant wine bars. Goethe's birthplace and an ensemble of Renaissance municipal buildings have been rebuilt around the Römerberg.

There are rich cultural offerings, many small avant-garde theaters, and a string of museums on the south bank of the Main. Trade fairs include international fairs in March and August; the

Frankfurt's alternative landscape.

Easter fur fair; and the world's largest book fair in early October.

At the center of the old town lies the **Römerberg square**, where restoration has created a historical document in stone rather than a living set of buildings. The graceful 15th-century Römer (city hall) contains a popular registrar's office. Behind it stands the gleaming replica of the imperial banqueting hall in use from 1562 to 1792; it contains a complete set of portraits of the 52 Holy Roman emperors from Charlemagne to Franz II. The middle of the square is

cally elected parliament met in the heady days of the 1848 revolution. The present structure, rebuilt from the ruins of the original one destroyed in the 1944 bombings, is used for ceremonies and exhibitions. Further northeast are several nicely restored patrician houses dating from the 15th to 18th centuries.

South of the Römerberg square, past the slender Gothic Nikolaikirche, you will find the **Historisches Museum**, which gives a good idea of what the old days were like. There is a scale model of the old city, and the exhibits of life from the 15th to the 20th century include an artisan's kitchen and the imperial banqueting table, set for a coronation feast.

A short walk eastward brings you to Frankfurt's **Dom** (cathedral), a red sandstone building with a tall 15th-century Gothic steeple. In the tower hall note the splendid sandstone sculpture of the Crucifixion by the Mainz artist Hans Backoffen (c.1470–1519). The church's interior is rather austere, but there are fine choir stalls, and to the right of the choir is the Wahlkapelle (election chapel), where the seven prince-electors met in conclave to decide on the new emperor.

Five centuries ago, Frankfurt already was one of Europe's main financial centers, to a large extent the work of the Jewish community. The changing fortunes of Frankfurt's Jews are evocatively illustrated at the **Jüdisches Museum** to the west of the Historisches Museum, appropriately installed in the neo-Classical Rothschild-Palais (1821), histori-

graced by a fountain (17th century) topped by the figure of the goddess of justice (blindfolded and holding a pair of scales); it used to sprout wine on coronation days. Opposite the Römer is the rather inconspicuous **Paulskirche**, which played a minor but important part in German history. It was here that Germany's first, short-lived democrati-

Frankfurt across River Main.

cal home of one of Europe's leading banking dynasties.

Goethehaus

Goethe described his birthplace as a spacious house, light and gay, with pleasant views of the garden. Handsomely reproduced at Großer Hirschgraben 23, slightly west of the Paulskirche, it does indeed have an atmosphere of ease and serenity. The furnishings of his study – his old mari-

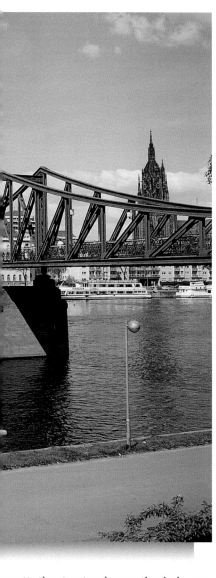

A puppeteer.

loves, and the impressive coronation ceremony of the new emperor Franz I. The adjoining museum displays documents on his life and work, with pictures and sculptures by well-known contemporary artists and friends.

The city's modern shopping center spreads out along the **Zeil**, a broad pedestrian street leading to the landmark clock tower of the Baroque **Hauptwache**, once a police station, now housing a café. The Goethestraße aspires to the elegance and glamor of London's Bond Street; both the shops and the shop assistants are much younger here. The Große Bockenheimer Straße, cobbled and lined with mouthwatering delicatessen shops and smart bistros, leads to the recently renovated

onette theater stands near the desk – are authentic, as are the blue Baroque dining room and the kitchen. Goethe lived here during the first 16 years of his life, and in his entertaining autobiography *Dichtung und Wahrheit* (Poetry and Truth) paints an unforgettable picture of a happy childhood, complete with minor domestic catastrophes, pranks, first

neo-Classical **Alte Oper** (old opera), an imposing stone-clad building with a surprisingly small area inside used for concerts and musicals. Frankfurt's new theater-land is around the Theaterplatz near the river.

Cross over to the left bank of the Main to find along the **Schaumainkai** promenade one long stretch of museums, conveniently grouped next to each other. It begins in the west with the **Liebighaus**, a museum of sculpture from different civilizations and epochs, starting with Egyptian and Greek statues, then covering the whole of Europe from the Middle Ages to the 19th century. The **Städelsches Kunstinstitut** houses one of Germany's most comprehensive painting collections. It is strong on Dutch and Flemish Primitives (Bosch, Memling, Van Eyck) and German masters of the 16th century (Altdorfer, Grien, Brueghel the Younger); also on view are works by Botticelli, Veronese, Rembrandt, Poussin, by French Impressionists (Renoir, Monet) and by 20th-century artists like Picasso, Klein and Tapies.

The **Bundespostmuseum** (postal museum) displays everything from mail coaches to rare stamps, including the most advanced telecommunication technology. Next to it, you find the **Deutsches Architekturmuseum** (German museum of architecture) and **Deutsches Filmmuseum**, emphasizing technical aspects of film production, with little about directors and actors, and the **Museum für Völkerkunde** (ethnology), with masks and other cult objects from native tribes.

Nearby, the white, box-like building, designed by the American architect Richard Meier (1985), houses the **Museum für Kunsthandwerk** (applied arts). The well-lit and spacious interior holds furniture from the Gothic onward, a large variety of glass, faience and sandstone, and works from Near Eastern and Far Eastern cultures. European porcelains from all the famous factories (Meißen, Berlin, Nymphenburg, Vienna, Sèvres) are displayed in the annex. If it is getting dark by the time you leave the last of the museums, explore the streets and lanes of surrounding **Sachsenhausen**, Frankfurt's boisterous nightlife center, full of bars and bistros and snug little wine taverns serving Äppelwoi and frankfurters on sauerkraut.

Slightly to the west of the city center – take the tram – lies the **Zoo**, famous for its rare species, which are encouraged to reproduce. The animals live in their natural habitat. Among the many wonders is an amazing beehive with thou-

Sachsenhausen, Frankfurt's drinking gallery.

sands of bees busy at work.

Wiesbaden's Warmth

From Frankfurt to Wiesbaden take the autobahn or a short detour across the foothills of the Taunus with its well-kept little towns and spas. **Wiesbaden** itself, the capital of Hesse, is pleasantly situated on hilly ground. It has retained much of the easy, confident air of its glorious days as one of Europe's most fashionable **spas**. The Romans were the first to use its healing waters, and built a forum; just one arch remains from that time. After the Romans left, nothing much happened until 1744, when Prince Karl of Nassau set up residence in his new palace of Biebrich, a suburb of Wiesbaden.

In the 19th century, the Nassaus endowed the city with stately public buildings, providing a splendid background to the high life of the international jet set congregating round the card tables and roulette wheels of the casino. Although the Russian nobles who were once the main patrons, have been replaced by wealthy Arabs and tanned, nouveau-riche Germans, walking around the city center affords some insights into old wealth and stately living.

The neo-Classical **Kurhaus** (beautiful park at the back) contains richly decorated halls and the Spielbank (casino). Gambling started here in earnest in 1771, and Wiesbaden's original casino provided the inspiration for the "Roulettenburg" in Dostoyevsky's novel *The Gambler*. It was suspended between 1872 and 1949, originally by order of Emperor William I after his son had formed an "unsuitable" attachment to a woman gambler. The south side of the Kurhaus square is taken up by the colonnaded theater.

Wiesbaden's main shopping street is the elegant, glitzy **Wilhelmstraße** running parallel to the municipal gardens, with some excellent, long established cafés. More lively is the area to the west, around the Langgasse and the small Altstadt with a number of distinguished-looking 19th-century houses and the sumptuous Schloß of the dukes of Nassau, which today houses the *Land* parliament.

Try the famous waters at the **Kochbrunnen**, a fountain a few steps east of the Kurhaus and sheltered by a neo-Classical arcade. Despite the much-vaunted healing properties you are advised to restrict intake to one liter per day. From Wiesbaden cross the Taunus range and descend on picturesque old **Limburg** with its cathedral set high above the Lahn. The building, begun in 1235, illustrates the transition in Germany from Romanesque to Gothic. The façade with its curious red, black and yellow stripes is Romanesque, but the lofty vaulted interior is Gothic, with black pillars, galleries and fine stained glass. The gem of the nearby museum is a 10th-century Byzantine reliquary cross.

The town also contains a delightful ensemble of old *Fachwerk* houses with festooned gables in the pedestrian zone around the Römer and Fischmarkt, some of which are said to date from c.1290. With their overhanging balconies almost touching others across the narrow alleys, these half-timbered buildings look like oversized gingerbread houses.

Upstream from Limburg, the wooded Lahn valley winds its way to Wetzlar. There are a number of sleepy medieval towns in the area, including Runkel and Braunfels, both watched over by hillside castles.

The old university town of **Marburg** north of Wetzlar, is well worth exploring. In the Middle Ages it was a famous place of pilgrimage because of the relics and shrine of St Elizabeth, daughter of the king of Hungary and wife of Landgrave Ludwig of Thuringia. She devoted herself to the town's sick and poor after her husband had died on one of the Crusades. In 1231 she herself died of exhaustion, at the age of 24, and very soon afterwards was canonized.

The **Elisabethkirche** at the north end of the Altstadt is Germany's first Gothic church (1235–83) and derives its typically German character from its three aisles of equal height – thus making it also the first church hall – and the homogeneity of the chancel and transepts, each terminating in an apse. Among the treasures is a statue of St Elizabeth (c.1470), showing a graceful, even slightly sexy young woman with a huge crown, dressed in a sable coat and olding a model of the church in her left palm. In the sacristy is St Elizabeth's shrine, a huge casket studded with semi-precious stones and decorated with scenes of the saint's life. Immediately to the left of the entrance is the tomb of Field-Marshal von Hindenburg (1847–1934), who as president of the Weimar Republic appointed Hitler Chancellor in 1933. Look out for several old pews which are constructed so as to tip forward suddenly if you lean too far back in them – a medieval device to stop people coming into the church to sleep during the day.

From the church follow the ascending **Steinweg**, a picturesque and well-scrubbed shopping street, until you find the **Marktplatz** on your right. Only the upper part still has original half-timbered houses dating from the mid-16th century. Built on the slope of a steep hill, they crowd together and leave room only for narrow, stepped alleys. The market square during term is the city's nightlife center, but outside term it is very peaceful.

On the hill stands the bulky **Schloß**, residence of the landgraves of Hesse from the 13th to the 17th century. The rooms include a graceful knights' hall and a small Gothic chapel with a ceramic pavement. Medieval works of art and documents on local history are on display at the **Museum für Kunstgeschichte**. The park affords pleasant walks, while from the south terrace you have marvelous views along the Lahn valley to the Taunus hills.

Episcopal City, Fulda

Its religious past has left the city of **Fulda** with a rich legacy of Baroque buildings and ornaments. In the 8th century St Boniface, an English missionary sent to convert the pagan Germans, ordered the foundation of a **monastery** that became highly influential and was a center of early German literature. The poem called *Hildebrandslied* (lay of Hildebrand) was written here by monks in about 810 on two spare pages of a theological manuscript. The saint's tomb lies in the crypt below the high altar of the Baroque cathedral, built on the site of the 8th-century Romanesque basilica. The adjacent **Dom-Museum** holds the relics of the saint – his head and sword, and the book that he used to try to ward off the heathens. Ironically, they martyred him in 754.

Outside the town, visit the huge Baroque **Schloß Fasanerie** of 1756. It has been converted into a museum, mainly for porcelain and Greek and Roman antiquities; but there are also many examples of furniture and decoration from the period 1740–1850 which give a good overview of contemporary German taste. Nearby it is the hilltop **Petersberg** church, a former Benedictine abbey (rebuilt in the 15th century) with a 9th-century crypt and covered with wall-paintings.

Northeast of Fulda lies the Schwalm region where folk traditions are still alive. The main town of **Alsfeld**, as

Hercules Monument in Kassel.

sleepy as it is picturesque, has several half-timbered Renaissance buildings. At the Marktplatz stands the **Hochzeitshaus** (1565) used for weddings, and opposite the tiny **Rathaus** (1516), set on arcades where stalls were set up on market days. Here the Brothers Grimm heard the story of Little Red Riding Hood, and to this day the girls' red folk-dresses are still worn at summer festivals; big bad wolves, however, seem to have dis-

appeared. The Schwalm region is also known for producing Hesse's most delicious sauerkraut.

Further east lies **Kassel** on several hills overlooking the Fulda valley. It was developed in the 17/18th century by the landgraves of Hesse who built the palace of Wilhelmshöhe and it also attracted industry. This indirectly became the undoing of Kassel during the last war, when it was heavily bombed be

ause of its large factories which pro-
uced tanks and locomotives. Most of
he elegant quarters were reduced to
ubble; the Altstadt disappeared and
as not been rebuilt, and therefore the
ity's present character is mainly mod-
rn and industrial. However, it is still
vorth a detour.

The **Friedrichsplatz** is adorned by
one of the region's finest neo-Classical
uildings, the **Museum Fridericanum**.
very five years (the next time in 1997)
t hosts the Documenta, a 100-day festi-
al of contemporary and futuristic art
hat has brought post-war fame to the
ity. Two noteworthy items in the square
n front of the museum are an almost
nvisible piece of sculpture, a 3,300-
oot-long (1,000-meter) brass rod driven
ertically into the ground by the artist
Valter de Maria; and some of Joseph
euys' 7,000 oaks which he planted all
ver the city and environs. The museum
nce housed the court library, where
akob and Wilhelm Grimm worked dur-
ng their mid-twenties.

It was at one of the markets on the
utskirts that they met Dorothea
iehmann, a housewife and gifted story-
eller who became a prime source for
heir fairy tales. Her father's inn, the
nallhütte on the road south to Frank-
urt, is still in business today. The
essisches Landesmuseum caters
nainly to specialized interests. It dis-
lays a curious collection of scientific
nd astrological instruments and globes
n the ground floor, and upstairs houses
a wallpaper museum, said to be the

only one of its kind, with wall-hangings
going back to the 16th century.

On the western edge of town, 15
minutes away by tram, lies a little gem,
in fact a large and very Baroque 18th-
century building, the **Schloß
Wilhelmshöhe** with its superb painting
collection (Rembrandt, Hals, Rubens,
Cranach, Dürer, Titian, Murillo, Poussin
and many lesser immortals) as well as
Greek and Roman antiquities, notably
the **Kassel Apollo**, a Roman copy of an
archetypal Greek bronze statue. The
building is surrounded by a beautiful
landscaped park full of Baroque temples and other delectable follies, fake
tombs and grottoes and the amazing
Löwenburg castle with fortress walls and
gray pinnacles, an artificial ruin and
pure Romantic fantasy (1793–97). In
summer the fountains behind the Schloß
play at regular intervals and supply a
riveting, poetic spectacle. At the top end
of the park stands a huge (230 feet [70
meters]) granite monument crowned by
a statue, a copy of the Farnese Hercules
in the Naples museum. From the top
you have a panorama of the château
with Kassel in the background.

Driving northward on a road that
for a while follows the placid Weser, you
reach the romantic **Sababurg**, said to
have been the castle that inspired the
Sleeping Beauty fairy tale. It is now a
hotel where Grimm fairy tales are sometimes read aloud during meals. The
adjacent zoo, Germany's oldest (1571),
has bears, buffaloes, penguins and other
likable creatures.

M u n i c h   &   B a v a r i a

Bavaria, the largest of the *Länder* (federal states), has the most beautiful landscapes dotted with Baroque churches and gaily painted farmhouses and is inhabited by a people as self-assertive as they are varied. A kingdom until 1918, it calls itself a *Freistaat* (free state) – as does Saxony – and everywhere you see its white-and-blue checkered flag flying. The typical Bavarians, sporting *Lederhosen* and *Dirndl*, are fond of gregarious beer-drinking and can be rough and gruff, though in general they are a warm and humorous lot.

All this is a product of history. The Wittelsbach dynasty ruled from 1180 to 1918 as one of the first German duchies, from its capital Regensburg (until 1255), then Munich. In 1805 Napoleon elevated the duchy to a

Linderhof Castle.

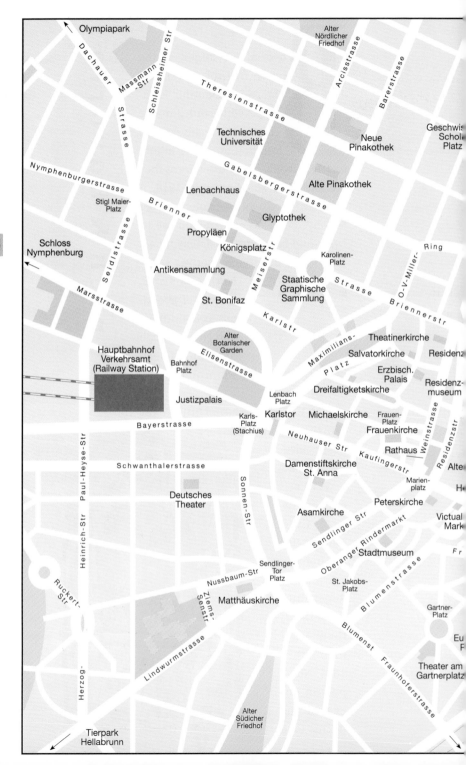

Olympiapark

Dachauer

Massmann-Str

Schleissheimer Str

Theresienstrasse

Alter
Nördlicher
Friedhof

Arcisstrasse

Barerstrasse

Strasse

Nymphenburgerstrasse

Technisches
Universität

Neue
Pinakothek

Geschwi
Schol
Platz

Gabelsbergerstrasse

Alte Pinakothek

Lenbachhaus

Stigl Maier-
Platz

Brienner

Glyptothek

Schloss
Nymphenburg

Seidlstrasse

Propyläen

Königsplatz

Meiserstr

Karolinen-
Platz

Ring

O.-V.-Miller-

Antikensammlung

Marsstrasse

Staatische
Graphische
Sammlung

Strasse

Brennerstr

St. Bonifaz

Karlstr

Alter
Botanischer
Garden

Theatinerkirche

Maximilians-

Hauptbahnhof
Verkehrsamt
(Railway Station)

Elisenstrasse

Bahnhof
Platz

Salvatorkirche

Residenz

Platz

Erzbisch.
Palais

Dreifaltigketskirche

Residenz-
museum

Justizpalais

Lenbach
Platz

Bayerstrasse

Karls-
Platz
(Stachius)

Karlstor

Michaelskirche

Frauen-
Platz

Weinstrasse

Residenzstr

Frauenkirche

Paul-Heyse-Str

Neuhauser Str

Kaufingerstr

Rathaus

Alte

Schwanthalerstrasse

Damenstiftskirche
St. Anna

Marien-
platz

He

Deutsches
Theater

Sonnen-Str

Peterskirche

Heinrich-Str

Asamkirche

Sendlinger Str

Victual
Mark

Oberanger

Rindermarkt

Stadtmuseum

Fr

Ruckert-
Str

Nussbaum-Str

Sendlinger-
Tor
Platz

St. Jakobs-
Platz

Blumenstrasse

Ziems-
Senstr

Matthäuskirche

Gartner-
Platz

Eu
F

Herzog-

Lindwurmstrasse

Blumenst

Fraunhoferstrasse

Theater am
Gartnerplatz

Alter
Südicher
Friedhof

Tierpark
Hellabrunn

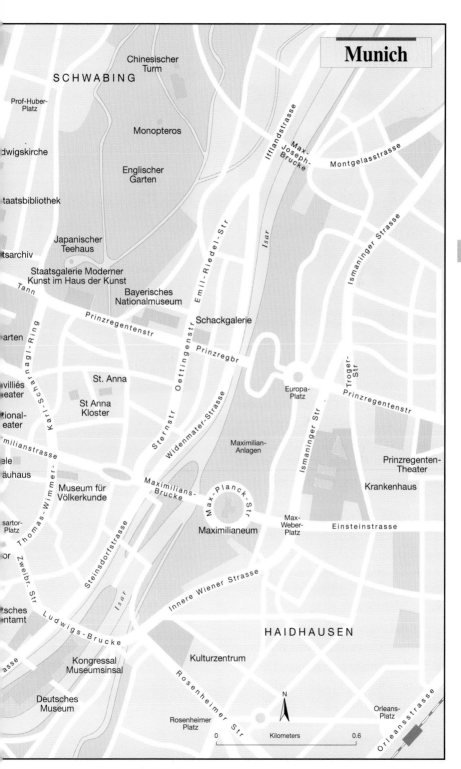

Munich

SCHWABING

Chinesischer Turm

Prof-Huber-Platz

Monopteros

dwigskirche

Englischer Garten

taatsbibliothek

Iffrandstrasse

Max-Joseph-Brucke

Montgelasstrasse

Isar

Japanischer Teehaus

tsarchiv

Emil-Riedel-Str

Ismaninger Strasse

Staatsgalerie Moderner Kunst im Haus der Kunst

Tann

Bayerisches Nationalmuseum

Schackgalerie

Prinzregentenstr

arten

Prinzregbr

Oettingenstr

Kaulbach-Schack-Ring

villiés eater

St. Anna

Sternstr

Troger-Str

Europa-Platz

Prinzregentenstr

tional-eater

St Anna Kloster

Widenmaier-Strasse

milianstrasse

Maximilian-Anlagen

Ismaninger Str

Prinzregenten-Theater

ele

äuhaus

Thomas-Wimmer-

Museum für Völkerkunde

Krankenhaus

Maximilians-Brucke

Max-Planck-Str

sartor-Platz

Steinsdorfstrasse

Max-Weber-Platz

Einsteinstrasse

Zweibr. Str

Maximilianeum

or

Isar

Innere Wiener Strasse

sches ntamt

Ludwigs-Brucke

HAIDHAUSEN

asse

Kongressal Museumsinsal

Kulturzentrum

Rosenheimer Str

Deutsches Museum

Rosenheimer Platz

Orleansstrasse

Orleans-Platz

N

0   Kilometers   0.6

A Bavarian smile.

kingdom, and in 1871 Ludwig II, the fairy-tale king, agreed to Bavaria being included in the new German Empire. In 1919 it became part of the Weimar Republic, and since 1945 has been continually ruled by the Christian Social Union (CSU), the right-wing sister-party of the CDU. Although modern light and high-tech industries have grown phenomenally since the war, Bavaria is still predominantly rural. Cereal-growing on the plains tends to be large and efficient, but of the dairy farms, many are still small and backward – which makes them all the more picturesque. There is still a notable "feudal spirit"; while the strong farmers' lobby is treated deferentially by the politicians, members of the nobility are almost everywhere treated

Green vista of the German Alps.

Lakes like the Chiemsee pepper the Alps region.

with reverence and awe; there even exists a small political party devoted to the restoration of the monarchy. In fact, Germany's nobility was shorn of its last remaining privileges in 1919, since then titles of nobility are officially treated as part of the surname.

The landscape of Bavaria is greatly varied, and so is the character of its people. The region south of the Danube with the high Alps, rocky and snow-covered and with skiing resorts and castles, is Germany's foremost tourist area, and it is here that you find the true, the storybook Bavarians. To the north are the wide rolling spaces, partly forested, cut by the valleys of the Danube, Lech, Isar, Inn and other smaller rivers. The area to the southwest, around Augsburg,

is part of Swabia, and the people are more like the Swabians of Württemberg in character, cuisine and dialect. In the east, Bavaria borders on the Czech Republic. The dark woods and narrow valleys of the *Bayrischer Wald* (Bavarian Forest) and the *Oberpfalz* (Upper Palatinate) are among Germany's poorest regions, with gray houses huddled around the village pond. Its main industries are glassblowing, basket-weaving and charcoal-burning. The whole of the north is the historic region of Franken (Franconia), which only became part of Bavaria in 1803 and where the natives do not consider themselves Bavarians at all. The area around Würzburg produces excellent wine sold in *Bocksbeutel* green bottles in the shape of a pouch.

Beer Gardens

The *Biergärten* (beer gardens, of course) are Bavaria's major contribution to the art of beer-drinking, apart from the beer itself. As soon as the last snows of winter have disappeared, you will find them being set up in every city, town and village as a meeting place for the gregarious Bavarians and a magnet for the tourist weary of sightseeing.

The essential props are a patio, an open court or backyard with a few horse chestnut trees, a couple of trestle tables and benches and beer on tap. The waitresses are all cut from the same cloth: they are invariably female, bosomy, strong, cheerful and quick-witted and wear *Dirndl* dresses and sensible shoes. Once you have got your *Maß* (a liter of beer served in a heavy glass or stoneware tankard), you just relax, take in the other guests, watch the sparrows swooping down from the trees to pick crumbs, and catch a glimpse of village life until the sun and the beer and the soothing uneventfulness of your surroundings begin to make you feel slightly drowsy.

Beer gardens are very popular with pensioners and office workers, who during their lunch break will go there for a short picnic, or for a longer one after work. Many bring their own food – the management does not mind in the least – and after ordering perhaps a *Radlermaß* (a shandy, "beer for the cyclist") or a *Spezi* (Coke and lemonade), they unpack their bags and spread out the goodies on the table: some *Laugenbrez'n* (salt pretzels), butter, a *Radi* (big white raddish), a bit of cheese and a few slices of warm *Leberkäs* (meat loaf made of liver, ham and pork). Such rustic fare was exactly what farmers and day-laborers took with them when they spent the whole day out in the fields during the harvest. This tradition becomes even more

A typical beer garden.

poignant when you see it celebrated in one of Munich's big beer gardens, in the Englischer Garten, for instance, which is patronized by a younger crowd, where you can picnic in the shadow of a "Chinese" pagoda, or the more intimate and traditional Hirschgarten, where deer graze within sight. More modest but equally welcoming are the beer gardens attached to inns in the city, with their leafy backyards illuminated at night by Chinese lanterns or strings of light bulbs suspended from the trees.

Bavaria has a profusion of fine Baroque and Rococo buildings, even down to village churches with their characteristic onion-shaped domes. Many churches and palaces are of Romanesque or Gothic origin, and were remodeled in the 18th and early-19th-century in the ornate styles which the Wittelsbach royal house favored. In vernacular architecture there is little half-timbering in the south. The ground-floors are usually whitewashed, the up-

A local in a traditional costume complete with felt hat.

per floors of slatted wood with flower-decked balconies and wide overhanging eaves. Traditional clothes and costumes are still much in daily use in upper Bavaria.

In rural areas women wear brocaded *Dirndl*, the men *Lederhosen* (leather trousers) and for ceremonial occasions felt hats with feathers or a tuft of chamois hair. In cities, elegant people also often wear elaborate *Dirndl* and jackets, suits and capes made of thick *Loden* cloth in green or black.

Bavaria is the paradise of beer-drinkers. Almost every small town has its own brewery, even in wine-growing Franconia, often with a tavern attached. The Bavarians were very proud of their strict brewing regulations, which per-

mitted only malt, hops, yeast and water to be used; these high standards of purity were enforced from 1516 until very recently; such that now even Bavarian breweries are allowed the use of "additional substances". Like the small breweries with their taverns, village butchers frequently have a slaughterhouse at the back and a restaurant in front, next to the shop. There you can order *Weißwürste* ("white" sausages of veal and pork, spiced with lemon, onions and nutmeg) or *Leberkäse* ("liver cheese", meat loaf – but no liver is used), *Schweinshaxn* (pigs' knuckles) with sauerkraut or the ubiquitous *Schweinebraten* (pork roast) and a stein of beer.

A Good-Time City

Munich, the capital of Bavaria and of German Baroque, is the most likable of Germany's metropolitan cities. Center of fashion and filmmaking, pilgrimage place of all serious beer-drinkers, it ranks culturally equal with Berlin as the main German center of the arts, and its range of museums is finer than even that of the reunited Berlin. Its people are extrovert and full of fun and feeling, with a quick temper and a short memory. In contrast to Frankfurt's glitzy skyscrapers, the city's skyline is deliberately kept free from high-rise office buildings (some have been put up in the outskirts), which provides an attractive intimacy and human scale to buildings and streets. The layout of the center, where most of

The enchanting glockenspiel is Munich's emblem.

the important and interesting monuments are, is clear and simple, with the old quarter around the Rathaus in the south and the long, broad avenue of the Ludwig- and Leopoldstraße terminating at the heart of Schwabing, Munich's artistic and arty heartland in the north. The whole area is of manageable size and can be easily explored on foot. The more distant sights are all served by the modern U-Bahn (underground) or S-Bahn (mainly above ground) and – best of all – by the rackety but efficient tram; if you prefer exploring by bicycle, look out for a *Fahrradverleih* to rent one.

Munich has long been called "Germany's secret capital", and even after the change of the official capital from Bonn to Berlin, its atmosphere, beauty and excellent geographical position will leave it without serious rivals. Its *Freizeitwert* (what the Germans term as leisure value) is very high, and it is the prime destination of the upwardly-mobile middle class, of big business and high-tech industries.

The continental climate guarantees hot summers and icy winters, the surrounding countryside is picturesque, the Alps offer marvelous skiing and hiking, and Italy – the vineclad hills of South Tyrolia, the shimmering beauty of Venice, the Mediterranean and Adriatic – is just a few hours away. So if it pours in Munich and you feel low, get in your car and head south.

Munich originated as a village in the 9th century near a monastic settle-

The Parliament House at night, Munich.

A couple in traditional costumes
during festival time.

Oktoberfest in Munich.

ment; its emblem, a child dressed like a monk, derives from this ("Mönchen" may be a corruption of "München", meaning "monks"). It was founded in 1156 by Henry the Lion, and in 1180 came under the rule of the Wittelsbachs, who in 1255 made it their ducal residence and in 1503 the capital of all Bavaria. Since the Thirty Years' War, Bavaria has been a stronghold of Catholicism, although Munich itself has for the last decades been governed by a moderate SPD coalition. During the 17th and 18th centuries the Wittelsbachs endowed it with palaces, of which the Residenz and Nymphenburg remain. Its greatest artistic flowering started under Ludwig I (r.1825–48), who drew artists and architects to his court before

his scandalous liaison with the Spanish dancer Lola Montez led to his abdication. His successors continued the good work, building and collecting in the grand style. In the aftermath of the First World War, disaffection with the established powers led to a short and bloody experiment in revolution and counter-revolution and years of political instability. Adolf Hitler, born in Braunau (Austria), came to Munich to study art and soon became the leader of the Nazi Party (founded 1919), staging an abortive putsch in 1923. Later when he ruled from Berlin, he often came back to the city he loved to hold major parades. Much of the Altstadt was destroyed by wartime bombing, and although there is a good deal of undistinguished post-

Marienplatz.

the best starting point for city tours and for excursions to the countryside, with an underground station for both the U- and S-Bahn, and also the center of the Bavarian topographical survey. The north side is taken up by the impressive neo-Gothic Neues Rathaus, topped by the figure of the city's emblem, the **Münchner Kindl**. Its famous gyrating glockenspiel has two sets of figures, depicting a ducal wedding (1568) and a coopers' dance (1517) and performing at 11 a.m. (in summer also at noon and 5 p.m.). The center of the relatively small square is graced by a tall red marble column and a figure of the Virgin on a crescent moon, a memorial erected at the end of the Swedish War (1632–35). There are outdoor cafés, huge

war architecture, planning and restoration of the historical substance has basically been intelligent and sensitive.

Munich is a major convention center, and also has a number of popular festivals and fairs which include the *Fasching* (carnival; early January to Shrove Tuesday); the *Auer Dult*, a well-stocked antiques and secondhand market (end of April, of July and of October); festivals of music and theater in summer; the celebrated *Oktoberfest* (mid-September to first Sunday in October); and a very attractive, atmospheric *Christkindlmarkt* with stalls crowding the Marienplatz square from the end of November to Christmas Eve.

The **Marienplatz** has been the focus of the city for many centuries; it is

The "U" for underground and "S" for streetcar are used nationally to denote transportation available.

Cultural history aside the Deutsches Museum is a trip into the age of space and technology.

flower boxes with blazing red geraniums, several beerhalls, stalls selling herbal confectionery, pavement artists and musicians and milling crowds. On the east side, the much-restored Altes Rathaus with its stepped-gable façade and pinnacled Gothic tower, is a fine example of 15th-century Bavarian secular architecture.

A few steps south stands the city's oldest church, the much rebuilt **St Peter**, its tower (1386) one of Munich's landmarks and affording superb views onto the maze of crooked lanes below. The nearby **Viktualienmarkt** (market for victuals) is known for its excellent produce, its cheeky saleswomen and its spartan eating houses and pubs frequented by the locals. The stalls are simple trestle-tables covered with all kinds of edibles and protected by huge striped umbrellas. Customers from all social strata do their shopping here, and wealthy elegant housewives, pensioners with string-bags, voluminous peasant women with headscarves, sprightly office-girls and taciturn Turks mix to examine the goods with a critical eye and probing touch.

Historical Devotions

Continue south and come to the remarkable **Stadtmuseum**, devoted to the history and culture of Munich and Bavaria. A huge vaulted late Gothic hall has medieval and later armor and weaponry, and there are sections dealing with puppets and brewing, cinema and traditional costume. The showpiece are the Moriskentänzer (Moorish dancers), ten carved figures, gilded and painted in 1480 by Erasmus Grasser. Further on, the fascinating Marionettentheater is a small temple of the muses for children, with evening performances of operas by Mozart, Orff and Egk, all acted out by marionettes.

To the northwest lies the delightful **Asamkirche** (1733–46), a late Baroque marvel of frescoes, sculptures and stuccowork and the masterpiece of the brothers Egid Quirin and Cosmas Damian Asam, who built churches all over southern Bavaria. Regaining the Marienplatz, to the left runs the Kaufingerstraße, the main pedestrian shopping street, rather down-market and with a number of huge subterranean beerhalls. Nearby stands Munich's oldest and most famous landmark, the **Frauenkirche**, with its eye-catching twin towers with green (oxidized copper) cupolas. The late Gothic cathedral (1488) is one of the largest hall churches in southern Germany. The interior is striking for its simplicity and lofty space. The top of the stalls in the chancel are decorated with 24 busts of Biblical figures by Grasser, while the south chapel contains a stunning altarpiece with paintings by Michael Pacher and Jan Polack, the greatest Munich painters of the Gothic period.

East of the Marienplatz, the **Weinstadl** (1552) in the Burgstraße is the oldest patrician mansion in Munich. The ornate wall-paintings outside are very fine examples of Renaisssance decoration; entering through the massive wooden portal, you find a simple, very civilized wine tavern.

The nearby **Alter Hof** (old courtyard) is an impressive example of a medieval city fortress built around a charming, echoing yard; this was the residence of the Wittelsbachs from 1253 until 1474. The tower passage leads to the Münzhof (courtyard of the mint), its three galleries showing Italian influence. A few steps eastward get you to the Platzl square with Munich's largest and best-known beerhall, the **Hofbräuhaus** (court brewery), where some 10,000 liters are consumed daily. Its history goes back to 1591, when the Wittelsbachs built their own royal brewery in the Alter Hof, then in 1644 moved it to the Platzl. After it was opened to the public in 1830, it proved so popular that the brewing-house had to make way. The present building in the style of an Old Munich patrician house dates from 1896. Though tourists greatly outnumber local people, the atmosphere re-

Goethestraße in Munich.

mains authentic.

To the north lies the broad, impressive Maximilianstraße, leading past the Siegessäule (victory column) to the huge, moody Maximilianeum where the Bavarian parliament meets. The Maximilianstraße together with the Maffei- and Theatinerstraße in the west, are the smartest of Munich's streets, lined with posh galleries, fashion boutiques, the two grandest hotels and discreet restaurants with indiscreet prices. This being the focus of Munich's wealth and glamour, caviar and fur coats are much in evidence.

At the beginning of the Maximilianstraße lies the **Residenz**, a vast complex of buildings (16–19th century) with seven inner courtyards. For 500 years this was the residence of the dukes, then the electors and lastly the kings of Bavaria. King Gustavus Adolphus was so taken by it in 1634 that he planned to transport the whole edifice back home to Sweden. The oldest part is the Antiquarium (1571), the biggest secular Renaissance hall north of the Alps, a magnificent vaulted chamber, the ceiling covered with lively frescoes. It is part of the Residenzmuseum, a succession of highly ornamented rooms full of portraits, porcelain and gilded furniture. The Schatzkammer (treasury) contains dazzling ivory crucifixes, sword pommels encrusted with rubies and diamonds, and vases and plates of jasper, agate and lapis lazuli

To the east is the intimate

Munich is also a city of lively fashion.

Cuvilliéstheater, a gem of Rococo playfulness, while the western front of the Residenz is taken up by the inconspicuous modern Residenztheater and the grand Nationaltheater, Munich's opera house.

The nearby **Feldherrenhalle** (Field Marshals' hall), modeled on the Loggia dei Lanzi in Florence, was where Hitler's 1923 putsch was nipped in the bud; while he served his subsequent prison sentence, he worked on *Mein Kampf*, his programmatic autobiography.

Next to the loggia rise the very tall towers of the **Theatinerkirche** (Church of the Theatine Order) with its rhythmic, sharply defined Baroque façade and grandiose, harmonious interior, richly decorated with very elaborate

stuccowork. The gateway opposite the church leads to the **Hofgarten**, one of the most charming city gardens in the Renaisssance style outside Italy. It is an oasis of peace and solitude. Chamber music is sometimes played in the small temple with a bronze Diana (1594), and under the western arcades you find a pleasant café.

If you follow the street opposite the Hofgarten gateway you soon come to the wide square of the **Königsplatz** with the three-arched Propyläen (Greek for "gateway") as its western termination. This memorial to the Greek War of Independence, which ended in 1833, exemplifies the Doric order of Classical architecture, while the two buildings flanking it are of the Ionic order (the Glyptothek) and Corinthian order (the Antikensammlungen).

The square with its colonnaded neo-Classical buildings was the brainchild of King Ludwig I and executed by Leo von Klenze (1784–1864), the architect responsible for most of Munich's great 19th-century buildings. The **Antikensammlungen** (collections of antiquities) contain one of Germany's most important collections of Greek and Roman antiquities, and are especially strong on vases. The **Glyptothek** (Greek for "stone library") was Germany's first museum of sculpture and is now devoted to antique sculpture only, with many world-famous pieces, including the languid marble Barberini Faun and the Aegina marbles. In summer, the inner courtyard turns into an open-air café, an enchanting spot for a rendez-vous.

Just beyond the Propyläen archway you find the **Lenbachhaus**, a municipal art gallery housed in the opulent mansion the "painter prince" Franz von Lenbach (1836–1904) built for himself in 1887–91. Modeled on Tuscan villas and furnished by the portraitist of popes, kings and opera singers, the museum is not at all as fustian as its pedigree would suggest. Devoted to painting produced in Munich since the late Gothic, it is particularly strong on the *Blaue Reiter* group of artists, with ten rooms full of Kandinsky, Klee, Marc, Jawlensky and Gabriele Münter; a few contemporary artists are also on show.

Nearby is the **Alte Pinakothek** with one of the world's greatest collections of Old Masters, all represented by some of their best work. The unprepossessing dark mock-Renaissance building (1826–36) was erected to house paintings that the Wittelsbachs had accumulated since the 16th century. They are all there: the Flemish and Dutch Primitives, the German Old Masters (Grünewald, Dürer, Altdorfer), the great Italians (Raphael, Titian, Tiepolo), Rubens, Rembrandt, Hals, Claude Lorrain, Poussin, as well as El Greco and Velásquez. Confronted with such a surfeit of riches, one has to pick and choose according to one's taste and temperament, and try to ignore other, equally deserving works. Across the road, the **Neue Pinakothek** shows European artists of the 19th century. The angular, fortress-like building (1975–81) by Al-

The multistorey bookstore in Munich.

exander von Branca looks post-modern from the outside but the interior follows a time-honored layout. Paintings range from the Nazarenes, the forerunners of the English Pre-Raphaelites, via Romantic (Böcklin) and Biedermeier (von Schwind) artists to modern German masters (Liebermann, Corinth), Jugendstil draughtsmen (Klimt) to a small but well-chosen selection of French painters (Corot, Manet, Daumier, Monet, Cézanne).

East of these two museums is the university and students' quarter of Munich with lots of specialized bookshops, cafés, simple rented accommodations, pubs, cinemas and jazz clubs. North of the neo-Classical university buildings with their huge fountains stands the

Englischer Garten, Europe's largest city park.

Siegestor, a triumphal arch crowned by Nike, the goddess of victory, on her chariot; the gateway, modeled on the Arch of Constantine in Rome, marks the boundary between the city center and **Schwabing**, famous pre-war haunt of artists, writers, journalists and other anti-establishment figures. Although past its heyday, it is still inhabited by many young and middle-aged intellectuals, filmmakers, designers and wheeler-dealers in cultural matters. It is full of leggy girls and shaggy boys, smoky students' taverns, fringe theaters and smart bars.

Gardens, Villas and Parks

Further east lies the wonderfully varied and very popular huge **Englischer Garten**, Europe's largest city park at $1^1/_2$ sq miles (3.7 sq km). It was begun by a multi-talented American, Benjamin Thompson, who later became Count Rumford and who, while he was serving as Minister of War to the Bavarian king, had this piece of marshy land drained and turned into an "English", i.e. informal park.

An arm of the Isar, a tributary of the Danube, runs through it, and there are woodlands and meadows, a Chinese-style pagoda with a beer garden, a lake for boating and a circular neo-Classical temple, the Monopteros. Sunbathing in the nude is all the rage here. At the southern end, the **Haus der Kunst** (house of art) shows a collection of 20th-cen-

Schloß Nymphenburg, an art galore.

tury painting (Munch, Picasso, Magritte, Warhol, Pop Art) and sculpture (Barlach, Giacometti, Moore), while further east, the **Nationalmuseum** has an astonishing range of medieval sculpture, folk art, tapestry, porcelain and icons.

The building itself is a wild and painful mixture of architectural styles from Romanesque to Baroque, and the display is cramped and old-fashioned, which partly explains the dearth of visitors.

Beyond the Isar, in the quiet residential district of Bogenhausen, stands

and technology and the one with the biggest number of visitors. Its well-displayed collection of airplanes, cars, boats, machinery of all periods, together with reconstructions of coal-mines, the Lascaux caves and astronomical devices can be exhausting in the company of enthusiastic children; a complete tour would cover 10 miles (16 km). Many of the models and dioramas are animated, and you can press buttons to see how things work.

In west Munich the beautiful palace and park of **Nymphenburg** are definitely worth a visit. Best to take a tram from Schwabing, which stops directly in front of the yellow-and-white Schloß. On your way, note the audacious tent-like roof of acrylic glass marking the Olympic Village (1972) and park with the TV tower and in the background the BMW headquarters in a building shaped like four linked cylinders.

Nymphenburg began life as a hunting park; the first buildings were put up in 1664, and it later became a summer residence of the Bavarian electors and kings. The Baroque main building with its monumental, almost 2,300-foot-long (700 meters) frontage has a splendid High Baroque to neo-Classical interior, of which several rooms are accessible on guided tours. Note the attractive Chinese lacquer room in the south wing, and in the south pavilion the royal apartments with the delicious *"Gallery of Beauties"*, commissioned by Ludwig I to depict the most beautiful women of his time. A descendant of the

the **Stuckvilla** (Museum Villa Stuck), the luxurious town house of a society painter of the turn of the century. It is a charming period piece with beautifully crafted furniture, Roman-style wall-paintings and fine decorative objects.

Further south, on an island in the Isar, you find the **Deutsches Museum**, Germany's prime museum for science

The Olympic Stadium in Munich.

Wittelsbach still occupies an apartment in the north wing. A long leafy avenue runs up to the palace; the canal in the middle, graced by ducks and swans in summer, in winter is transformed into a curling-alley.

Behind the Schloß lies the splendid park, parts of which are very formal with Grecian urns (Resnais filmed *Last Year in Marienbad* here), others are wildly romantic. It is dotted with delightful pavilions in Chinese style (the Pagodenburg) or used as royal baths (the Badenburg). The supreme jewel is the outwardly modest former hunting-lodge Amalienburg (1734–39; designed by Cuvilliés the Elder), sumptuously decorated with a stunning hall of mirrors. An interesting botanical garden

and a café housed in the Orangerie are to the north.

To round off an excursion to Nymphenburg, walk along the quiet, leafy Hirschgartenallee (southwest corner of the palace) to the **Hirschgarten** (deer park), a huge beer garden much frequented by the locals, and watch the herds of deer beyond the fence.

One of the most attractive lakes south of Munich is the **Starnberger See**, easily accessible by S-Bahn. It stretches out for more than 12 miles (20 km) in a setting of wooded banks interspersed by villas, castles and small resorts.

A popular road along the west shore goes through some trim little towns. It was at Berg Castle (3 miles [5 km] from Starnberg) that the deposed king Ludwig

I was sent to pass his last hours. The day after he arrived at Berg, where he was to be interned on grounds of insanity, he drowned in the lake under mysterious circumstances, on 13 June 1886.

Renaissance Enclaves

Augsburg, Bavaria's third largest city and during the Renaissance one of Europe's greatest commercial and cultural centers, has an impressive array of fine churches and palaces and also some of Germany's grandest Renaissance ensembles.

The city was founded in 15 BC by the family of the Roman emperor Augustus, but today is almost completely devoid of Roman remains – the vandals, whether Vandals, Goths or Huns, did a thorough job during the 5th-6th century. It became a Free Imperial City in the 13th century, and by the 15th century was about the richest town in Europe, largely due to two dynasties of financial geniuses, the Fuggers and the Welsers. The Religious Peace of Augsburg (1555) established, at least for a time and a place, the principle of peaceful co-existence of Catholics and Protestants, to which the city's "double churches" still bear witness. Here Hans Holbein the Younger, the great portraitist, was born in c.1497, and Diesel invented the fuel engine in 1897. Its best-known native son, the left-wing playwright and poet Bert Brecht (1898–1956), only recently and after much altercation was honored

with a small museum. Rebuilding after wartime bombing has been sadly uninspired; but if the city lacks cozy charm, it partly makes up for it by the purity of its impressive Renaissance architecture and the congenial atmosphere of its smart cafés and wine taverns.

Augsburg's resplendent Maximilianstraße and its continuation, the Hohe Straße, leading right through the center of the Altstadt, are lined by grand public buildings and proud mansions. At the south end, the 15th-century **St Ulrich and Afra** is one of the so-called double churches, where the two religions worshipped side by side; the Catholic part with its caissoned vaulting and opulent Baroque altar is magnificent; one of the north chapels has a balcony topped by expressive terra-cotta statues of saints. Southeast of the church stands the **Rotes Tor** (red gate), a fortified group of 16th-century buildings with a central courtyard. At the foot of the tower, an open-air theater has been laid out. The nearby Heilig-Geist-Spital (1631) houses the famous Augsburger Puppenkiste, a museum of puppetry with frequent theatrical performances.

Passing St Ulrich and Afra, follow the Maximilianstraße to the **Schaezler-palais** (1770), until fairly recently the family home of a dynasty of silversmiths. The sprawling building now houses two intimate museums, one devoted to German Baroque masters, the other to local painters of the 15th-16th century, including Holbein the Elder with a touching votive painting, and Dürer with the

Tradition is preserved in the volksfest parade.

famous portrait of Jakob Fugger the Rich.

Turn left at the second bronze Renaissance fountain and you come to a narrow, busy shopping street and the church of **St Anna** (1321), a former Carmelite monastery, whose flamboyant Gothic architecture contrasts with the Rococo stucco and frescoes. The heavy, sombre *Fuggerkapelle* (funerary chapel of the Fuggers), considered the first true example of the Italian Renaissance style in Germany, and three paintings by Cranach are among the many notable works of art in this church. The Goldschmiedekapelle with its 15th-century wall-paintings is a reminder that the work of the Augsburg goldsmiths is still regarded as the finest in Europe

during that period.

To the east, fronting the Maximilianstraße, is the massive Renaissance **town hall** by Elias Holl (1615) with a beautifully proportioned façade. Its famous *Goldener Saal* (golden hall) is a symphony in gold and brown, with elaborate ceiling paintings (open during office hours). The square in front of the Rathaus leads into a maze of pretty lanes with pubs and wine bars and family restaurants. Just east of the center lies the **Fuggerei**, a complex of eight streets lined by 66 gabled houses, founded by Fugger the Rich in 1519 to house the town's poor. It is the world's first social settlement, and still takes in citizens in need, as it did in the 16th century. Reputedly five times as rich as the Medicis, Jakob Fugger was only the most successful member of the Fugger dynasty, the "Rothschilds of the Renaissance". From here it is just a few steps to the old town ramparts, mainly 15–16th century, offering secluded walks and views down tiny gardens and orchards of half-timbered 17th-century craftsmen's houses.

The tall white **Dom** north of the old center has much work to admire: a Gothic doorway dedicated to the Virgin, Romanesque bronze door panels, several religious paintings by Holbein the Elder and very early (12th century) stained-glass windows with highly stylized figures of the prophets. Further down the main street stands Mozart's father's birthplace, now a small museum; Mozart is still a common name in Augsburg.

Haflinger horses take part in the volkfest parade.

Nürnberg, the capital of Franconia, with its fortifications and old town houses, picturesque fountains, imperial castle and great museum, is after Munich the culturally richest city in Bavaria. It owes its legacy to an extraordinary moment in artistic history, when several Renaissance geniuses were at work here at the same time: the mastersinger Hans Sachs (1494–1576); cobbler-cum-poet extraordinary, the sculptor Adam Kraft; the woodcarver Veit Stoß; Peter Vischer the brazier; Willibald Pirckheimer, jurist and Humanist; Martin Behaim, who invented the first globe in the early 1490s; Peter Henlein, who allegedly made the first pocket watch (dubbed the "Nürnberg egg"), and Albrecht Dürer (1471–1528),

son of a goldsmith and among the greatest and most inquisitive of artists.

Nürnberg's rise to fame began in the 11th century, when two emperors built castles on the slopes above the Pegnitz river. From 1356, each new emperor of the Holy Roman Empire was expected to hold his first diet here in the Kaiserburg fortress; so it was a kind of German capital.

This distinction attracted a lot of business and wealth which in its train encouraged intellectual and artistic skills, until the 15–16th century became the golden age of Nürnberg's innovative culture and science.

Its great medieval ensemble remained intact until a bombing raid in January 1945 wiped out 90 percent of

View from Albrecht Dürer's house encompassing Dürerplatz and the 11th century fortress, the Kaiserburg.

the Altstadt. Rebuilding the city, the old irregular street layout has been preserved, and a great many old buildings have been painstakingly restored. Despite all this loving attention and lavish expenditure, the Altstadt retains a certain flatness and uniformity, since the stone has not been aged by time and the weather, but through the hand of man.

Among Nürnberg's notable fairs and festivals, there are the toy fair (February), the international bardic meeting (August), the German inventors' fair and Altstadt festival (September) and the colorful, old-fashioned Christkindlesmarkt, Germany's largest pre-Christmas market, full of delicious smells and glittering tinsel from the bakeries and stalls filled to the beams with traditional toys and Christmas decoration.

Exploring Nürnberg

Nearly everything worth seeing is within the Altstadt. A good starting point is the **Kaiserburg**, an awesomely grand building where burgraves and emperors held court from the 11th to the 15th century. The oldest part is the high pentagonal tower (c.1040), relic of an earlier castle long destroyed. The imperial chapel (12th century) has an upper part for the emperor's use, a gloomy lower one for his footlings. The **Rittersaal**, where the knights gathered to deliberate and drink, has beautiful 16th-century paintings

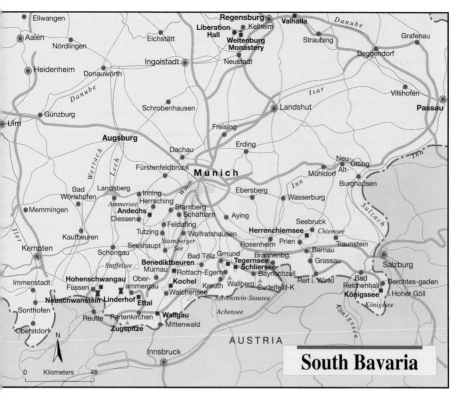

South Bavaria

and is used for concerts. Good views of Nürnberg and its hilly environs can be gleaned from rooms and windows, the most extensive panorama from the top of the Sinwellturm. The galleried inner courtyards are most appealing.

Below the fortress you find the most picturesque part of the old town, the houses huddling as if for protection against the ramparts. Here is the 15th-century **Dürerhaus** where the artist lived from 1509 until his death in 1528. Its beautiful interior, largely authentic, is now a museum with some original woodcuts, first editions of his treatises and many copies of his other works. All around this area are quaint half-timbered houses, narrow alleys opening on

to courtyards with pubs and wine taverns and restaurants carefully rebuilt. This is the best spot to try the long, slim *Nürnberger Bratwürste* (pork sausages) spiced with herbs and patterned by black stripes from the charcoal grill. Few of the rich merchants' houses have been rebuilt, save the pink gabled Renaissance Fembohaus, now a museum of city history. Nürnberg's patrician families have vanished from the limelight, although they still do exist.

South of the Fembohaus stands the handsome Renaissance **Altes Rathaus**, modeled on Venetian palazzi, with fine doorways and an underground dungeon. Beside it, note the very popular bronze Gänsebrunnen (1555), a foun-

Detail of the beautiful fountain Schöner Brunnen built from 1385-96.

tain with the figure of a farmer carrying to market two geese that spout water. Opposite the Rathaus stands the **St Sebalduskirche**, Nürnberg's oldest (13th century) church and one of its two finest. Works by three of the city's famous craftsmen can be seen inside: Peter Vischer is represented with a bronze shrine (1519) and a self-portrait in apron and skullcap on a silver sarcophagus. There is also a sculptured tomb by Adam Kraft and a crucifixion by Veit Stoß.

Cross the Weinmarkt in front of the church, and a few houses further south you come to the **Spielzeugmuseum** (toy museum), installed in a 17th-century house, with displays of dolls' houses, pewter figures and other toys.

The focus of the Altstadt, however,

is the **Hauptmarkt** (main market); most of the buildings are new and dull, but the Gothic Liebfrauenkirche has a mechanical clock with historical figures appearing daily at noon, while the best known of Nürnberg's fountains, the **Schöner Brunnen** (beautiful fountain) is decorated with worldly rulers and Biblical prophets. South of the market lies the pink **Heilig-Geist-Spital**, a hospital built in the 14th-15th century on two arches straddling an arm of the Pegnitz. Its central courtyard (open to the public) with wide arcades surmounted by wooden galleries gives an idea of what the mansions of Nürnberg used to look like.

The Altstadt south of the river is mostly modern, but has a few highlights. The Gothic **Lorenzkirche**, Nürnberg's loveliest church, has a façade broken by an outstanding rose window, a ravishing *Annunciation* by Veit Stoß, a stone tabernacle with a self-portrait of the sculptor Kraft supporting the balustrade and in the ambulatory very fine stained glass (1487). Outside the church the startling **Tugendbrunnen** (fountain of virtue; 1585-89) is graced by the statue of a lady whose breasts sometimes spout water.

A few streets south you come to one of Germany's greatest museums, the huge, rambling **Germanisches Nationalmuseum**, its glory a collection of great masters of the German Renaissance, who were often both painters and engravers. There are penetrating portraits by Dürer and Holbein the younger, crowded scenes by Altdorfer and fervent religious works by Grien and his Protestant counterpart Cranach. Among objects of the minor arts there is a stunning piece of table decoration, a three-masted ship (1503), witness to the pre-eminence of Nürnberg in the gold-smiths' craft in Dürer's time. Major works by German Renaissance (and earlier) wood and stone sculptors are shown in the chapel of the former 14th-century Carthusian monastery which now forms part of the museum building.

A promenade leads further east to the **Handwerkerhof** opposite the rail-way station, a replica of a medieval craftsmen's village where tourists can watch toymakers, blacksmiths and the like at work. Have another *Bratwurst* here at the famous restaurant "Das Bratwurstglücklein", a warm *Krapfen* (doughnut) or a *Lebkuchen* (ginger-bread), also one of Nürnberg's famous produce; and at the end of the tour treat yourself to a short, pleasant walk along the riverbank to the Weinstadl, the most idyllically pretty spot in the city and a wine tavern to boot.

Ultra-picturesque **Rothenburg ob der Tauber** ("above the river Tauber"), one of Germany's best-known small towns, looks almost too good to be true. Protected by its ramparts, it commands the winding course of the Tauber. Touring its paved streets, old houses, fountains and quaint back alleys, visi-tors are plunged into the atmosphere of the 16th century.

In the 12th century two castles stood successively upon the terrace overlook-ing the river. After an earthquake de-stroyed the castles in the 13th century, the wealthy burghers devoted themselves to building and embellishing public monuments such as the town hall and the churches, not forgetting of course their own half-timbered and gabled mansions. After the Thirty Years' War and its economic hardships, the town was reduced to the status of an obscure regional market; without much new building going on, it preserved its medi-eval appearance for centuries, only to suffer from bombing raids at the end of the last war. Carefully rebuilt, it is now often used for location work on films set in the Middle Ages.

The **town hall** dominating the daz-zling ensemble of the market square is partly Gothic (the belfry dates from the 14th century), while its front section is Renaissance. There is a small museum in the former imperial hall, and the top of the tower offers a stunning view on the roofs and walls of Rothenburg in the shape of a wine glass. North of the Marktplatz can be seen the gable of the old Ratstrinkstube, whose clock jacks enact the famous *Meistertrunk* (bumper of wine) episode. The story goes that during the Thirty Years' War Protestant Rothenburg was unable to resist the imperial army under Tilly, who was determined to raze the town. The gen-eral said he would relent, however, if a leading citizen could down a 3-liter tank-ard of local wine, which one ex-mayor managed to do. In commemoration,

Markus Tower in Rothenburg ob der Taubes.

there is a pageant on this theme at Whitsuntide.

North of the market stands the **St-Jakob-Kirche** with a superb altarpiece by Riemenschneider (1504) in the south aisle, and a very fine high altar, a masterpiece of late German Gothic art with highly detailed narrative paintings, including one of the earliest town views in Western art (1466). The broad pedestrian street going south from the

Marktplatz runs past the Renaissance **Baumeisterhaus** (master-builder's house), whose stepped gables are occupied by dragons, and the façade is decorated by the seven cardinal virtues (faith, hope, charity, prudence, moderation, fortitude, justice) and the seven deadly sins (pride, covetousness, lust, envy, gluttony, anger, sloth) higher up. Nearby is a picturesque corner formed by the juncture of two streets which both end at a

A wrought-iron sign typical of the many beautiful ones displayed throughout Germany.

fortified gateway. The most handsome mansions are found in the Herrngasse leading from the market to the ramparts. Following the battlements, you come to the beautiful Burggarten overlooking the bend of the Tauber; the splendid views takes in the two-tier bridge, the Topplerschlößchen, a tower bizarrely topped by living quarters, and the village of Detwang.

Würzburg and Wine

North of Rothenburg, **Würzburg**, the wine-capital of Franconia, is pleasantly situated on the Main amid vineclad hills. The people are friendly and outgoing and like to join up for drinking in spacious subterranean wine taverns, the equivalent of Munich's beer cellars. The city acquired its plan and general appearance between 1650 and 1750 under the supervision of three prince-bishops, members of the Schönborn family, who built most of the Baroque churches and the Residenz palace. Matthias Grünewald the painter (c.1465–1528) and the master-builder of the Baroque, Balthasar Neumann (1687–1753), are closely associated with the city; the "master of Würzburg", however, is Tilman Riemenschneider (1460–1531), the sculptor who came to live here in 1483. What makes his wood-carvings especially appealing is that his interest centered entirely on people whose faces, hands and clothes served as the means

The Marienberg in Würzburg.

to express emotion and sensitivity.

The city is dominated by two grandiose buildings of the prince-bishops: the hilltop fortress **Marienberg** in the west, and the Residenz with its lovely park in the town center. The massive, thick-walled fortress, floodlit at night, provides a fine sight. It was the prince-bishops' residence from 1253 to 1720, its fortifications dating from the 16th century. It houses the Mainfränkisches Museum with several Riemenschneider statues. There is also a dungeon to explore and a tiny fortified church (706), one of Germany's oldest, built shortly after St Kilian, the "apostle of the Franks", was put to death in 689. From the terrace you have a marvelous view over the city and its surrounding vineyards.

From the fortress there is a pleasant walk down into town. Cross the 15th century Mainbrücke adorned with statues of twelve saints, monumental in size and Baroque in conception, and continue to the **Dom**, rebuilt after 1945 and preserving its Romanesque exterior.

The interior, a mixture of various styles, has three Riemenschneider sculptures, and against the pillars in the nave the tombs of the prince-bishops are lined up side by side. Opposite stands the Neumünster with an elaborate Baroque façade. The 18th-century church was built over the graves of St Kilian and two fellow apostles; inside is the shrine to Franconia's patron as well as a font (7th century) believed to have been used by the saint to baptize. Straight ahead lies

Tiepolo ceiling detail in the Residenz, Würzburg.

the **Residenz**, one of the largest and most splendid Baroque palaces in Germany, built from 1720 to 1744 after designs by Neumann. The grand staircase ends at the vestibule, whose vaulted ceiling is decorated by an enormous Tiepolo fresco glorifying one of the prince-bishops (1753).

In the oval *Kaisersaal* (imperial hall) the Venetian artist has illustrated various episodes from Würzburg's history. One wing of the palace is taken up by the dazzling fantasy – Neumann's again – of the **Hofkirche** (court church). From here enter the terraced gardens for a good view of the elegant palace buildings.

Strolling back to the city center, you pass the Lusamgärtlein on the north side of the Neumünster; here the minstrel-poet Walther von der Vogelweide, who died c.1231, is said to be buried. A few steps further you enter the Marktplatz with the Marienkapelle, a fine Gothic hall church at the north side, and to the left the Haus zum Falken, which houses behind its graceful Rococo façade the tourist office. Twisting alleys lead to the Main and numerous wine pubs serving a cool glass of Frankenwein.

The enchanting city of **Bamberg**, east of Würzburg, presents a strange contrast: while it is graced by some of the most exuberant Baroque buildings in Bavaria, its atmosphere is that of a typical self-effacing small Franconian town. It was founded in the 10th century

Rococo detail in the Residenz,
Würzberg.

by the counts of Babenberg, who gave it their name. It owes its importance mainly to the Emperor Henry II (r.1002–24), who added to its status of an imperial residence that of a flourishing episcopal town. It straddles the rushing river Regnitz, which from the 12th century divided the episcopal city on the hill from the burghers below. This explains why the quaint Altes Rathaus with its trompe-l'oeil painted façade was built on an islet in the river, strategically placed to serve the town's two parts. The riverbanks are lined with charming gabled cottages, while narrow streets wind up to the great cathedral with its four green spires.

This **Dom**, built in transitional Gothic style – the eastern apse still fol-lows Romanesque patterns – has beautiful doorways leading into the spacious interior dominated by the raised chancels on both ends. Among its many masterpieces of German Gothic sculpture, the most famous is perhaps the equestrian statue of the *Bamberger Reiter* (Bamberg horseman; c.1230), the representation of a knight-king who symbolizes an ideal of the Middle Ages. Next to it is a sensitively sculptured group of the Visitation. The center of the nave is taken up by a virtuoso work by Riemenschneider, which took him 14 years to complete: the tomb of Henry II, the Saint, and his wife Kunigonde, decorated with many narrative scenes from the life of this saintly couple, including an operation for gallstones, performed by St Benedict on the emperor. Note also the late 14th-century choir stalls and, above the entrance, the Adam door with representations of Henry and Kunigonde, St Stephen and St Peter and Adam and Eve – the first nude sculptures of the Middle Ages.

On the Domplatz next to the cathedral stands the former episcopal and imperial palace, the Alte Hofhaltung (old residence) with its Renaissance façade of carved gables, oriel window and corner turret. The picturesque inner courtyard (open until dusk) is lined with half-timbered Gothic buildings with sloping roofs and dormer windows.

The adjacent **Neue Residenz**, Bamberg's largest edifice, displays paintings by German Renaissance masters; the imperial apartments are sumptu-

Swans along the Regnitz River lined with old fishermen's homes
now known as "Little Venice", Bamberg.

ously furnished with Baroque furniture, parquet floors and authentic Gobelin tapestries; the emperors' hall is outstanding for its allegorical frescoes and portraits. The serene rose garden at the back offers a fine bird's-eye view of the city. From the Domplatz, the Karolinenstraße leads to the old burghers' town spread along the Regnitz; from the bridge at the lower end of the old town hall there is a good view of the idyllic old fishermen's houses along the riverbank.

On the road north to Coburg, you will notice two remarkable buildings facing each other in solitary splendor from two hills separated by the young Main, here in its upper reaches more a brook than a river. On the north side

rises the vast former Benedictine abbey of **Banz**, founded in the 11th century and rebuilt in the 18th to designs by Johann Dientzenhofer, a member of the famous dynasty of Baroque masterbuilders. Banz itself is the "holy mountain" of Franconia, and its tradition goes back to the Franks who, having defeated the Thuringian tribes in 531, settled in the region and introduced to it the cult of St Denis, protector of the Merovingian dynasty. The *Klosterkirche* (abbey church) is remarkable for the complexity of its roofing and the magnificent painted ceiling. The terrace affords a grand view of the Main valley and of the church opposite: **Vierzehnheiligen**, though dull from afar, has an interior even more splendid. Balthasar Neumann, that most subtle and inventive of Baroque masterbuilders, is responsible for the breathtaking interior, a succession of three oval bays framed by colonnades and covered with low inner cupolas. Its masterpiece is the Nothelferaltar, an altarpiece dedicated to a group of 14 saints who help people in need, executed in 1764 by stuccoworkers from the famous Bavarian Wessobrunn School. The altar, a Rococo pyramid with a pierced baldachin and with all lines swirling cloud-fashion, was erected on the spot where in 1445–6 a shepherd boy had a vision of the Infant Jesus among the 14 saints of intercession. A local cult developed, a pilgrims' chapel was built, and then slowly (1743–72) this magnificent edifice was realized.

Compact Coburg and Remarkable Regensburg

The dreamy little town of **Coburg** is well-known for its dynastic links to the royal houses of Belgium and Great Britain and its well-preserved castle with an excellent museum of prints and drawings. The Coburgers have yet to capitalize on the illustrious genealogy of their former rulers. The town center between the Marktplatz and the Ehrenburg bears a late Renaissance imprint, bestowed on it mainly by the most enterprising member of the House of Saxe-Coburg, Duke Johann Casimir (r.1596–1633). Here the Coburgers take advantage of

the slightest provocation to organize pageants and communal festivals; around Christmas-time, the market is transformed into an old-time bazaar with dozens of stalls selling hand-blown glass decoration and all the traditional trinkets that turn the humble fir or spruce into a resplendent ornament without which no German family can truly celebrate. All year round you can try at one of the market stalls the delicious *Bratwurst* grilled over pine kernels.

At **Schloß Ehrenburg**, the gray, formal Renaissance palace that was home to the Saxe-Coburg family until 1918, the rooms where Queen Victoria stayed on several occasions can be visited: her modest bedroom, the Giants' Hall with heavy Italiante stuccoes and the neo-Baroque throne room. Most rooms are smallish and have a lived-in feeling. The Saxe-Coburgs, who lived in the town from the 16th century onward, by the 19th century were related through marriage to the English, Belgian, Portuguese and Bulgarian royal families, and were nicknamed the "royal stud farm". Princess Victoria met Albert, one of her numerous cousins, for the first time in 1836, a few days before her 17th birthday. They married four years later, and by the time Albert died (1861), Victoria had borne him nine children who in turn married into most of the remaining royal houses of Europe.

Set high on a hill above Coburg, the **Veste** (fortress) is one of the largest castles in Germany, with a double ring of fortified walls. The present buildings late from the 16th century and, with high roofs broken by dormer windows, are grouped around an inner courtyard. The half-timbered *Fürstenbau* (princes' palace) holds memories of Luther's stay in 1530; the Music Room contains four paintings by Lucas Cranach. The treasures of the Veste's rich and important *Kunstsammlungen* (art collections) are displayed in several wings of the castle; in this ambience, works from the Renaissance period acquire an added poignancy. Like with many castles, the Veste's stark exterior forms a strong contrast with the charming, prettily half-timbered courtyard with its obsolete cannons and ornamented well.

To the southeast of Nürnberg, **Regensburg** is one of Germany's loveliest old cities. Founded by the Romans, by the 13th century it had become one of the largest and richest cities in southern Germany, a trading center with particularly strong links to Venice. Its legacy from those days are not so much great buildings and palaces, as an atmosphere and charm of artistic intimacy and civilized living. After the 14th century it was overtaken by Augsburg and Nürnberg, but retained some political importance: in 1663, when the Holy Roman Empire's Imperial Diet became permanent, its seat was at Regensburg's Rathaus and remained there until its dissolution by Napoleon in 1803. In 1810 Regensburg became part of the Kingdom of Bavaria. It escaped unscathed from the last war and is today a booming industrial center with a new

university (1967).

The majestic **cathedral** is regarded as south Germany's finest Gothic church; its high lace-work spires are a good landmark for orientation. Inside there is some beautiful stained glass (14th century), and the chapel has traces of Romanesque frescoes. A few steps east lies the picturesque Alter Kornmarkt with a Romanesque tower on its north side and the Alte Kapelle (old chapel) to the south. This was also originally Romanesque, but was later completely redecorated in Rococo style; elegant tall windows and much gilded stucco make this a light and serene place of worship. Take a look at the massive stone slabs of the **Porta Praetoria** to the northeast of the Dom, built by the Romans in AD 179 as part of their defenses against the wild tribes beyond the Danube. East of the Alte Kapelle stands the huge Stadtmuseum, housed in a former Minorite monastery; it is devoted to local history and culture and its displays include paintings by members of the Danube School, of which Albrecht Altdorfer (1480–1538), who sat on the city council, is the best-known representative. There are several other fine old churches around here.

West of the Domplatz lies the Gothic **Altes Rathaus** with its magnificent Reichssaal, where the Diet met; the hall, lit by a slender oriel window, has lovely painted ceilings and a 13th-century minstrels' balcony. In this quarter of town you notice the famous patrician towers, a feature unique in the north of the Alps. In the Middle Ages, the rich

Young tourists taking a break.

burghers built themselves town mansions with towers, modeled on Italian domestic architecture (there is a marvelous ensemble at San Gimignano in Tuscany). Regensburg used to have 60 of them, of which 20 survive. The towers, symbols of wealth, were up to 12 stories high and decorated with loggias. The highest of those extant, the nine-story Goldener Turm, has a wine-bar on the top floor (fine views).

After the Dom, the most interesting church is **St Emmeram** south of the Altstadt; parts of it are 8th century, and it is decorated with some of Germany's earliest Romanesque carvings, while the interior is lavishly Baroque. The church forms part of a former abbey that since 1812 has been the residential palace of

the princes of Thurn and Taxis. This dynasty pioneered the European mail service in the 15th century, then held the monopoly of German postal services right until 1867. Today the family owns vast timber forests in Bavaria, the largest private Bavarian brewery, 17 percent of Regensburg's buildings as well as huge tracts of land in South America. When the family is not staying here, some rooms of the palace are open to the public.

For a splendid view of the busy Danube and the old quarter, walk to the Steinerne Brücke (stone bridge), where a salt warehouse with a vast roof flanks a fortified gateway. To the west lies the small Fischmarkt square with a fish market held each morning, and a few

View at sunrise over Passau encompassing St Stephan's Cathedral and the Danube River.

steps eastward bring you to the Historische Wurstküche, said to be Germany's oldest cooked sausage house (c.1140).

East of Regensburg, on a hill above a bend in the Danube, stands the **Walhalla**, a Doric temple built by Ludwig I in 1842 to honor Germany's greatest men; Walhalla or Valhalla, in Nordic mythology was the final resting place of the heroes' souls. The concept may be unfashionable today, but in summer the place is crowded with tourists inspecting some 200 busts and plaques of soldiers, artists, scientists etc.

South of Regensburg, the little river **Altmühl** flows into the Danube at Kelheim, where three towers and three city gates remain of the 13/14th-century fortifications. The Altmühl valley, prettily pastoral and lined with charming villages, is still undiscovered by mass tourism. A journey up it from Kelheim to Eichstätt, where the castle was rebuilt by Elias Holl in 1593 and the cathedral has stained-glass windows designed by Holbein the Elder, is definitely a delightful excursion.

On the Austrian Edge

Passau lies right on the Austrian border and is very picturesquely situated on a narrow strip of land, where the broad Inn and the lesser Ilz flow into the Danube between wooded hills. The city is a center of staunch right-wing Catholicism, of which the profusion of shops selling devotional articles is an indication. During the Middle Ages it was a powerful bishopric, and later became a Free Imperial City. The legacy of these glorious times is a number of notable buildings, chief among them the lofty **cathedral** with green cupolas. Originally late Gothic, it was rebuilt in Baroque style and contains the world's largest church organ, with 17,388 pipes and 231 registers; performances are given at noon in summer. The best view of its flamboyant Gothic façade is from the lovely old Residenzplatz, lined by handsome Renaissance mansions, one of which houses a toy museum. At the Rathausplatz by the Danube stands the ornately painted 14th-century town hall, whose main halls are decorated with frescoes of Nibelung legends. Opposite is a large museum of glass.

Passau's narrow streets flanked by well-preserved old houses offer peaceful walks, and the public gardens at the junction of the three rivers are a good spot to watch the busy traffic on the Danube. Across the river, the big white hilltop fortress, Veste Oberhaus, built in the 13th century by the local prince-bishop, affords fine views of the old town. Further south, close to Mozartian Salzburg in Austria, lies the popular mountain resort of **Berchtesgaden**. The historic center around the Schloßplatz is marvelously preserved with granary, accounting house and the royal castle, a former Augustine priory. It is now a museum with a rich display of weapons,

porcelain and tapestries, much of it collected by Crown Prince Rupert, son of the last Bavarian king, who lived here from 1923 until his death in 1955. On a tour of the **Salzbergwerk** (salt mines), active since 1515, you are provided with miner's clothes before sliding down a 1,650-foot-long (500 meters) chute to the salt rock below, where a train takes you through galleries and tunnels of glistering salt crystals. For an awesome view of the Alps, take the bus to Obersalzberg, where Hitler had his country house (now destroyed). An elevator takes you up to the Kehlstein peak (6,000 feet [1,800 meters]). A more tranquil and very pretty excursion would be to the nearby Königssee, dramatically enclosed between the towering heights of the Kahlersberg and Watzmann. Walking along the shore, you will find the very picturesque lakeside chapel of St Bartholomä.

Germany's leading ski resort, **Garmisch-Partenkirchen**, lies some 60 miles (100 km) south of Munich in a flat valley with mountains all around. Partenkirchen is the older and more interesting part of the twin town, with a Heimatmuseum devoted to local history, and a fine parish church. During skiing season from November to May many big events are held at the two giant Olympic ice and skiing stadia built for the 1936 winter games. Then, too, bars sculpted in ice line the streets of this elegant, fashionable place. The star local attraction is the mighty **Zugspitze** (6,500 feet [2,000 meters]), Germany's

The cross on the east peak of the Zugspitze.

highest peak. A road west from Garmisch leads to the charming, dark-blue Eibsee; either from here or from the town itself a log-railway takes visitors to the Schneefernerhaus, from whence a cable-car crosses dizzying chasms to the summit. The wide views over the Austrian and Swiss Alps are sensational.

Close by is the pretty little resort of **Mittenwald**, a very active center of violin-making. There is a technical school that teaches the craft and a small museum displaying old violins and other string instruments; even the local liqueur is sold in violin-shaped bottles. The picturesque old village has also some of the best examples of a quintessentially Bavarian art called *Lüftlmalerei* (airy painting): many of the traditional houses with overhanging eaves boast a richly painted façade showing rural scenes and other folklore motifs. Among skiers, Mittenwald is known for its abundance of snow even at times when other resorts are completely bare. A 45-mile (75-km) round-trip from Garmisch will get you to two of Germany's most extraordinary castles and a solitary pilgrim church of Baroque splendor.

Leaving Garmisch northward, you pass the former Benedictine monastery **Kloster Ettal**, founded in 1330 by Emperor Ludwig of Bavaria. The vast abbey set in Alpine solitude, mostly 18th-century Baroque, has a venerated statue of the Virgin attributed to the Italian artist Giovanni Pisano (c.1250–c.1314). The small cream-colored **Schloß**

Hohenschwangau Castle.

Linderhof to the west was built by Ludwig II deep in the forest of a wild valley, in a hunting area reserved for the Wittelsbachs. The park, laid out in Italian villa style, is especially charming, with pools, cascades and terraces. The road to the town of **Füssen** leads across Swiss territory. Füssen, an important trading center at the approach to the Tyrol, has a 15th-century castle rising high above, the former summer residence of the bishops of Augsburg. It also has a casino much frequented by the Swiss, who are not allowed such pleasures at home. East of Füssen lies the castle of **Hohenschwangau** (1832–38), an impressive neo-Gothic edifice reflecting Maximilian II's taste for troubadour Romanticism. The castle still has the warmth of a palace that was once lived in. Among its highly ornate furnishings are the vast mural paintings with medieval scenes that had a dramatic and lasting influence on Ludwig II, who grew up here. Nearby he built his own castle, stupendous **Neuschwanstein**, rising on a spur and bristling with towers and pinnacles. The designs were sketched by a theatrical decorator and not by an architect, which explains the dream-like atmosphere. Ludwig lived here only for 170 days, before he was dethroned. From the unfinished Romanesque-Byzantine throne room there is an unforgettable view of wooded mountains and lakes.

Further north lies the charming **Wieskirche** in solitary splendor. Simple

Painted facade of a house in Oberammergau.

from the outside, the Baroque interior – executed by an artist from the famous Wessobrunn School – is overwhelming through the unity and harmony achieved by the adaptation of the decoration to the architecture. On the way back to Garmisch, you pass the attractive little town of **Oberammergau**, full of traditionally painted houses. It is a center of wood-carving, but its chief claim to fame is the *"Passion Play"* performed every ten years. It originated in 1633, when a terrible plague miraculously stopped just short of Oberammergau, and the villagers vowed to put on a passion play every decade. Today the more than 100 performances attract about half a million visitors.

This region in the southwest corner of Germany has some of the loveliest scenery and romantic sights of the country, with medieval towns, hilltop castles, extensive vineyards and gently and not so gently sloping wooded hills.

The wide bed of the Rhine and the sunny Black Forest mark its borders with France, the Bodensee (Lake Constance) in the south is partly Swiss, while the plains in the north, through which the peaceful Neckar winds its way, towards the southeast give way to the windy heights of the Swabian Jura.

The flowery portal prevalent in Germany.

Baden and Württemberg are ancient regions with marked differences in climate and character, and were merged only in 1951 after a popular referendum. Baden, whose contours closely follow the east bank of the Rhine, was settled in the 3rd century by the Alemanns, a Germanic tribe. It has much in common with neighboring France, its people being largely Catholic, fun-loving, easy-going and fond of festivals and folklore.

Württemberg forms the main part of an ancient territory known as Suabia, and the Swabians, descendants of another Germanic tribe which settled between the Neckar and the Bodensee, are by repute ponderous, slow, very

271

**Heidelberg &
Baden-Württemberg**

The gentler Black Forest landscape.

hardworking, gently humorous as well as somewhat pious and puritanical. Stuttgart, formerly Württemberg's capital and now the region's, lies in the center of a highly industrialized area. Most of its businesses are light industrial (engineering, optics, electronics), which are clean and relatively unobtrusive. Much of the countryside, indeed, looks charmingly rural with orchards, tobacco fields and much cabbage grown for sauerkraut.

Among the region's many attractions are Heidelberg Castle, the epitome of German romanticism; the elegant spa Baden-Baden; picturesque Freiburg; Konstanz with its tropical gardens; and the Swabian Jura with more castles than any other part of Germany save the middle Rhine.

A Big Small Town

Stuttgart, said to be the richest city in Europe, is at once impressively industrial and amiably low-key and gentle. Its central part lies in a hollow, cradled by wooded hills with sumptuous villas peeping from behind dark foliage. It is the world's leading producer of luxury, high-performance cars: both Mercedes-Benz and Porsche have their headquarters in the outskirts and car museums worth visiting.

Its opera and theater are among the most exciting in Germany, and the museums of art and ethnology contain

The Black Forest.

great and evocative displays. Although not usually thought of as a spa, its mineral springs produce more mineral water (18 million liters a day) than any other European city except Budapest; it is even piped into the local fountains and swimming-pools. The old spa town of Bad Cannstadt just across the Neckar and now a suburb of Stuttgart, puts on the *Cannstadt Was'n* in late September, Germany's biggest annual beer-festival after Munich's *Oktoberfest*.

Part of the modern downtown area is taken up by the Schloßgarten, a broad ribbon of a park that extends more than $1^1/_2$ miles (3 km) from the Schloßplatz to where the Neckar snakes its way out of the city. Start your walk at the Schloßplatz with the **Baroque Neues**

Schloß and the **Kunstgebäude**, the city's art gallery, housing good examples of modern and very modern German art. Southward lies the small and graceful Schillerplatz, the city's only old-world square, with a bustling fruit and flower market held three times a week. All around are historic buildings well restored after wartime bombing. South of the Schillerplatz lies the clumsily rebuilt former Altstadt.

One of the few surviving older buildings is the modest house where the philosopher Hegel, Karl Marx's main inspiration, was born in 1770. The restored Stiftskirche (15th century) nearby has an octagonal tower and inside, eleven vivid Renaissance statues of medieval Württemberg rulers. The most impor-

Farmer's wife in front of the farmhouse in the Black Forest region.

tant of the historic buildings is the Altes Schloß just east of the Stiftskirche. It is in part the remains of a 14th-century moated castle, the rest a fine Renaissance ducal palace with a lovely arcaded courtyard. This is now the **Landesmuseum**, whose important historical collection include the Württemberg crown jewels, Gothic playing cards, much Swabian religious sculpture and various local Roman and Frankish antiquities.

Just east of this part of the park and its lake with swans is the magnificent **Staatsgallerie**, the area's main art gallery. Its large new wing was designed by the late Scottish architect James Stirling; now that the public outcry against it has died down, the building is generally admired as one of Germany's most successful and satisfying examples of contemporary architecture.

Horse riding in the Black Forest.

The museum's holdings start with 16th-century Old Masters, Swabian, Dutch and Italian, but its forte is the more modern era, featuring scores of great artists from the last 150 years from Monet to Moore and Beuys, with several memorable paintings and sculptures by the Stuttgart-born Oskar Schlemmer (1888–1943), a leading member of the Bauhaus movement.

Southeast of the Schloßgarten you find the Bohnenviertel, an area devoted to nocturnal pleasures, where intimate though slightly seedy pubs and restaurants are making way for chic boutiques and wine bars open into the small hours. The university quarter lies a bit further west, and with it the ethnographic Lindenmuseum. Its many imaginative displays include African masks and costumes, Javanese shadow-puppets, a Near Eastern bazaar and several Japanese tea-houses.

On the hill behind it is the very well-designed Killesberg park with an open-air theater and beer-garden, flamingo pond, miniature railway and tower with panoramic views. The nearby Weissenhof Siedlung comprises a group of houses designed in 1927 by Gropius, Le Corbusier, Mies van der Rohe and other famous architects as part of the Bauhaus movement; badly bombed in the war, it has since been rather poorly rebuilt.

A pleasant excursion from Stuttgart leads through rolling woodland and past the Pfaffen and Bären lakes (there is a good pub at the Bärensee) to the well-known **Schloß Solitude**. This elegant little cream-colored pavilion in Hellenistic style was built in the 1760s by the Duke of Württemberg for his mistress, siting it so that he could see it on its hilltop from his own palace at Ludwigsburg, 9 miles (15 km) to the north. Or go by boat from Stuttgart to pretty **Marbach**, Schiller's birthplace, where the large and interesting Schiller Nationalmuseum houses the foremost German literary archive. This stirring, radical poet-dramatist is the second most frequently performed of all playwrights in Germany, after Shakespeare.

Heidelberg.

Heidelberg: Spirit of Germany

Most visitors enter **Heidelberg** from the west, by way of its modern quarter with research towers and high-tech industries. Do not be disappointed but drive straight through to the Bismarckplatz, the city's present-day center. A walk along the Hauptstraße takes you progressively back in time into the Altstadt, where medieval lanes on both sides frame glimpses of looming green hills. On the Hauptstraße you find the Kurpfälzisches Museum, prettily housed in an 18th-century palace with a courtyard café.

Its glory is Riemenschneider's altar-piece (1509) of Christ and the Apostles, its realistically carved faces gaunt with pathos; important, too, is its big collection of paintings and drawings by leading German Romantics. Further along the main street you come to the L-shaped **Universitätsplatz**. The key event in Heidelberg's history was the founding, in 1386, of Germany's first university, which provoked an exodus of German scholars from the prestigious Paris Sorbonne back home. When the university's rapid growth caused a space problem, the simple solution decided upon was to drive out the city's Jews from their houses and synagogues and convert the buildings to faculty housing. In 1563 members of the university composed the Heidelberg Catechism, the defini-

A student's pub in Heidelberg.

tive statement of reformed Christian faith. The medieval buildings were destroyed at the end of the 18th century, the present Baroque Old University dating from 1728. Heidelberg is one of Germany's most popular universities, both on account of its great tradition (seven Nobel laureates in modern times) and its warm and sympathetic ambience; students account for one quarter of the city's population.

At the far end of the square stands the library, the **Bibliotheca Palatina**, with splendid medieval manuscripts; its most famous treasure is the *Codex Manesse*, a beautifully illuminated 14th-century collocation of earlier love lyrics, with portraits of all the great minnesingers (facsimile display). A few

steps past the university square and up the Augustinerstraße brings you to the *Studentenkarzer* (student goal), in use from 1712 to 1914, where scapegraces were locked up for their pranks, like swimming naked in the Neckar or letting a pig run loose in the streets; the walls are covered with their plaints and witticisms.

The Hauptstraße soon widens for the Marktplatz with the Hercules fountain, the late Gothic Heilig-Geist-Kirche, and the **Haus zum Ritter** (knight's mansion), a glorious late Renaissance masterpiece with a bust of St George in knightly armor; it has been converted into a hotel.

From the Marktplatz take the signposted route through crooked alleys up to Europe's quintessential romantic ruin, surrounded by green terraces, remnants of the Renaissance garden. Architecturally most beautiful are the north and east walls, the latter now only a façade but with a wealth of ornament. The **Schloß**, former seat of the princes and electors of the Palatinate, is an assemblage of various centuries and styles from the late feudal period (14th century) to the Renaissance-Baroque transitional period (early 17th century). The story of its ruination is almost as poignant as its present grandeur. In 1671 the young Princess Elizabeth-Charlotte was commanded by her father, the elector, to marry the gay duke of Orléans, brother of Louis XIV.

Over the ensuing 50 years "Liselotte", as was her popular nickname, who had been born in the castle, wrote some 4,000 homesick letters about her life as a "royal slave" in Paris. When his brother died without an heir, the Sun King used her supposed claim to the Palatinate as a pretext for invading it. Heidelberg was captured in 1689, and in 1693 French troops razed the city and demolished the castle. In 1774 a fire completed the destruction. The survival of the ruin in its present form owes much to the French immigrant nobleman Count de Graimberg, who in the 19th century – while the castle was being carted away stone by stone for building material – battled for 50 years to save and restore it.

The Schloß's chief beauty is its site and overall appearance. But take a

guided tour and note, among other curious and delightful bits, the Elizabeth Gate erected in a single night (1615) as a surprise for the elector's wife. You cannot miss the Großes Faß (great vat; late 18th century) with a capacity of 220,000 liters (49,000 gallons), guarded by the figure of the dwarf Perkeo, who was court jester and cellarman, a great

Heidelberg Schloß and town at night.

drinker himself and the inventor of a curious clock. The **Deutsches Apothekenmuseum** (German pharmaceutical museum) contains fine 18/19th century furniture and a collection of ancient prescriptions; an alchemist's laboratory has been reconstructed in the Apothecary Tower.

Back in town, take a look at the **Alte Brücke** (old bridge), which Goethe considered a world wonder; its twin towers at the south end were the medieval city's main gate. Today, crowned with Baroque helms and graced with a neo-

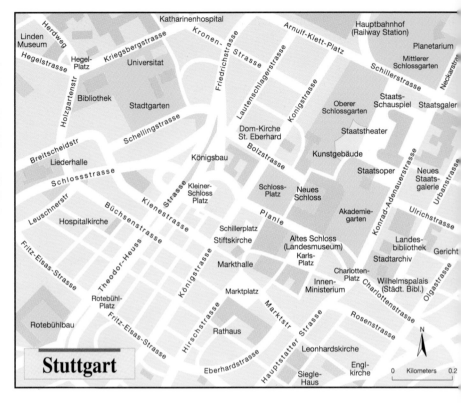

Stuttgart

Classical arch, the gate and bridge have become a famous landmark. Cross the bridge and climb the *Schlangenweg* (snake path) zigzagging steeply through vineyards and orchards, until you reach the famous *Philosophenweg* (philosophers' walk), for more than six centuries a favorite place for ratiocination with professors and students.

The winding path affords superb views of Heidelberg with the enormous red and white ruined castle on its green hillside and the Neckar flowing swiftly below, and past graceful towers and bridges, and onto steep rooftops capping boisterous beer and wine taverns and down quaint alleyways of a city left unscathed by wartime bombing (except

for a few bridges).

Southeast of Stuttgart, wonderful **Ulm** on the Upper Danube offers the visitor some medieval marvels with natural grace. A river-walk along the Jahnufer on the far side of the Danube, in the suburb of Neu-Ulm, which belongs to Bavaria, offers lovely views of the soaring cathedral and old gabled houses along the banks. The **Metzgerturm** (butchers' tower) flanking the bridge is the only surviving gateway of the old ramparts. The town's glory is the **Münster** (cathedral), whose sweeping vertical lines and lightness of pierced architecture are very beautiful. The 530-foot spire (161 meters) is the tallest of any church in the world. The great Gothic building dates from 1377, although the spire was finished only in 1890. The energetic may climb its 768 steps and be rewarded with a stunning view as far as the Alps, on a clear day. The cathedral has a beautiful porch with three arcades and high interior fan-vaulting. The pulpit is surmounted by a 15th-century sounding board above which is a kind of second pulpit for the Holy Ghost, the invisible preacher. Note especially the exceptional wood-carved choir-stalls (1469–71) by Jörg Syrlin; they are decorated with two series of personages, one Biblical, the other of pagan antiquity, men on the left, women on the right.

South of the Münster stands the graceful town hall with an astronomical clock (remodeled in 1580) on the west front. The nearby Marktplatz is graced with the vividly-colored **Fischkasten** (fish-crate) fountain, also by Syrlin (1482). A few steps east, the Ulmer Museum has Picassos and Klees as well as works by Syrlin and other early Ulm masters. The city's famous sons are the physicist Albert Einstein (1879–1955) and – much more a figure of folklore – the Tailor from Ulm. This was a certain Albrecht Berblinger who during a visit by the Württemberg king in 1811, decided to demonstrate his flying machine to the public. In front of some 10,000 onlookers, he leaped from the town wall with his weird-looking wings and proceeded to plummet like a stone into the Danube; his earlier attempts at hang-gliding had been more successful.

Fashionable Spa
Baden-Baden

Sheltered by the Oos valley between the Black Forest and the Baden vineyards, **Baden-Baden** is the most luxurious resort in Germany. In Roman times the Emperor Caracalla came to Baden-Baden to cure his rheumatism; during the 16th century the great physician and alchemist Paracelsus (c.1490–1541), who established the role of chemistry in medicine, came to look after the health of the local margrave. In the 19th century the town became the summer capital of Europe because it was a pioneer in the new craze for casinos, just ahead of Monte Carlo. The casino was operated by a Frenchman; the opera house was inaugurated in 1862 with a work by Berlioz, directed by the composer himself; and the Iffezheim races, run in August and still a grand affair, were organized by the Jockey Club of Paris. Napoleon III, Bismarck and Queen Victoria were among those who rode along the elegant Lichtentaler Allee, while more humble visitors walked, like members of the Russian colony (Gogol, Turgenev, Dostoevsky) and the French colony (Balzac, Hugo, Dumas), and ferociously played the tables.

Since 1900 the number of beds has dropped from 15,000 to 4,000, partly due to the much reduced retinue of today's wealthy visitors. It is still a very fashionable and expensive place. Whereas most German spas rely mainly

A spa in Baden-Baden.

on routine guests paid for by national insurance, at Baden-Baden some 95 percent come privately, and most are well-to-do; over 40 percent of overnight visitors are foreign. The most beautiful promenade is the Kaiserallee and its continuation, the long Lichtentaler Allee; it runs beside the Oos which flows over an artificial bed. The Kurhaus (1821) with portico and white Corinthian columns, contains rooms where glamorous balls are held, and gaming rooms. Nearby is the Trinkhalle (pump room) with wall-paintings illustrating legends of the Baden-Baden countryside. The promenade is profusely planted with azaleas, magnolias, maples and silver poplars, tulip trees and Chinese gingkos, and in summer presents a riot of colors.

On its south end is the Gönneranlage where pergolas and fountains flank a rose garden.

A short walk of about four miles (6 km) from the town center takes you to the **Yburg ruins**; from its tower (110 steps) the vast view takes in the Rhine plain with the Baden vineyards in the foreground. A wonderful excursion (45 miles [75 km] round trip) leads through vineyard villages; follow the signposts of the Badische Weinstraße (wine road) to Sasbachwalden, a famous ceramic center, and the Mummelsee, then return on a winding route to Baden-Baden.

The road south from Baden-Baden runs parallel to the wide Rhine plain, full of wild fowl and rare birds, and ideal for cycling; beyond lies the tempting

ridge of the French Vosges with fine wine and good food and the city of Strasbourg with its famous lacey cathedral. Thus you reach youthful, lively **Freiburg** at the point where the Black Forest meets the Rhine plain. Cradled by green hills, with lots of culture and an easy-going ambience, it is easy to understand why many visitors place it even above Munich as the favorite German town. Founded by the local duke in the 12th century, it had a very peaceful history, was ruled by Austria from 1368 to 1805 and thereafter became a part of Baden. Last war's bombing destroyed large parts of the Altstadt, but these have been well rebuilt.

The old town is full of alleyways, small shops and wine taverns; **Zum alten Bären**, dating from 1311, claims to be Germany's oldest inn. Some streets are graced with mosaic paving, using pebbles from the Rhine, and a network of tiny streams runs down many narrow Altstadt lanes. The Gothic **Münster** is one of Germany's finest cathedrals, with a Romanesque transept (c.1200) and a towering lacework steeple (380 feet [116 meters]). Inside are several original stained-glass windows (13/16th century), which had been hidden during the war and so escaped damage. There are luminous paintings by Cranach the Younger and a superb high-altar triptych by Hans Baldung Grien (1511). In the west porch, note the expressive 13th-century sculptures of the Wise and Foolish Virgins.

Three notable buildings have sur-

Art on the street in Baden-Baden.

vived on the south side of the Münsterplatz, where a daily market is held: the Baroque archbishop's palace (1756), the house that the painter Christian Wenzinger built for himself in 1761, and the Gothic **Kaufhaus** (as the name implies, a medieval department store) flanked by watchtowers with pointed roofs. The most delightful quarter lies just south of the cathedral, between it and the picturesque **Schwabentor** (13th century), part of the old ramparts. Nearby is Freiburg's best museum, the **Augustiner**, a former monastery; this provides an ideal setting for its superb display of 13/15th century religious art from the Upper Rhine area, notably an altarpiece by Grünewald (1517); it also houses a rich collection of stained glass.

Colorful Freiburg.

Cuckoo Clocks

Cuckoo clocks.

Contrary to the old joke that Switzerland after centuries of peace had produced nothing but the cuckoo clock, these clocks in fact trace their origin to Germany's Black Forest. There, in the mid-17th century, peasants started clock-making. All parts were cut from wood except for those like the verge, where metal was indispensable. The earliest ones had weights of stone and only a single hand.

Opinion is divided as to who invented the curious and playful contraption. The popular candidate for the honor is Franz Anton Ketterer from Schönwald, a town northeast of Freiburg. Probably his first models only imitated the call of the cuckoo and did not include the characteristic small bird that emerges from a shuttered window. The invention is said to date from about 1730. The musical striking work was then a novelty on Black Forest clocks, and is thought to have derived from the astronomical and performing clocks in the minster of Villigen near Freiburg. The popular chalet type of today's design seems to date from the mid-19th century. The essential features include a small house decorated with carved leaves, birds, stags and other Romantic ornaments, and the dial shows white Gothic-style figures on a dark background with white carved hands.

Clock-making in the Black Forest started as a home handicraft. In summer, a member of the family would fill his pannier and tour the markets and fairs in the vicinity to peddle the clocks which the family had made during the winter. Cuckoo clocks quickly became very popular, and their production was soon organized along industrial lines. Distribution was also improved, and many clocks were sold in England. In the 1830s, the Kammerer family established a trading house in London which even survived the fierce competition from the cheap American clocks of the mid-century.

If you fancy buying one, explore the "kingdom of the cuckoo clock" in the central Black Forest between Freudenstadt and Freiburg, and combine the quest for the perfect traditional specimen with a drive through beautiful countryside and old, half-forgotten villages.

To the west are a number of remarkable houses grouped around the Rathausplatz. The elegant **Haus zum Walfisch** (1516) with its red-and-gold façade, was built by the treasurer of Emperor Maximilian I and offered refuge in 1529–31 to the philosopher and moralist Erasmus of Rotterdam, who was fleeing the Reformation in Basle. The **Neues Rathaus**, partly dating from the 16th century, originally consisted of two patrician houses which were linked in 1901 by a central arcade to become the town hall. South of the Rathausplatz lies the main campus of the university which was founded in 1467 and is one of Germany's oldest; it has two Rococo courtyards and a Jugendstil lecture hall.

Just south of Freiburg lies the famous Black Forest vantage-point Schauinsland ("view the countryside"; at 4,200 feet/1,286 meters), reachable from the city by road or by train and cable-car, which affords a majestic panorama. Northwest of the town, the slopes of the Kaiserstuhl produce some of the finest Baden wines. If you follow the Badische Weinstraße via Müllheim, you come to **Badenweiler**, Germany's most fashionable spa after Baden-Baden. Here the Roman emperor Vespasian took the waters in A.D. 1st century (remains of the baths have been excavated), and the great Russian playwright, novelist and doctor Anton Chekhov used to spend his summers here and died at the Park Hotel in 1904. A more cheerful note is supplied by the graceful Kurpark with a smart new Kurhaus.

On the Swiss Border

Southeast of Freiburg, on the shores of the Bodensee (Lake Constance), lies the busy town of **Konstanz**, said to have been founded in the 3rd century by the father of Constantine the Great. It became a bishopric very early (c.590), and enriched itself on linen trade; the historical background of this industry is well documented at the *Haus zum Kunkel* on the cathedral square, a museum of silk and linen manufacture. The Bohemian Reformer Jan Hus was burned at the stake in 1415 in what is now the Tägermosstraße, where his former rooms have been turned into a museum. The French essayist Michel de Montaigne stayed at what is today the **Gasthof zum Adler** in 1580 on his way to Italy; his diary of this tour provides interesting insights into the modes of traveling and sightseeing in those days.

Konstanz' major church is the **Münster Unserer Lieben Frau** (Cathedral of Our Lady), built on the site of a Roman fort. The crypt dates from c.1000, but only in 1856 was church construction really completed with the addition of the pyramidal tower. There are beautiful panels (1470) on the main façade doorway, and several fine works of art inside. The Holy Sepulchre of c.1280 is an excellent example of High Gothic, while the staircase (1438) with scenes from the Old and New Testaments is late Gothic. Further south in the **Rosgartenstraße**, the late 13th-century Church of the Holy Trinity has noble wall-paintings depicting the history of the Augustian Order (1417), while the nearby **Rosgarten Museum** is devoted to prehistory, cultural history, folklore and coinage. The Altstadt has been very thoroughly renovated recently south of the cathedral; at the Obermarkt, formerly the place of public execution, note the **Malhaus**, a Renaissance building housing a pharmacy that has been

Wooden huts on stilts, revealing early lake settlement, were found at Unterhildingen.

in business since the 14th century.

To the east of the cathedral, right on the shores of the lake, you find the **Konzilsgebäude** (not open to the public), a 14th-century warehouse. Its name erroneously implies that this was where the famous Council of Konstanz met,

which between 1414 and 1418 attempted to heal the schism caused by the Avignon papacy; in fact the council met at Münster in Westphalia. Vivid pictures of council meetings and daily life in Konstanz at that time by Ulrich Richental (1460) can be seen at the Rosgarten

famous for its exotic flora. The Baden princes and members of the royal house of Sweden started to grow brushwood and tropical plants here. Due to the very mild climate, an astonishing variety of trees and flowers flourish: there are palm, orange and lemon trees, hibiscus in the rose garden, banana trees with their immense drooping leaves and Mexican daturas displaying huge trumpet blossoms.

The island of **Reichenau**, accessible by boat or car, in the 10th–11th century was one of the most important monastic centers of the West; today it concentrates on market gardening with glasshouses glinting among the crops. The church of **St George** in the village of Oberzell is a late 9th-century edifice, its stepped buildings of remarkable harmony. The glorious wall-paintings (c.1000) are concerned exclusively with Christ's miracles. The **Münster** (old abbey) at Mittelzell of the 8/12th century has a robust Romanesque tower decorated with Lombard pilasters and friezes, a timbered vault (also Romanesque) and a Gothic apse much pierced with windows. Its treasury includes an early-14th-century reliquary of St Mark of beaten silver enriched with enamels.

To travel around the south side of the Bodensee from Konstanz means crossing into Switzerland via Massenbach – which has numerous 14th-century palatial mansions, the most important housing a museum devoted to Napoleon – and Stein am Rhein, a most beautiful Swiss medieval town.

Museum. The southern part of the city belongs to Switzerland; and Konstanz' casino is very popular with the Swiss, who cross the frontier for a night at the tables, a pleasure forbidden in their own country. Konstanz is a favorite starting point for round-trips along the shore of the Bodensee. For a shorter excursion, take the boat or car to **Mainau** island,

T he mighty Rhine is impressive wherever you come upon it: at the foaming cataract in Schaffhausen just across the Swiss border; in the wide Baden plain where it is bordered by broad sweeps of almost impenetrable woods and marshes; along the edge of the industrial Ruhr area, where its dark waters cut a swathe through densely built-up conurbations; or near the Dutch border, close to its estuary, where its wide bed seems already part of the sea.

From its source at the base of the Gotthard massif in the Swiss Alps to its mouth near Rotterdam it covers a distance of 820 miles (1,320 km), of which slightly less than half goes through Germany; it is Europe's third-longest river and its busiest waterway, being navi-

Burg Eltz, all we imagined a castle to be.

gable for 550 miles (880 km) to Rheinfelden near Basle. As a natural frontier it has often been fought over (mainly between French and Germans) since Julius Caesar in 55 B.C. built the first bridge across it near Andernach, north of Koblenz, thereby drawing the unruly Germanic tribes inexorably into the whirlwind of history.

The "Real" Rhine

Attractive though it may be in many places, by far the most beautiful stretch lies between Koblenz and Mainz; this is what both Germans and foreigners think of as the "real" Rhine: steep cliffs and fast currents, hilltop castles and picturesque ruins, vineyards and small valley towns with half-timbered houses and beckoning taverns.

The discoverers, if not the inventors, of the grandeur and beauty of the Rhine with all its historical and legendary associations were the English travelers of the 18th century on the Grand Tour to Rome, who journeyed by horse and boat, by coach and on foot straight across half of Europe. Byron with his *Childe Harold* and Turner with his numerous drawings and paintings were only the best-known propagandists of the Rhine. The words of Mary Shelley, wife of the poet and author of *Frankenstein*, conjure up the quintessential attractions of this part of the Rhine, then as now. In 1817 she wrote: "We were carried down by a dangerously

rapid current, and saw on either side of us hills covered with vines and trees, craggy cliffs crowned by desolate towers, and wooded islands, where picturesque ruins peeped from behind the foliage, and cast the shadows of their forms on the troubled waters, which distorted without deforming them. We heard the voice of the vintagers,

A cruise along the Rhine.

and...memory presents this part of the Rhine to my remembrance as the love-liest paradise on earth."

The waters are less troubled today, and many of the "desolate towers" have been renovated and now welcome visi-tors, offering splendid views, authentic dungeons, delicious food and soft beds. If you want to prolong your stay, you can rent a whole castle or – better still – buy one; a dozen or so between Cologne and Mainz are in private hands. Most of them date from the Middle Ages, when the Rhine was the most important wa-

Confluence of the Rhine and Moselle Rivers.

terway in Europe and even busier than now; the castle owners – noble and ignoble knights, dukes and archbishops – levied tolls from the boatmen and fishermen, or used their fortresses as places of refuge in times of war and rebellion.

The best time to travel is autumn; from August to October the wine harvest is celebrated in all the towns and villages along the river and its hinterland with traditional costumed processions and much jollity; many places put on special shows like the *"Rhein in Flammen"* (the Rhine ablaze) with great fireworks, tolling of church bells and vinous *Gemütlichkeit* in the taverns.

There are two ways of touring the Rhine. In summer, cruise boats run daily between Cologne and Mainz with many

stops in between. The stretch between Cologne and Koblenz is a little dull, for the countryside is flattish and the river sluggish. If you go by car, you need to decide along which bank to travel.

On the road by the right bank some of the most spectacular castles are out of sight. The most popular route is along the left bank between Koblenz and Bingen; heavy lorries, which used to be a nuisance on the rather narrow riverside road, now prefer to take the autobahn further west through the Hunsrück hills. In Bingen get ferried across to Rüdesheim for the final leg to Mainz.

Situated at the confluence of the Rhine and the Moselle, **Koblenz** is an important wine and traffic center; it has been rebuilt after the war – when more

A sundial in the Moselle wine valley.

than 80 percent of the city was bombed – in rather pedestrian fashion. There are a few interesting spots to visit, and it makes a good starting point for a Rhine tour.

At the point where the sweet-tempered Moselle joins the gruff Rhine lies the *Deutsches Eck* (German triangle), an open square with a stone monument for William I (1897); the equestrian statue has been demolished, but the base remains, and from its top (107 steps) you have a good view. This is where the Teutonic Order of Knights set up their first post on German soil in 1216. A delightful promenade runs along the Moselle bank.

Turn left at the Balduinsbrücke, built across the Moselle in 1343, and enter the Altstadt. At the Münzplatz you find the Metternich-Hof, birthplace of the Chancellor of Austria and architect of post-Napoleonic Europe, who came from an old Catholic Rhineland family. Sprinkled between modern buildings, some very old houses have miraculously survived: Kastnerstraße no.2 dates from c.1300, while at the corner of Am Plan and Löhrstraße stands the 17th-century *Vier Türme* (four towers) with four projecting oriel bays.

The Romanesque **Florinskirche** at the north side of the Altstadt has a Gothic chapel, and the nearby Mittelrhein-Museum is housed in a Renaissance building. The Florinsmarkt itself is an enchanting small restored square with many taverns serving sim-

Moselle villages of Kinheim and Losnich.

accessible by car or chairlift. It dates from the 10th century and was the residence of the archbishops of Trier till sacked by the French in 1799; the present fortifications, battlements, gateways and maze of long tunnels were erected by the Prussians in 1816 when the left bank was still French.

Along the Moselle

Before journeying along the Rhine you may want to make an excursion up the serene Moselle valley to the venerable old city of Trier. The Moselle valley is nothing but light and clear, presenting a striking contrast to the Rhine. It has its share of pretty villages and old towns, and its wines are highly regarded, especially by the French because of their affinity with the wines of Alsace.

Follow the river and turn off at Moselkern for the spectacular setting of **Burg Eltz**, a fairy-tale castle of the 12/16th century, embodying all the fantasies anyone ever had about castles – towers, soaring granite walls, turrets, half-timbered gables, lookouts and pointed roofs like witches' hats.

The main town on the Moselle is **Bernkastel-Kues**, famous for its wines and as the birthplace of the great theologian and philosopher Nikolaus von Kues (1401–64); the *Haus zum Krebs* where he was born is now a small museum. The market square is the focus of town life. Note the old pillory and iron chain in the northwest corner. The Ren-

ple but tasty food.

To the west lies **St Castor**, also Romanesque, with interesting early Gothic wall-paintings. The neo-Classical Schloß (with park) to the south was completely gutted by fire-bombing, and only the façade has been restored.

Nearby on the Rhine embankment is the *Weindorf*, a relic of the 1925 wine fair and a replica of a typical wine village with a square enclosed by a vineyard and four half-timbered houses. It seems bizarre to fake a wine village when the whole region is full of authentic ones; but the wine is good, and the place is crowded in summer.

From here you can see the vast fortress of **Ehrenbreitstein** towering over the opposite bank of the Rhine; it is

Bernkastel-Kues, the main town in the Moselle valley.

aissance town hall overlooks an octagonal fountain (1606) graced by the town's patron, St Michael. Nearby the top-heavy *Spitzes Haus* (pointed house) seems to defy gravity.

Following the winding course of the Moselle, you eventually reach **Trier**, which has better-preserved Roman remains than any other town in northern Europe. It is the center of the Moselle wine trade, and its huge underground wine cellars can be visited. Yet its people are not as jolly and fun-loving as those in the Rhine wine towns, and tend to be a bit heavy and solemn, in temperament closer to their Luxembourg neighbors.

The legendary founder of the city was the son-in-law of Semiramis, the fabulous Queen of Assyria; that is the conceit behind the Latin inscription on a 17th-century house at the Hauptmarkt (main market square): "Trier existed 1,300 years before Rome came into being." More prosaic and more likely is its foundation by Emperor Augustus in the 1st century B.C. It reached a high standard of craftsmanship, trading practices and intellectual activity – the museums supply tangible evidence of this – before a Germanic assault in the 3rd century. However, it was soon after declared an imperial residence, and the first Christian emperor, Constantine (r.306–37), commanded massive ramparts to be built and magnificent religious and secular monuments.

Trier thus became a Christian metropolis in the West, on an equal footing with Rome. In 314 the first German bishopric was established. In the 5th century, the Frankish invasion led to its downfall, but by the Middle Ages it was again important in political and religious affairs (the two being almost synonymous at the time), its archbishop ranking as one of the seven electors, the dignitaries who decided on each new emperor of the Holy Roman Empire. Today the city is a bastion of conservative Catholicism.

Walking Tour

Almost all the important buildings lie within the Altstadt. A walk may start in the north, at the impressive **Porta Nigra**,

Trier dates back to Roman times.

the "Black Gate", so called since the Middle Ages on account of its dark patina of soot and grime. Part of the Constantine ramparts, it is the largest and probably finest Roman relic in Germany.

The central building with double arcades and flanked by protruding towers, is an imposing example of military architecture. In the 12th century it was transformed into a two-story church, of which the Romanesque apse can be seen on the east end. Napoleon in 1804 had it restored to its original appearance. The terrace affords a grand view over the city.

The **Hauptmarkt** to the south is a busy pedestrian shopping area with some outstanding medieval monuments and gabled, half-timbered and Baroque

houses, mostly restored after bombing. The 13th-century *Dreikönigshaus* (house of the Three Kings, sometimes known as the Magi) is an early Gothic dwelling tower built for security and defense: the original front door can still be seen on the first floor level, high above the street. Close by is Germany's oldest pharmacy, the 13th-century Löwenapotheke.

The square is the focus of city life and presents a colorful picture with its flower and vegetable stalls, a Celtic cross erected in 958 and an ornate Renaissance fountain. On the west side stands the *Steipe*, a replica of Trier's 15th-century banqueting hall and now a restaurant; under its arcades public trials used to be held.

A few steps to the east, the fortress-like **Dom** on the site of Constantine's palace shows its daunting façade and squat square towers. From the outside the different stages of its construction are plainly visible, dating from the 4th (central section) to the 12th century (east end).

The Baroque interior contains interesting altarpieces, while from the Gothic cloister you have an attractive view of the cathedral and the adjoining Liebfrauenkirche. This is the earliest Gothic church in Germany (1235–60). Designed in the form of a Greek cross, the addition of two chapels has resulted in an almost circular building which is highly original. The treasury contains precious ivory and goldwork as well as much-venerated relics: a part of St Peter's chain and what was thought to be Christ's Holy Tunic, recently redated to the 13th century and rarely shown.

The finest exhibit at the **Bischöfliches Museum** (episcopal museum) are the 4th-century frescoed ceiling paintings rescued from Constantine's palace which he himself had destroyed to make way for a church. The panels, only discovered in 1946, have remarkably fresh colors; the figures are said to represent Constantine's mother, his eldest son and his wife.

The exhibition galleries, opened in 1988, are wonderfully bright and inviting in the best manner of modern museum design. The huge brick basilica south of the museum was built by Constantine as part of his palace; 100 feet (30 meters) high and 250 feet (75

meters) long, with no pillars or buttresses, it is the largest surviving single-hall structure of the ancient world. Since the 19th century it has been used as a Protestant church, and after wartime bombing destroyed its Roman marble floor it has been restored very plainly.

Still moving southward, you soon come upon the enormous **Rheinisches Landesmuseum**, with prehistoric exhibits and splendid Roman antiquities, intricate mosaics and finds from a treasure trove at Neumagen, including the famous sculpture of a ship loaded high with wine barrels and propelled by oarsmen. The adjacent palace gardens offer quiet walks past pools, flower-beds and Baroque statuary.

Nearby you can explore the ruins of the famous **Kaiserthermen** (imperial baths), which were among the largest in the Roman Empire. The arrangement follows the usual gradations in temperature from hot to tepid to cold pools, ending in a gymnasium court for physical exercise. The system of water heating and circulation is admirable and well above the standards of many European dwellings today.

Westward lies Trier's second set of Roman baths, the 2nd-century **Barbarathermen**, of which the subterranean part presents a seemingly endless maze of passages, channels and chambers. To the east you come upon the amphitheater, situated on the slopes of the Petrusberg above the city. Carefully restored, it retains a sense of its original grandeur when it seated 20,000 spectators. Some of the cages where the animals were kept are almost completely intact.

Castle Country

From Trier, take a scenic drive back to Koblenz. Driving south from the city past a modern brewery in its outskirts, you will come to a footpath right up to **Stolzenfels**, a vast ocher castle on the hillside. It was rebuilt in neo-Gothic style (1836) inspired by English country houses and Spanish castles, by King Frederick William IV, who added the battlements. The lavish interior is now a museum; the keep offers good views down the river. In 1845, during her royal Rhine cruise, Queen Victoria met the great Metternich here, by then a very old man who, as the queen noted, "was laying down the law very much"; meanwhile Prince Albert talked to his boyhood hero, the explorer and naturalist Alexander von Humboldt, sharing gloomy thoughts about the situation in Ireland and Poland with him.

On the right bank, soon the high-towered silhouette of the **Marksburg** comes into view, the only castle on this route which was never captured or even partly pulled down. What survives, therefore, is more or less its original 15th-century form; building of the castle started c.1283 under the counts of Katzenelnbogen, and the battlements were rebuilt in 1479.

Since 1900 it is the headquarters of the Deutsche Burgenvereinigung (German castle society) and has been expertly refurbished. Here you get an excellent introduction to medieval life and customs. Bedrooms are stocked with cradles and looms; the chapel has lovely 13th-century wall-paintings; a display of armor includes authentic medieval pieces as well as copies of what Greek and Roman soldiers wore; there is a torture chamber, and even a medieval lavatory open to the terrace below. The kitchen can be hired for medieval banquets, at which small oxen are roasted whole on the spit. On the hill behind the castle rise three tall chimneys belonging to the Braubach silver-mining works.

Beyond the Marksburg the river makes a big bend, just north of **Boppard** on the left bank. It is the largest of all Rhineside resorts and very jolly during wine-festival times. Roman foundations can still be seen south of the Marktplatz at the top of the Kirchgasse.

The local museum, housed in 17th-century wings of the old archbishops' residence, has graceful bentwood furniture created by Boppard's best-known native son, Michael Thonet (1796–1871), founder of the firm that for more than a century has been furnishing the coffeehouses of Vienna, Paris, Brussels and the rest of the world with the familiar chairs and tables he first designed. Boppard's $1^1/_2$-mile-long (3 km) elegant and colorful promenade is lined by hotels, wine taverns and boat landings.

The river valley narrows to a defile and reaches **Rheinfels**, biggest of all the

St Goar, a charming medieval town.

Rhine castles between Koblenz and Mainz. Built in the 13th century, it was extended during the 16/17th century to make it virtually impregnable.

In 1796 the castle surrendered to Napoleon's troops without a shot being fired, and for the next three years the soldiers did their best to demolish it. The towering frame of its great vaulted hall survives, and the castle museum has a model of how it looked in 1607. Stroll through its maze of ruins to inspect the clock tower, pharmacy, brewery, even the gallows.

Just below Rheinfels, **St Goar** is a very touristy town. The old Gothic Stiftskirche with charming frescoes (15th century), was built over an 11th-century Romanesque crypt, matched in size and splendor only by those of Speyer Cathedral and St Maria im Kapitol, Cologne.

Opposite St Goar lies **St Goarshausen**, overlooked by **Burg Katz**, a partially reconstructed 14th-century fortress of the counts of Katzenelnbogen; it can be visited by prior arrangements at the tourist office in St Goarshausen. It was built to rival another castle some miles downstream which belonged to the archbishops of Trier and was inevitably nicknamed "**Burg Maus**"; after extensive restoration, "Mouse Castle" now houses an aviary and there is a daily display of falconry.

From St Goar, the curving river passes the **Loreley**, just above Oberwesel. The high wooded bluff holds a notable place in German romantic lore. One

The Pfalz, a medieval toll house on the Rhine.

legend relates that it held the treasure of the Nibelung; in another, the subject of poems by Heine and others, a lovely siren sat on the cliff, singing songs that lured boatmen to their death.

Before the recent dynamiting of bedrock, treacherous currents made this a particularly dangerous turn of the river. It is more pleasant to admire the almost perpendicular rock-face from the left bank than to drive up from the back for a mediocre view.

Beyond the Loreley, **Oberwesel** is a pleasant wine-town with towers and half-timbered houses; the Gothic Liebfrauenkirche has remarkable altar-pieces and a triptych showing the 15 cataclysms ending the world. One hundred fifty years ago, salmon fishing was an important source of income for the inhabitants of this area. Then the Rhine became more and more polluted from chemical effluvia, and now the tide is turning again: because of strict regulations, the water quality is fast improving; eel-farming has already restarted and Rhine salmon probably will be available at restaurants again soon.

Forests and Fortresses

High above Oberwesel towers the impressive medieval **Schönburg**, former triple fortress of the dukes of Schönburg; part is now a Catholic holiday center, part of a delightful hotel with four-poster beds and a balcony overlooking the Rhine. Its owners have painted one of the outside walls bright red, as it was in the 16th century, when painted walls were a symbol of wealth.

Soon you see a white-walled toll fortress standing on a mid-river island; its five-cornered central tower dates from 1327, while the many-turreted outer wall was added later.

The little castle is called Pfalzgrafenstein, usually shortened to "the **Pfalz**". It acquired historical fame when Field Marshal Blücher, the Prussian general who saved the day at Waterloo, here crossed the Rhine during an earlier campaign against Napoleon.

On the right bank, Kaub is a small town with well-restored houses and a broad promenade. On a precipice above it stands **Burg Gutenfels**, a late 19th-century reconstruction of the 13th-century castle in which Gustavus Adolphus lived during part of the Thirty Years' War.

Continuing on the left bank, you reach charmingly quaint **Bacharach**, shielded from river, road and railway by a line of ramparts with gateways and tall towers. It probably derives its name from a Roman altar stone sacred to Bacchus, the god of wine, which once stood in the Rhine. Bacharach's market square is graced by flower-decked wooden houses, and its narrow streets are lined with ancient half-timbered dwellings now in use as hotels, wine pubs and craft shops where artisans can be seen at work.

High above Bacharach, **Stahleck** is

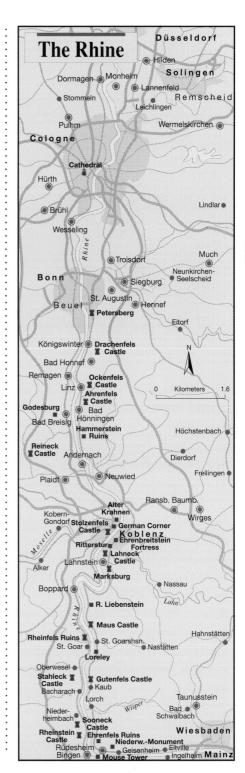

Burg Klopp, a former stronghold of the archbishops of Mainz.

a much-restored yet imposing old fortress. It now houses a youth hostel; the steep drive up is worth it for the fine view over the river from the terrace.

On the opposite bank lies the old village of Lorch with a notable Gothic church and the gabled and profusely decorated Hilchenhaus, a Renaissance mansion. Beyond Stahleck, steep terraced vineyards cover the rocky ground on both banks, sometimes sloping at a dizzying angle of 60°. The road passes two more high-perched old castles, both much restored: **Sooneck** with garden terraces and a tall tower, and **Reichenstein** with a display of hunting trophies and old armor.

A few minutes later, the small castle of **Rheinstein** comes into view, set on a high hill almost sheer above the river, and alluringly floodlit at night. It was bought in 1975 by a retired Austrian opera singer, who has restored it tastefully and sometimes organizes opera seminars or stages knightly plays. On the opposite bank, the small resort of **Aßmannshausen** is famous for its red wine, one of Germany's best burgundy.

Bingen, at the confluence of the Nahe and the Rhine, is not a resort but a workaday town with some interesting features. It is overlooked by the turreted **Burg Klopp**, a former stronghold of the archbishops of Mainz and now the town hall; the museum inside displays some gruesome surgical instruments left behind by Roman army doctors. There is a splendid view from its terrace, taking in

Drosselgasse, Rüdesheim, lined with wine taverns.

ing beggars. A prosaic explanation suggests that "Mäuseturm" is a corruption of "Mautturm", toll tower. On the opposite bank stand the romantic ruins of Ehrenfels, a 13th-century castle.

Wine Towns

From Bingen, cross by passenger or car ferry to **Rüdesheim**, wine capital of the Rheingau, Germany's most productive wine-growing region. It contains some picturesque old houses and vintners' mansions, but is overcrowded and very touristy, especially its famous alley, the Drosselgasse (thrush alley), lined with wine taverns dating from the 18th century. The clock tower halfway down has a tinkling set of performing figures.

Most of the more than 3 million annual visitors ignore Rüdesheim's two interesting museums: the Brömserhof exhibits early mechanical instruments, while the square and fortified Brömserburg shows a great variety of wine-presses and other vinous objects, some very ancient. Nearby is the well-known brandy factory Asbach, whose owner in 1907 coined the German word for brandy, *Weinbrand* (distilled wine); where tastings are held in summer.

High above Rüdesheim rises the huge Niederwald memorial, erected after 1871 to celebrate France's defeat and Germany's unification; it is accessible on foot, by car or by cable-car. The centerpiece is a monumental 35-foot-high ($10^1/_2$-meter) figure of Germania, a

the hills of the Hunsrück and Taunus ranges and the huge vineyards of the Rheingau, as well as the ruins of Ehrenfels castle and the Niederwald monument across the river.

At Bingen's hilltop chapel of St Rochus, there is a procession and fair in August to celebrate the town's deliverance from the Black Death in the 14th century; Goethe came as a visitor in 1814 and wrote a short account of it. The town is chiefly known for the small yellowish **Mäuseturm** (mouse tower) on an island, a former toll station with a romantic legend attached to it. The story goes that the fiendish Hatto, archbishop of Mainz, fled to the tower and there was eaten by mice in divine retribution for burning to death some starv-

Riesling grapes from the Moselle
Valley.

The architecture is austerely grandiose
the fine leafy half-timbered cloister, the
13th-century dormitory with ribbed
vaulting, very impressive and almost
devoid of decoration; and the plain Romanesque church now used for concerts. The abbey was secularized in 1803,
and with its adjoining vineyards is now
owned by the *region*, which uses it for
wine-tastings and wine-auctions.

On the way back to the Rhine, you
pass improbably medieval-looking
Kiedrich, a village dominated by the
ruins of Scharfenstein castle.

The **St Valentinuskirche** (15th century) has flamboyant decor and intricately carved pews with wine motifs; its
other treasures are the "Kiedrich Madonna" of 1330 below the rood screen
and Germany's oldest working organ
(c.1500). Gregorian chants have been
heard here since 1333 and are now
performed during mass on Sundays and
religious holidays.

Join the Rhine again at the village
of **Eltville**, famous for its sparkling wines.
There are several very picturesque houses
and mansions of the 16–17th century,
and the ruins of a former moated castle
by the riverbank. The parish church
(15–17th century) stands on the site of a
Romanesque basilica and contains a
baptismal font of 1517 from the workshop of the Mainz sculptor Backoffen as
well as a delicate Madonna on a crescent moon (16th century).

Thomas Mann in his novel about
the urbane con-man Felix Krull, called
the landscape around Eltville "one of

most Teutonic lady brandishing the imperial crown. The terrace offers a more
peaceful view of vineyards, monasteries
and the Rhine as far upstream as Mainz.

From Rüdesheim, make a detour
inland and head for **Johannisberg**, a
handsome hillside palace surrounded
by vineyards, and with a shop that sells
its distinguished wines. The 18th-cen-
tury building was given to Prince
Metternich in 1816 and still belongs to
the family. From the terrace and the
excellent restaurant there are fine views.

To visit **Kloster Eberbach**, you join
the riverside road again and then turn
off at Hattenheim. The lovely monastery in a secluded setting up a green
valley, was founded by Cistercian monks
in 1135 as a companion to Clairvaux.

Gutenberg

Very little is known about Johannes Gensfleisch, called Gutenberg, the inventor of European printing with movable types. Most of his life and the circumstances of his invention are still shrouded in obscurity, despite the searchlights of many scholars and historians. He was born in Mainz at the very end of the 14th century and was apprenticed to a goldsmith.

Towards 1440, living in political exile in Strasbourg, he began experimenting with printing work; in great secrecy he tried out ways of setting a page from individual wooden or metal letters. Compared to woodblock printing, the great advantage of using movable type was that you could edit, sub-edit and correct a text before printing it in bulk and with every copy being identical.

Gutenberg returned to Mainz sometime between 1444 and 1448, and by 1450 had perfected his invention far enough to start exploiting it commercially. To get his business afloat, he borrowed some money from the lawyer and printer Johannes Fust and then borrowed some more, before Fust foreclosed the loan in 1455. Immediately the bulk of his presses and types went to another printer; Gutenberg seems to have given up printing for good around 1460. He died in Mainz in February 1468 and was buried at the Franciscan church, which was pulled down in 1742.

The only book undoubtedly printed by him is the 42-line Bible, of which some 180 copies were printed and almost fifty copies, each slightly different, have come down to us. One of them is kept in the strongroom of the Gutenberg Museum in Mainz, and it looks truly splendid. Two columns with some 3,700 characters in brilliant black print fill the page, and there are 1,280 pages altogether. The initials and borders are decorated by hand in luminous colors, and the paper, made purely from rags in northern Italy, has lost none of its crispness.

Gutenberg's printing process, although it looks laborious and complicated now, was of a technical efficiency not materially surpassed until well into the 19th century. At the Museum, there are frequent demonstrations of this fascinating early version of the "black art".

the loveliest spots of the world's inhabited regions".

Beyond Eltville, follow the sharp bend of the Rhine to Mainz.

Romanesque Wonder

Over the centuries **Mainz**, the capital of Rhineland-Palatinate, has played many roles. It has been a key part of the Roman empire's defenses, a historic stronghold of Catholicism, a major trade center during the Middle Ages, a gathering point of German Humanists, focus of intellectual ferment in Germany's rise to national unity, and a Rhenish city going madly merry during carnival.

Situated beside the Rhine on a broad, fertile plain, it is a place with much character and an attractive well-restored Altstadt; one of Germany's grandest cathedrals; an excellent museum dedicated to its famous son, Johannes Gutenberg, the pioneer of modern printing; and a jolly, easy-going atmosphere as befits the city that is the country's leading wine market. It has some flourishing industries, and the second German television network, ZDF, has its headquarters here.

From the Roman period, which lasted from 38 BC to roughly AD 400, little remains except for what is exhibited in the museums. In 742 St Boniface created the archbishopric and made Mainz the main center of the Church in Germany. Archbishops – and later archbishop-electors – were the moving force behind Mainz' commercial expansion and artistic and cultural flowering. During the late 15th century some of Germany's leading Humanists (Reuchlin, Celtis, Hutten) made the university, founded in 1477, a center of intellectual research, which focused on the rediscovery of Greek and Roman literature and thought, and its application to the religious and political situation of their own times. Goethe witnessed the short-lived heady period when Mainz, inspired by the ideals of the French Revolution, had a Jacobine, left-wing government, which was quickly snuffed out by the French occupation forces who also closed the university in 1798; it was reopened only in 1946. After annexation by France, the city never quite recovered its importance, but it is still often regarded as the most French of German towns, and many French families settled here.

The Mainz carnival is second only to Cologne's, and more political. It be-

gan in the 1830s as an expression of student disaffection with the harsh conservative regime of the time, epitomized by the Austrian chancellor Metternich's Carlsbad Decress (1819); the carnival organizers then often risked arrest. After 1918 the festival was appropriated by the bourgeoisie and the focus shifted from Left to Right, where it remains today. After the pre-Lenten carnival, Mainz' other great time of jollity and raucous fun is the wine festival from the last weekend in August to the first weekend of September.

The **Dom** in the city center epitomizes the character of the town and its people – plump, ruddy-complexioned, and despite its massive proportions somehow cozy and intimate. Typically for the Rhineland, the Romanesque basilica has chancels at either end, each with a majestic tower, the eastern one an austere construction of the 12th century, the western one a more ornate synthesis of Romanesque, Gothic and Baroque. Enter by the 13th-century Marktportal (market porch) with its 1000-year-old bronze doors. Of the 29 monumental archiepiscopal tombs, the

Drinking and dancing in Rüdesheim.

most important one is at the west end of the nave, profusely decorated with 16th-century sculpture. Note the elegant Rococo choir stalls in the west chancel.

The lively market square next to the cathedral is lined with some highly decorative rebuilt Renaissance houses. The square's fountain is genuine, in fact the oldest Renaissance one in Germany (1526); it is a splendidly intricate artifice commemorating Charles V's victory over the French at Pavia.

A few steps east stands the marvelous museum devoted to Johannes Gutenberg (c.1398–1468) and the history of printing. It is housed in a modern building which cleverly incorporates an old 17th-century inn. There are reconstructions with demonstrations of sev-

eral early printing shops, and a strong-room holds the museum's prize possession, the Gutenberg Bible of 1452–5 with 42 lines to the page. The Chinese had invented block-printing and movable letters centuries earlier, but as nobody seems to have heard of this, these techniques had to be invented all over again in the West, where their cultural impact went much further.

The Mainz Rhine quay has been turned into a highway, but the **Altstadt** south of the Dom is pedestrianized and ideal for strolling. There are several alleys lined with half-timbered houses, looking proud and pretty with geraniums and vine overspilling from window-boxes.

From Leichhof square you get a fine

view of the soaring cathedral, while little Kirchgarten is a lovely old cobbled street lined with restored 16–18th-century houses. Note the undamaged Baroque **Augustinerkirche** and the **Frankfurter Hof**, a cradle of Europe's 1848 revolution.

Between the Altstadt and the Rhine you find Mainz' oldest surviving house, the 12th-century **Wohnturm** (residential tower), built by a Jewish family and still lived in by Jews. This serves as a reminder that in the 12th century Mainz was a Jewish intellectual center, specializing in Talmudic studies and influential as far away as France, Italy and Spain.

To the north lies the electors' Schloß, which is an enormous late Renaissance building with a Baroque extension; it now houses the Römisch-Germanisches Museum with a disappointing and confusing collection of Roman and German antiquities.

Across the road stands a copy of the famous Jupitersäule, the most important Roman triumphal column in Germany. The original is exhibited at the nearby Mittelrheinisches Landesmuseum (museum of the central Rhineland), occupying the old imperial stables and displaying fine examples of Roman sculpture.

Going South

South of Mainz, on the undulating hills running parallel to the Rhine, some excellent wine is grown. The area is full of defensive-looking villages, some rather pretty and all devoted foot and claw to wine-making. At places like Nierstein and Nieder-Olm, Lörzweiler and Oppenheim it is easy enough to follow the traditional taverns signs, usually a wreath of vine-leaves, a jug or a grape, to receive a friendly welcome, sensible advice and a glass of honest and deliciously cool white wine.

Like Mainz and Speyer, **Worms** was an imperial residence on the Rhine. The hill which with its cathedral dominates the town, was the site of one of Rome's earliest bases on the Rhine; later the Frankish kings held court on this historic hill, and Charlemagne celebrated two of his five marriages here as well.

The magnificent 12th-century cathedral's exterior is one of Germany's finest examples of the Romanesque, while in the north aisle are five beautiful Gothic reliefs. In the first chapel on the right as you enter, a very old carving shows "Daniel in the Den of Lions".

It was at the Schloßplatz north of the Dom where the Nibelungs and the Franks held court, and where on a spring day in 1521 Martin Luther faced the Diet of Worms under Emperor Charles V and refused to retract his criticism of the Catholic Church, uttering the famous (but apocryphal) words: "Here I stand, I have no other choice. May God help me. Amen." His subsequent excommunication eventually led to the Reformation.

Worms was also an important Jewish center from the 10th century onward, with a great Talmudic school. The history of the Jews of Worms reflects the fate of their brethren all over Germany. The community survived for 1,000 years despite sporadic attacks throughout the centuries.

In 1096 fanatical Crusaders destroyed the synagogue and the Jewish quarter, and during the Black Death, which ravaged Europe between 1347 and 1351, the Jews of Worms were attacked by their fellow townsfolk who accused them of having poisoned local wells.

Only in the 19th century did things start to improve: the Jewish ghetto was opened, and Worms even had a Jewish mayor from 1849 to 1852. It was not until the Nazis came to power that Worms' ancient Jewish community was systematically destroyed. The old synagogue was rebuilt in 1961, and another poignant reminder is the Heiliger Sand (holy sand), the oldest Jewish cemetery in Europe (11th century) which contains over 1,000 ancient gravestones with Hebrew inscriptions.

The Gothic Liebfrauenkirche (Church of Our Lady) in the northern suburbs has given its name to the well-known *Liebfraumilch* (Milk of Our Lady) wine produced in the surrounding vineyards. To the southwest of Worms the vineyards of the Palatinate begin. The zigzag route linking many wine villages is clearly marked "Deutsche Weinstraße".

A visit at harvest-time is best of all; but nearly all the year the attractive *Weingüter* (wine estates) are kept open in the villages, where in October you can drink the new, barely fermented wine called *Federweiße*.

South of Worms, where the Neckar joins the Rhine, lies **Mannheim**. The city, now one of Europe's largest river ports, was conceived in 1606 as a fortified residential town and follows a strict plan: the central part is built on a grid pattern, each of its 144 blocks being denoted by a letter and number. Although often damaged during later wars, this chessboard pattern remains as a conspicuous feature and gives the city center a strange formal beauty. Schiller lived here from 1782 to 1785 and three of his plays premièred at the Nationaltheater. An early bicycle without pedals and driven by kicking the ground, the "dandy horse", was given trial runs on the road between Mannheim and Schwetzingen by its inventor, the forester Baron Drais, in 1817; 70 years later, Carl Benz demonstrated his first motor vehicle here.

Just west of the city ring lies the **Kunsthalle**, one of Germany's finest museums of painting and sculpture of the 19/20th century. It includes Manet's *"Execution of the Emperor Maximilian"* as well as superb works by French and German Impressionists and modern sculpture by Rodin, Brancusi, Giacometti and Moore. The Reiss-Museum documents local history and has an attractive collection of local porcelain.

Between the grid-patterned center and the Rhine lies the massive **Schloß**

(1720–60), begun by Elector Carl Philipp, under whose reign Mannheim became one of the commercial and cultural centers of Germany. With more than 400 rooms and some 2,000 windows, the building is one of the largest Baroque palaces in the country.

Today it is part of the university, but its Rococo library and ornately decorated *Rittersaal* (knights' hall) are open to the public, and concerts are frequently performed in splendid setting. Mannheim also hosts the colorful Upper Rhine regatta in June. Across the river lies another industrial city, **Ludwigshafen**, home of the BASF chemicals firm; an elegant suspension bridge connects the two cities.

Already from a distance, **Speyer**'s red sandstone **Dom** with its massive Romanesque domes and towers is a majestic sight. The town, originally a Roman fortification, became a bishopric in the 7th century and first assumed importance in the 11th century, when Emperor Conrad II began with the building of the cathedral (1030).

From its steps on St John's Day in 1146 Bernard of Clairvaux summoned Conrad III to set off on the disastrous Second Crusade. Here the second Diet of Speyer in 1529 annulled the religious freedoms previously granted. This caused the protest of six princes and 14 cities, followers of Martin Luther, who were from that time on known as "Protestants".

Inside, the bare walls and massive columns emphasize its airy, clean pro-

portions. On the right in the porch stands an impressive statue of Rudolph of Habsburg (r.1273–91), the first of the great Salian dynasty. The graves of the Salian emperors were only revealed during excavations in 1900, when Conrad II and his descendants were identified by their wooden orbs and copper crowns.

The transept is a masterpiece of unity and balance, where the lack of ornamentation brings out the natural grace and rhythm of the architecture. The splendid crypt, one of the most beautiful north of the Alps, shows Romanesque groined vaulting, which spreads out like a net supported by archstones cut alternately of pink and white limestone.

The 13th-century tombstone of Rudolph of Habsburg stands at the entrance to the sombre vault where four emperors, three empresses and four German kings rest in stone sarcophagi.

A few steps south of the Dom stands the heavy towered and turreted **Historisches Museum der Pfalz** (Palatinate museum); its greatest treasure is the Golden Hat, a Bronze Age cult object of pure gold (c.12th century B.C.). The wine museum in the cellars holds the world's oldest surviving bottle of wine still in a liquid state – it dates from about AD 300. To the west lies the remodeled Altstadt, a picturesque quarter of half-timbered houses and cobbled streets.

East of Speyer, on the road to Heidelberg, you come to **Schwetzingen**, famous for its asparagus and its Schloß. This was the summer residence of the Palatine electors and is a rather ordinary castle building with an extraordinary park, full of surprises, where an international music festival takes place every summer.

The park, landscaped by the Lorraine architect, Nicolas de Pigage (1723–96), combines the formal French style with the natural greenery popular at the end of the 18th century, to which were added symbolic monuments, fake ruins, temples, grottoes. There is a lovely court theater (1752) for summer concerts, a delightful trompe l'oeil bath pavilion and a Temple of Mercury with a grand view across an artificial lake and the minarets of a "mosque".

Saarland

In a small corner to the southwest lies Germany's smallest region, apart from Bremen, and its poorest in the west; it has 1.1 million inhabitants and covers 1,000 sq miles (2,571 sq km). The Saar is a region of coal-mining and heavy industry, and the long-term depression of this branch of the economy has cast a gloom over the whole area.

Its capital, **Saarbrücken**, lies in the center of the industrialized south and has little to offer the tourist. Most historic buildings have been much altered or restored over the centuries or have been blandly rebuilt after the last war. In the center you find the **Moderne**

Galerie, the city's best museum, with a big collection of 19–20th century art including works by Picasso, Dufy, Monet and Rodin.

Southeast of the Altstadt, the Gothic 13th-century church of St Arnual is remarkable for its many tombs of counts and their families of the Nassau-Saarbrücken line, especially those of Count Johann III and of Elizabeth of Lorraine, who died in 1456. Being a university city, the presence of students provides some color and gaiety to cultural and social life.

Every May a festival of young French theater is held here, and in January an avantgarde film festival takes place. Nearby France has recently had some noticeable influence on the local cuisine, traditionally always a poor man's fare consisting of a thousand and one potato variations.

To the north of the Saar valley and towards the Hunsrück range are lovely rural areas. **Mettlach**, the "pearl of the Saarland", has some picturesque old houses and a park with a Romanesque mausoleum; the entrance to the park is marked by a grand neo-Classical fountain by Schinkel.

St Wendel in the northeast is a pleasant little market town. Its main attraction is the Gothic church of St Wendelinus, with three towers and richly decorated interior. It is named after a 7th-century Irish missionary, patron of shepherds and farmers, who is buried in a stone sarcophagus (c.1360) behind the high altar.

North-Rhine Westphalia is the most populous of the region, and one of the most affluent. It embraces the vast Ruhr conurbation and the fertile agricultural plains to the north of it. Its present configuration dates only from 1946, with the joining of the north Rhineland and Westphalia which had belonged to Prussia since the 19th century.

Occupied by Caesar c.53 BC, the Rhineland remained under Roman occupation for almost half a millennium, before the Franks c.450 ended Roman rule along the Rhine. Under Charlemagne, Aachen became a center of European civilization.

During the Middle Ages, its major principalities were those of Kleve (Cleves), Jülich and Berg. Prussia gained

Highrise containing the offices of Bundestag deputies in Bonn.

Bonn, Dusseldorf, Cologne & Westphalia

315

Out and about in Westphalia.

its first foothold in the late 17th century, and at the Congress of Vienna (1814–15) the whole Rhineland came under Prussian rule. The Treaty of Versailles (1919) made the west bank of the Rhine a demilitarized zone to weaken Germany's industrial heartland. Its illegal occupation by Hitler in 1936 met with Anglo-French acquiescence, a reaction which indirectly paved the way for World War II.

The region north of the Ruhr area consists of pleasant pastures studded with black-and-white cattle, vast vegetable fields, lonely windmills and, towards the Dutch border, a succession of picturesque water castles. In the early 19th century, after the discovery of huge deposits of brown coal (lignite), the Ruhrgebiet rapidly developed into an iron-and-steel working center characterized by tall chimneys rising above endless rows of tenement houses. Today there is a trend toward cleaner and more versatile industrial set-ups, and steel giants like Hoesch, Krupps and Thyssen are concentrating more on mechanical engineering and advanced technologies.

The area south of the Ruhrgebiet with the notable cities of Cologne, Bonn and Aachen, is again farming country and the beginning of Germany's main wine-growing region.

Westphalia's best-known contribution to German food are its tasty smoked hams with a juniper aroma and served on wooden platters together with *Pum-*

The Dom in Münster.

pernickel, a coarse, black, moist rye bread. You wash this down with light beer (Dortmund is a big brewing center) and *Steinhäger*, a clear juniper schnapps distilled since 1688 in the village of Steinhagen.

The traditional dishes of the Rhineland are hearty and plain, heavily based on meat, mainly pork. Düsseldorf and Cologne produce top-fermented *Altbier* (called *Kölsch* in Cologne), while Aachen, Cologne and Neuß are centers of chocolate production. Chocolate, by the way, was introduced to Europe from Central America by Spanish seafarers in the 16th century, and was first consumed only as a healthy and sophisticated drink, before its transformation into a sweetmeat.

University Town

One of the most distinguished episcopal and university cities in Germany, smart and prosperous **Münster** has an enthralling center of light modern brick buildings, nicely restored historical houses and a strange sprawling Dom with beautiful stone and wood carvings. An island of staunch Catholicism in the sea of Protestant Westphalia, it was raised to a bishopric by Charlemagne in 805. Its main claim to historical fame is that the Peace of Westphalia, which ended the Thirty Years' War in 1648, was negotiated and signed here and in Osnabrück.

Until 1803 it was the seat of prince-bishops who endowed Münster with many fine Baroque buildings; in 1806 it became the capital of the Prussian province of Westphalia. More than 90 percent of the city center was bombed, because the Allies believed that the Nazis were using the university to train their élite.

Its bishop from 1933 to 1946 was Count von Galen, a noted opponent of the Nazis. Its university (founded in 1780) is the largest in Germany after Berlin and Munich; most of its 45,000 students use bikes to get around.

In March, June and October a five-day popular fair, the *Send*, is held. It is said that the best Westphalian ham comes from the Münsterland, the area around Münster, because farmers here feed their pigs with acorns.

The old circular layout of the city is still discernible, with the cathedral at the heart, and a ring avenue of lime trees planted on the line of the old ramparts. The **Dom** on the wide open cobbled Domplatz is an impressive construction, rather low with huge transepts surmounted by ornamental ironwork. Built between 1172 and 1265, it is a mixture of Romanesque and Gothic. In the narthex you are met by statues of the ten Apostles in Paradise.

The interior has many fine wood panels and memorial tablets full of narrative scenes, reliquaries, marble tombs and other noble furnishings, as well as an astronomical clock of 1420 with performing figures which come alive at noon.

Sculpture detail from the Dom in Münster.

South of the cathedral lies the **Prinzipalmarkt**, both a square and a street, first built up in 1150 and since then the center of municipal activities. It is fronted by well-restored houses with Renaissance gables. Because during the Middle Ages much tension existed between the city's merchants and the episcopal bigwigs (in the end, the latter won), the townhouses used to show their backs to the cathedral in a deliberate gesture of contempt.

This is now the main shopping area, largely traffic-free and graced by many elegant arcaded shops. Here lies the town hall, one of the most important buildings of German Gothic, with the Friedenssaal (peace hall), furnished with paneling and a chandelier of 1577, where the Peace of Westphalia was signed. Next to it stands the historic **Stadtweinhaus** (1612–15; now partly a restaurant), formerly the municipal wine cellars.

Turn into Alter Steinweg; the grand building to the left with its richly decorated façade is the Renaissance **Krämerhaus** (1586), the former grocers' guildhall. Nearby stands St Lamberti (1375–1460), the most perfect of Westphalia's Gothic hall churches. Near the top of its neo-Gothic tower (1898) hang the cages in which the corpses of the three leading Anabaptists of Münster were displayed in 1536. The Anabaptists were the most radical, left-wing sect of the Reformation. When its Münster branch, preaching a fierce apocalyptic message, tried to realize its utopian ideals, a war erupted which after much bloodshed ended in the defeat of the religious zealots. Pacifist sections of the Anabaptists have survived in large numbers under the name of Mennonites all over the world.

To the west of the city center lies the Baroque **Residenzschloß**, the palace of the former prince-bishops, with a well-kept park and smaller botanical garden, all now part of the university but open to the public. In the outskirts, visit the beautifully situated Haus Rüschhaus, which a local architect built for himself as a moated villa (1745–48). The Romantic poetess Annette von Droste-Hülshoff (1797–1848) lived here for 20 years, and the house is now a museum devoted to her life and writings.

A Picture Book Comes Alive

The friendly, intimate town of **Lemgo** was a thriving trade center in the 15–16th century, and its legacy consists of numerous gabled mansions in the delightful Altstadt. In 1927, the novelist Ricarda Huch stated that "walking through Lemgo is like leafing through a picture-book", and this largely remains true today. The unusual Rathaus is composed of eight buildings placed side by side, with unique oriel windows, gables and arcades. Under the central arches witch trials took place c.1670. Most houses along the main street date from the second half of the 16th century; the most notable are no.17 with a carved and painted façade, and no.36, the "House of Planets". Bear left into the Breite Straße to admire the **Hexenbürgermeisterhaus** (house of the witches' burgomaster) of 1568, a large patrician building with one of the most beautiful façades in town. It houses a museum of local history, in which instruments of torture seem to have played a large role: the witch craze of the 17th century, part of the Catholic Church's fight against popular magic and superstition, is one of the sad chapters of the Counter-Reformation.

Lemgo's modest claim to fame is its being home to German yogurt-making. Engelbert Kaempfer (1651–1716), a native of Lemgo and noted traveler – he was one of the first Europeans to visit Japan and write about it – is said to have

Düsseldorf, a leading center of fashion.

brought back from Turkey a recipe for yogurt. The refreshing, slightly acid milk product only became really popular in Germany early this century.

The oldest city in Westphalia, **Soest**, was once a major partner of the Hanseatic League and has retained much authentic medieval and Renaissance architecture. Beside the pink Rathaus stand two pale-green Romanesque churches, St Patroclus with a splendid west front and handsome square tower, and St Nicholas with a remarkable altarpiece of c.1400 by the great Konrad von Soest. Walk north through narrow streets with quaint old houses to the Wiesenkirche (14th century). Among its fine stained-glass windows is a curious one of the Last Supper (1520); it

shows Christ and the Apostles eating Westphalian food: boar's head, ham and rye loaves, with jugs of beer. The most important work of art is the altarpiece (1525) by H. Aldegrever of the Virgin between St Anthony and St Agatha; the latter was a Sicilian martyr who resisted the advances of a Roman officer, who then had her tortured. During this trial her breasts were cut off, a circumstance reflected in her iconography. Soest's biggest fair takes place on All Saints' Day.

On the way to Düsseldorf you cross the northern foothills of the **Sauerland** (bitter land), a wild schistous massif cut by deep valleys and partly covered by forests; it is a rough terrain with poor soil. Day-trippers from the densely populated Ruhr area come to the rivers and artificial lakes for fishing and watersports, while the highlands to the east offer good hiking and skiing opportunities.

Düsseldorf, Living Extravaganza

Düsseldorf, the capital of North-Rhine Westphalia, is – after Frankfurt – Germany's leading center of international banking and finance as well as of fashion design. More than 400 firms from Japan alone are represented, and the resident colony of Japanese citizens numbering some 6,000, is the largest outside Japan. It is said to have more millionaires than any other German city; its

The Alstadt in Düsseldorf.

smart society loves ostentation more than elsewhere in the country, and judges you by your money and how well you display it.

Although little notable architecture remains, Düsseldorf's long cultural tradition goes back to the splendor-loving Elector Johann Wilhelm (1679–1716), who drew musicians and artists to his court; Brahms, Mendelssohn and Schumann lived and worked here for a time, as did Goethe. Today its theater and opera are among the best in Germany. Its most famous native sons are

The old town hall in Düsseldorf.

the poet and writer Heinrich Heine (1797–1856) and the conceptual artist Joseph Beuys (1921–86).

Walk along the famous, elegant **Königsallee**, simply known as the "Kö", full of pretty girls and glamorous ladies. A canal runs down its middle, carrying ducks and swans on its back. The west side is rather somber, whereas the east side with its pastry shops and street cafés catches the afternoon sun and is known as the "chocolate side".

The main points of interest are spread fairly close to the Rhine, on the

Cologne on the Rhine with the Dom at night.

east bank. The Altstadt presents itself as a heady mix of the smart and the tawdry. Watch urchins performing cartwheels, for which the town is also known. At the north end of the Altstadt is the **Kunstsammlung Nordrhein-Westfalen** with a glorious collection of 88 paintings and drawings by Paul Klee (1879–1940), shown in rotation; after his Bauhaus years, Klee taught at the Düsseldorf Academy until sacked by the Nazis in 1933.

There are also good works by Picasso, Braque and the Surrealists, and by American artists like Kline and Rauschenberg. East of the museum lies the pleasant **Hofgarten** (royal park) with lakes and fountains, and in the far north corner the **Baroque Schloß** **Jägerhof**, housing a small collection of Goethe souvenirs.

At the south end of the old center stands the **Kunstmuseum**, the second of the city's two great museums. It houses a magnificent collection of glassware together with some 5,000 works of art from antiquity down to the present, with special emphasis on post-1900 arts and crafts.

Among its paintings are two remarkable Rubens and many fine examples of German Impressionism and Expressionism as well as of contemporary artists like Beuys and the group "*Zero*" of the 1960s and '70s.

Attractive walks line themselves up along the west bank of the Rhine, and from the TV tower near the

Cologne's twin-towered cathedral.

Rheinkniebrücke (bridge at a "knee" or bend of the Rhine) there is a splendid panoramic view. This residential district called Oberkassel (upper castle) has many tall Jugendstil villas, and pubs and bistros patronized more by locals than by tourists.

Cathedral City, Cologne

Cologne (Köln), capital of the Rhineland and one of Germany's largest cities, has a majestically attractive Rhine frontage, a lively Altstadt, a grand cathedral

Front portal of the Dom.

and artistic center of the Rhineland, and many of the magnificent works of art held by its museums and churches today date from this period. Most of its places of chief interest lie within walking distance from the Dom, as does the tastefully modernized Altstadt between the banks of the Rhine and the banking district to the west.

The best-known and most conspicuous of Cologne's treasures is the dark twin-towered **Dom**, keeping a watchful and censorious eye on the city from its site close to the river. Its building history spans more than 600 years. In 1164 Emperor Frederick Barbarossa offered important relics to the archbishopric of Cologne, and immediately the town became a major pilgrimage place. In 1248 building of a new cathedral started, its design influenced by Gothic buildings in Picardy. In 1437 work on the south front was stopped, to be taken up again only after 1842 in the then fashionable neo-Gothic style; in 1880 the completed Dom was finally inaugurated.

It is a structure overwhelming in size and decoration. After you have found your breath again, enter and feel its grandiose space. At the north aisle are five stained-glass windows of c.1500, and in one of the northern chapels of the ambulatory hangs the Gero-Kreuz (10th century; Gero was a margrave who advanced the eastern frontier of the empire during the Ottonian period), a massive oak crucifixion and an unique example of Ottonian art. In a glass case behind the altar stands the glittering

and several first-rate museums. It was founded c.40 BC as a Roman colony; there are some Roman remains in situ. Its patron saint is St Ursula, daughter of a 4th-century king of Britain, who on her return from a pilgrimage to Rome together with her virgin companions – either 11 or 11,000, depending on how you interpret the Latin numerals XIMV – was murdered by Huns somewhere close by. During the Middle Ages Cologne was an important political and commercial center and the largest city in all Germany, with some 40,000 people living within its fortified walls. For a time it rivaled Lübeck in the Hanseatic League; the Cologne Fair was first held in 1360. During the Renaissance it was the enlightened religious, intellectual

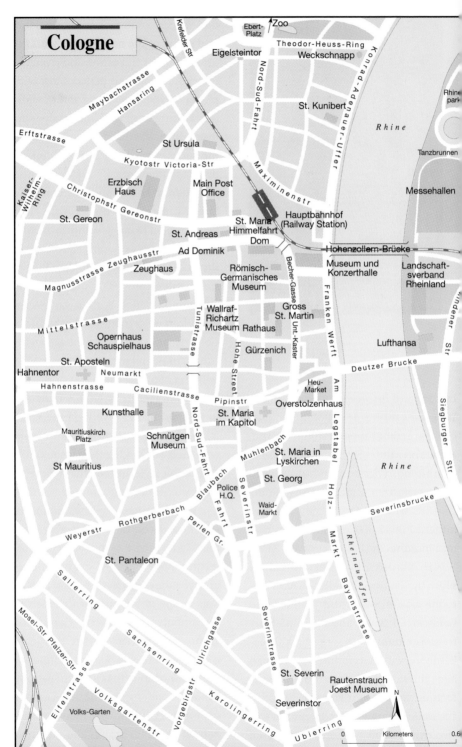

Cologne

Krefelder Str

Ebert-Platz

Zoo

Theodor-Heuss-Ring

Eigelsteintor

Weckschnapp

Konrad-Adenauer-Uffer

Maybachstrasse

Hansaring

Nord-Sud-Fahrt

St. Kunibert

Rhine park

Erftstrasse

Rhine

Tanzbrunnen

St Ursula

Kyotostr Victoria-Str

Maximinenstr

Messehallen

Kaiser-Wilhelm-Ring

Erzbisch Haus

Main Post Office

Christophstr Gereonstr

Hauptbahnhof (Railway Station)

St. Gereon

St. Andreas

St. Maria Himmelfahrt Dom

Ad Dominik

Hohenzollern-Brücke

Magnusstrasse Zeughausstr

Zeughaus

Römisch-Germanisches Museum

Becher-Gasse

Unt-Kaster

Franken Werft

Museum und Konzerthalle

Landschaftsverband Rheinland

Mittelstrasse

Tunisstrasse

Wallraf-Richartz Museum

Gross St. Martin

Windener Str

Opernhaus Schauspielhaus

Rathaus

Gürzenich

Lufthansa

St. Aposteln

Hohe Street

Deutzer Brucke

Hahnentor

Neumarkt

Siegburger Str

Hahnenstrasse

Cacilienstrasse

Pipinstr

Heu-Market

Am Legstabel

Kunsthalle

Nord-Sud-Fahrt

St. Maria im Kapitol

Overstolzenhaus

Mauritiuskirch Platz

Schnütgen Museum

Muhlenbach

St. Maria in Lyskirchen

Holz-

Rhine

St Mauritius

Blaubach

Severinstr

St. Georg

Markt

Rheinauhafen

Police H.Q.

Waid-Market

Severinsbrucke

Weyerstr

Rothgerberbach

Perlen Gr.

Fahrt

St. Pantaleon

Salierring

Bayenstrasse

Mosel-Str Pfalzer-Str

Sachsenring

Ulrichgasse

Severinstrasse

Eilelstrasse

Volksgartenstr

Vorgebirgstr

Karolingerring

St. Severin

Rautenstrauch Joest Museum

N

Volks-Garten

Severinstor

Ubierring

0   Kilometers   0.6

A band in Cologne.

Dreikönigsschrein (shrine of the Three Wise Men; 12th century). The splendid altarpiece showing the Adoration of the Magi is by Stefan Lochner (c.1400–1451), who is one of the most attractive German painters before Dürer. The Domschatz (treasury) holds fine gold and silver plate, episcopal vestments and manuscripts.

The **Römisch-Germanisches Museum** (Romano-German museum) next to the cathedral is the best of its size in Germany. Its exhibits are arranged by themes and include remains from public monuments, a port, a system of drainage, villas, tombs and all sorts of artifacts discovered in the region. Some of the works of art were commissioned by wealthy Romans from as far away as

Egypt and Greece. The museum is a cornucopia of beautiful and interesting objects and makes the historical period it is devoted to come alive.

Between the cathedral and the Rhine are two more museums not to be missed. The **Wallraf-Richartz Museum** and **Ludwig Museum** are conveniently housed under one roof. The first is devoted to Old Masters from the 14th down to the 19th century, with special emphasis on Rhineland art of its greatest period (14–16th century). Also well-represented are Lochner, Dürer, Cranach, Rembrandt and Rubens. The Ludwig Museum houses excellent paintings and graphics by modern and contemporary artists, donated by Germany's biggest and most controversial collector, whose wealth – like that of the equally munificent Sprengel family in Hanover - derives mainly from the manufacture of chocolate. German Expressionism is represented by many artists from the *Blaue Reiter* and *Brücke* groups, while of more recent vintage are the works of Warhol, Rauschenberg, Beuys, Saint Phalle, the Minimalists and the Photorealists. The huge photographic exhibition Foto-Historama Agfa is also worth a visit.

South of the cathedral runs the Hohe Straße, the city's main traffic-free shopping street, modern and ugly but lively. Between here and the Rhine lies the **Altstadt**, a network of small, almost provincial-looking streets. The imposing Altes Rathaus (14th century) is fronted by a lovely Renaissance loggia. A few steps further on you enter the wide space of the Alter Marktplatz where two 16th-century houses have survived the war. Right next to the town hall you can visit two subterranean curiosities: the Mikwe, a 12th-century Jewish ritual bath, relic of the former ghetto; and the vaulted Roman sewer below the Praetorium, remains of the Roman governor's palace. On the east side of the square rises one of the grandest of Cologne's Romanesque churches, Groß-Sankt-Martin, now used by the Hispanic community. Of the parishes in the old town which have kept their local autonomy and traditions, the most original is St Severinus, its narrow streets lined with small shops and cafés; here try the top-fermented *Kölsch* beer served in slim glasses.

The best view of Cologne is from the vast Rhine park on the right bank; take the cable-car from near the zoo, northeast of the cathedral. The Cologne carnival, during which the city is dizzy for days, starts on the Thursday before Shrove Tuesday with the *Weiberfastnacht* (women's carnival) and reaches its height on Rose Monday in a processional pageant parodying topical themes and personalities. The Corpus Christi procession in May/ June is solemn and at the same time sumptuous in character; it winds around the Dom and then embarks by boat on the Rhine.

A Small Town in Germany

While much money was lavished on Berlin before the Wall fell because it could not be Germany's capital, **Bonn** was subsidized because it had to be. Now that each city reverts to its original status, nobody quite knows how Bonn is going to handle its legacy of huge government buildings, high property prices and political shrinkage. Before the move to Berlin has been physically completed, govern-

Musicians performing in Bonn.

ment and parliament are still working out of Bonn.

Bonn grew around a Roman fortress founded in 11 B.C. It was incorporated as a city in 1244, and in 1597 became the residence of the archbishop-electors of Cologne. In the mid-18th century members of the Bavarian royal house remodeled the town into a Baroque residence. The palaces and churches of this period suffered much

from wartime bombing, but have been excellently rebuilt.

Well into the 20th century Bonn remained very much a typical Rhineland town, friendly, charming, something of a spa and a favorite place of retirement for civil servants and businessmen. This Sleeping Beauty was roughly awoken in 1949, when Konrad Adenauer, Germany's first post-war chancellor, maintained against competition from better-

The Museum of Modern Art in Bonn.

endowed cities like Hamburg, Frankfurt and Munich, that it would make an ideal interim capital – meaning until Germany's reunification – because it was geographically central and also obscure, without ambitions to a permanent role. Perhaps not by accident, Adenauer had a home close to Bonn and was a native of Cologne, so that this was his *Heimat*.

The **Altstadt**, although a bit commercial, has some pleasant pedestrian streets lined with 17–18th century houses. The pink Rococo town hall (1737) on the market square was used for state receptions. Kennedy, de Gaulle and

a stately Romanesque cloister and some Baroque furnishings.

A few streets further north you come to **Beethoven**'s birthplace where he lived until the age of 22, before leaving for Vienna to escape his alcoholic father. The small, attractive building has been turned into a museum; among its memorabilia are one of his grand pianos, a viola and the ear-trumpet he used to fight his deafness.

West of the train station, the **Rheinisches Landesmuseum**, one of the best regional museums, displays the skull of the Neanderthal man, found in 1856 near Düsseldorf. There are delightful 15th-century Rhenish paintings and numerous beautiful Roman antiquities, including a 3rd-century mosaic dedicated to the sun. A section on 19th-century landscapes of the Rhine Valley should put you into the right romantic mood for a cruise.

The impressive **Poppelsdorfer Allee**, a broad avenue lined with chestnut trees, was laid out by the electors to link their residence in the Altstadt with the Poppelsdorfer Schloß (1715) to the southwest. That building with its gabled façade influenced by French taste, belongs to the university and is closed to the public; but the curious, tranquil botanical garden at the back is open on weekdays.

The village of **Schwarz-Rheindorf**, $1^1/_2$-mile (3 km) east of Bonn, has an unusual 11th-century church built on two levels and with unique 12th-century wall-paintings showing scenes from

Queen Elizabeth were among those who addressed the crowds from its balcony. Nearby is the former electors' residence, a long orange-and-gray Baroque building, now part of the university.

The area is much enlivened by students who use the adjoining Hofgarten as their favorite meeting-place. Opposite the university is Bonn's finest church, the elegant 12th-century Münster, with

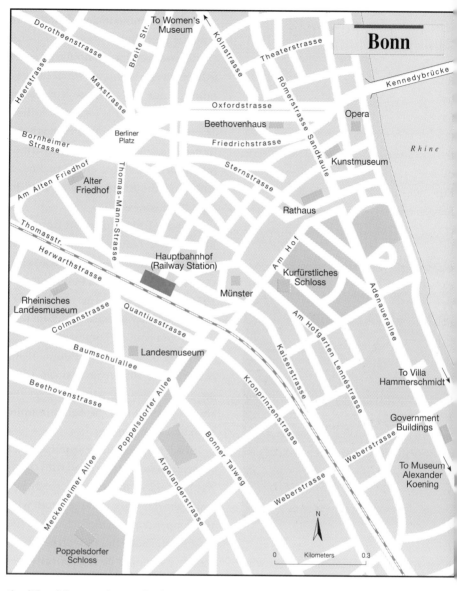

the life of the prophet Ezekiel. South of Bonn lies the pleasant wine-growing town of **Königswinter** and behind it rises the Siebengebirge (seven hills), a group of rounded volcanic hills covered with thick forests.

There are splendid views from the rocky Drachenfels peak, accessible on foot or by Germany's oldest rack-railway of 1883. From the slopes of these hills comes some fine wine, the best-known being the *Drachenblut*; according to a Nibelung legend, Siegfried killed the dragon that haunted this hill, then bathed in its blood and became invulnerable.

Entering Borderland

Right at the Dutch and French frontiers lies **Aachen** (Aix-la-Chapelle), first and foremost the city of Charlemagne and the center of the Frankish empire during the 8th and 9th centuries. Between 939 and 1531, thirty princes were crowned King of Germania in the cathedral, before the town lost its status of coronation city to Frankfurt. Building of the **Dom** began in c.800 by order of Charlemagne, as a domed octagonal basilica modeled on the churches of the Roman Empire of the East. After the addition of a Gothic chancel (mid-14th century), the building was finally consecrated in 1414. It deserves closer inspection. The portal on the Domhof is graced by two bronze doors of grand simplicity (9th century). Inside note the magnificent brass chandelier and at one of the pillars before the chancel a much venerated statue of the Virgin, to which many emperors and kings made offerings. The Pala d'Oro, a gorgeous altar frontal decorated with scenes from the Passion, and a crucifix (11th century) adorn the Carolingian high altar. Charlemagne's relics are placed in a wooden coffin at the end of the chancel. To see his throne of plain marble slabs, apply to the keeper of the treasury. The treasury itself houses one of Germany's richest ecclesiastical collections, including the Cross of Lothair (c.1000) encrusted with precious stones, a 2nd-century marble sarcophagus with relief work and, among several reliquaries, a bust of Charlemagne (1350).

Slightly north of the cathedral lies the **Couven Museum,** formerly a merchants' town house, which exhibits a collection of 17/18th-century household furnishings from aristocratic homes, as well as toys and Dutch faience tiles. From the museum it is just a few steps to the town hall (14th century) on the site of Charlemagne's palace, of which the squat Granus Turm may still be seen at the corner of the Krämergasse. Slightly set back in the same street is the **Postwagen** (mail coach) inn of 1657. You have to visit a café, however, if you want to try a local speciality, *Aachener Printen*, a kind of gingerbread, originally impressed with a saint's image. Further east near the Kaiserplatz lies Aachen's second important museum, the **Suermondt-Ludwig-Museum.** Its holdings include religious sculpture from the Lower Rhine and southern Germany as well as German and Flemish paintings from early times to the 17th century. Aachen was a favorite health resort already in Roman times, and Charlemagne also took advantage of its ancient baths; the waters from the hottest springs in northwest Europe are especially good against rheumatism, gout and sciatica. It was at Aachen that Paul Julius von Reuter (1816–99) founded his famous news agency, using carrier pigeons. Next door to his house is the interesting **Internationales Zeitungsmuseum** (international newspaper museum), which contains some 120,000 newspapers and fascinating exhibits.

Proud, lively Bremen, Germany's smallest region, is an old shipping town with a small, carefully restored old city enclosed by 17th-century ramparts. Narrow streets lead past tall old mansions in local Weser Renaissance style, and the people display great outdoor vitality and a fine civic spirit, a devotion to old customs and communal celebrations, with no less than 200 annual street-festivals.

335

Detail of Roland statue in the town square.

Bremen's origins date from the 8th century, when it became a bishopric. It soon grew into an important trading post, and in the 13th century was able to liberate itself from episcopal supervision to become a self-governing community. In 1358 it joined the Hanseatic League and continued to prosper, becoming a Free Imperial City in 1646. At the end of the Thirty Years' War (1648)

it was made a Swedish duchy and later came under Hanoverian domination. Industrialization and the growth of international trade during the latter half of the 19th century restored to Bremen a similar position it had enjoyed during the later Middle Ages; the city and its docking facilities were much enlarged. Heavy wartime bombing took its toll. Today Bremen is a thriving city, with big industrial areas in the outskirts, and a liberal, innovative SPD-led government.

Magnificent Marktplatz

The impressive **Marktplatz** (market square), one of the finest urban ensembles in Germany, is dominated by the magnificent arcaded Gothic **Rathaus** (1405) with a Renaissance façade added in 1612, decorated with statues of German emperors. Its elegant banqueting hall, the Oberer Saal, has a splendid roof-beam ceiling hung with monumental models of sailing ships. Every year since 1545 a fraternity dinner for local shipowners and other bigwigs has been held here, excluding "lesser mortals" like women and non-Bremens. The basement, Ratskeller, with charming 17th-century cubicles for private parties, offers 600 different German wines, said to be the best selection in the country; its oldest vintage is a *Rüdesheimer* of 1653. Giving the lie to the idea that northern Germans only drink beer and *Korn* (schnapps), a French chronicler in 1730 noted that in Bremen "one drinks Rhenish wine, the people drink Bordeaux". This restaurant is a good place to try the traditional dish named *Kohl mit Pinkel*, *Kohl* being kale, and *Pinkel* a sausage made of grits, lard, onions and hot spices.

At one side of the market square stands a giant 32-foot (10-metre) statue of the knight **Roland**, Charlemagne's nephew, erected in 1404 as a symbol of the city's independence. Other Roland statues have survived in former Hanseatic towns, but Bremen's is particularly well preserved and by far the best-known. Nearby is a delightful modern bronze pyramid of a cock on a cat on a dog on a donkey representing the "Street Musicians of Bremen" from the famous Grimm folktale and sculpted by Gerhard Marcks, a native son, in 1953. The twin-towered Protestant **cathedral** facing the Rathaus is much rebuilt and sombre inside; note the 16th-century organ and a fine 13th-century bronze font. The Bleikammer (lead chamber) exhibits nine mummies in open coffins recovered over the centuries along the banks of the Weser.

Near the banks of the river, the delightful **Böttcherstraße** is an alley rebuilt in 1920 in a curious stylistic mixture of Jugendstil and neo-Gothic. The tall red-brick gabled houses show great variety and contain cafés and bistros as well as workshops where you can watch gold- and silversmiths and other craftsmen at work. The street was the brainchild of the coffee magnate Ludwig Roselius (1874–1943), who invented

St Peter's Cathedral in the town square, Bremen.

decaffeinated coffee and made pots of money; his brand, Kaffee Hag, is still going strong. His collection of medieval art and furniture is exhibited at the Roselius-Haus, a 16th-century merchant's mansion. A second small museum in the Böttcherstraße is devoted to Paula Modersohn-Becker (1876–1907), the best-known member of the Worpswede artists' çolony, and her sombre Expressionist paintings. Although the village's heyday was in the 1880s to 1920s, it is still inhabited by numerous craftsmen and a delightful place to visit, situated at the edge of the Teufelsmoor (devil's moor) 16 miles (25 km) north of Bremen. In the southeastern corner of the Altstadt lies the charming village-like **Schnoor** quarter, a network of narrow, flowery streets lined with some of the city's oldest buildings (16/18th century), now housing cafés, bars, toy shops – touristy but attractive.

Multi-Museums

Bremen's three main museums all lie beyond the Altstadt. The **Kunsthalle** displays a rich collection of masterworks from the 14th to the 19th century, mainly German (do not miss Altdorfer's *Geburt Christi*); but Flemish and Dutch artists are also well represented, including a *Noli me tangere*, for which Rubens painted the figures and Jan Brueghel the rest, and some fine French Impressionists. The **Ostertorsteinweg** east of the museum is a colorful little street with bou-

tiques, health shops and a flea market catering to Bremen's youth; it is also strong on nightlife.

The **Überseemuseum** (overseas museum) near the train station shows an array of interesting ethnographic material, often collected by Bremen traders on the spot, including a reconstructed Papuan village, a Chinese house and a Japanese temple in a traditional garden setting. Bremen's long history comes alive in the large and spacious **Focke Museum** in the northeastern district of Schwachhausen. The quality of the objects and the way they are presented make a visit particularly attractive. To see how the harbor is doing today, take a boat trip (April to October) round the port past miles of masts and funnels, cranes and refineries and the handsome schooner "Deutschland", now a training ship.

The big port of **Bremerhaven** lies 35 miles (60 km) downstream from the North Sea. It was founded in 1827 as Bremen's deep-sea harbor and is now Germany's busiest fishing port. Since the disappearance of the luxury liners, the famous half-mile long embarkation point **Columbuskaje** has lost much of its glamor, although cruise ships and ferries still dock here. The city's main attraction is the splendid **Deutsches Schiffahrtsmuseum** (navigation museum), which traces German maritime history from ancient to modern times. It has models of old harbors and boats and a real Hanseatic trading ship from 1380, dredged up in Bremen port in

Helgoland is also a haven for birds.

1962. Its open-air section includes historic vessels moored at the quayside and some 500 models which you can steer yourself. Another interesting sight is the **fish auction**, held at 7 a.m. on weekdays in the **Fischauktionshallen** sheds.

Where Many Feared to Tread

On a round-trip from Bremerhaven you can visit the island of **Helgoland** with its impressive limestone cliffs. During the 14th century it was a pirates' lair, much feared by the Hanseatic cog ships, and in the war-ridden history of Europe it was always a vulnerable spot. Great Britain annexed the island in 1807, then in 1890 exchanged it for one of Imperial Germany's few colonial possessions, the island of Zanzibar in the Indian Ocean. During the last war, the islanders were evacuated to the mainland and only returned in 1952. Passenger ships visiting Helgoland are not allowed to moor alongside the quay; local boatmen, exercising an ancient and fiercely guarded right, transfer visitors to the shore for their four-hour stay. The island offers cliff walks, sea bathing from the lonely but sheltered Düne sand beach as well as tax-free tobacco, sweets and spirits.

Lower Saxony

As the name implies, the countryside of

The legendary piper of Hameln.

this region is predominantly flat, even dipping below sea level in some places. Its sparse beauty can, however, be quite addictive. It also has some of the most picturesque medieval towns of northern Germany, several treasure-packed museums, the finest Baroque gardens in the country, and islands haunted by pirates and hogged by holiday-makers.

It covers the whole western part of northern Germany except for Schleswig-Holstein, taking in the broad tongue of land between Hamburg and Bremen, East Frisia with its island-studded coast and naval and industrial center of Emden. Its most conspicuous natural features are the Lüneburg Heath full of sheep and birdlife and little else, and the Weser Bergland (Weser mountains), a hilly outcrop of the central German highlands. Here, in the vicinity of Hameln and Goslar and along the Weser, you encounter the dark, still quite forbidding forests in which some of the best-known German folk and fairy tales are set.

Lower Saxony's documented history starts with the military conquests and religious settlements masterminded by Charlemagne in the 9th century. During the Middle Ages the Welfs (Guelphs) ruled large parts of the region from their bases in and around Goslar, Braunschweig, Celle and Hanover. Henry the Lion (1139–80), one of the most controversial figures in medieval German history, had his chief residence at Braunschweig, from where he directed the colonization drive to the northeast into Slav territory.

Thanks not least to shrewd marriage politics, the Welf dynasty managed to intertwine its lineage with the Hanoverian Elector Georg Ludwig, who succeeded Queen Anne as Britain's King George I (and who never learned proper English). For the next 123 years Hanoverian monarchs held sway simultaneously in Westminster and their home duchy (later kingdom). During the years of foreign rule over Hanover (1803–13), many thousands of Hanoverians fought under British colors

in all the theaters of war against Napoleon, contributing significantly to Wellington's victory at Waterloo.

Hanover's History

Hanover (Hannover), the capital of the region, is a big, modern commercial city, yet at the same time its central area is full of interesting secular and religious buildings, intimate little squares with half-timbered houses and lively cafés and pubs. There was little history before the 17th century, when a branch of the Welf House of Braunschweig moved its princely residence here and built a palace at Herrenhausen. The arts flourished under the Elector Ernst August and his cultured wife Sophia, who encouraged Händel (1685–1759) to give concerts and the philosopher Leibniz (1646–1716) to look after the royal library for 40 years. Sophia was a Stuart, granddaughter of James I. The English Parliament chose her as successor to Queen Anne; as she died before that queen, in 1714, it was her son who became George I. In 1866 Hanover was annexed by Prussia and ceased to be a separate kingdom.

To the outside world, Hanover today is chiefly known for its international trade fairs, of which there are roughly 40 each year. The main one, the Hanover Fair, takes place in late April when it becomes difficult to find accommodation. In early June, a major *Schützenfest* (riflemen's festival) takes

The outdoor café is part of Germany's social landscape.

place, claimed to be the world's largest, complete with fireworks, parades and floats. The city is also a center for automobile, rubber, audio-visual and biscuit industries.

The main downtown area, centering on the **Kröpcke** piazza, a favorite rendezvous point, has been well rebuilt, with some quite striking new buildings. Next to the neo-Gothic Neues Rathaus of Wilhelmine grandiosity and with a high central dome (good views) stands the **Kestner Museum**, where a modern concrete latticework has been wrapped over the original 1889 façade in order to preserve it. The museum houses a good collection of medieval works of art as well as Egyptian, Greek and Roman antiques. South of the Rathaus you find

two other major museums.

The chief interest at the **Landesmuseum** is a varied collection of paintings from the Florentine Primitives and Cranach altarpieces to late-19th-century Germans. One of the finest collections of modern art in Germany is held by the **Sprengel Museum** (its main benefactor being the eponymous chocolate tycoon): there are roomfuls of Klee, Léger, Picasso, the Surrealists Ernst and Schwitters (a native son) as well as attractive works by Dali, Magritte and Kandinsky.

Walk past the **Leineschloß** (remodeled by local architect Laves in neo-Classical style) to the banks of the river Leine with its three exuberant sculptures by French artist Niki de Saint Phalle.

Behind the Leineschloß you enter the charming **Altstadt**. At the Marktplatz stands the 14th-century **Marktkirche** dominated by a four-gabled tower topped by a pointed bell turret. Inside are beautiful 14th-century stained-glass windows and a carved multicolored altarpiece (15th century).

Take the narrow Krämerstraße to the Holzmarkt and Burgstraße with the **Leibniz-Haus**, a copy of the house this major thinker of modern times, both philosopher and mathematician, occupied from 1678 to 1716. Some of the *Fachwerk* (half-timbered) houses have been assembled here after the war to form an ensemble of "old Hanover", an artificial but enterprising and attractive solution.

Past the **Historisches Museum** (excellent displays of the history of the town and of Lower Saxony) you come to a delightful little square graced by the half-timbered **Ballhof**, built in 1650 as a badminton hall and now a theater. This quiet residential area around the **Kreuzkirche** is sprinkled with pleasant cafés and restaurants.

Pleasure Grounds

On the northwest side of town lies the celebrated **Herrenhäuser Gärten** (Herrenhauser gardens), probably the finest Baroque gardens in Germany. They consist of four separate areas, of which the most interesting and soothing is the Großer Gärten, transformed and enlarged by Princess Sophia between 1680 and 1710. It is surrounded in the Dutch style by a moat, and contains a formal French pleasure garden, a fountain and a maze. There are several other fountains mesmerizing to watch; the central one, the Große Fontäne, has a plume of 270 feet (82 meters), the highest jet in Europe. Open-air concerts are given in summer from June to August.

The Berggärten (mountain garden) has many varieties of orchids and the mausoleum of the House of Hanover in which is found the tomb of George I. Southeast of the park, a small museum is devoted to the artist and poet Wilhelm Busch (1832–1908), an originator of the comic-strip and still hugely popular in Germany for his illustrated comic tales such as *Max und Moritz*.

Some 25 miles (40 km) northeast of Hanover lies **Celle**, one of the noblest old towns in northern Germany. From 1378 to 1705 it was the residence of the Lüneburg branch of the Welf dynasty, distant relatives of the British royal family. The **Altstadt** consists of a grid of streets with 16–18th-century red-and-white timbered and gabled houses, some of whose upper floors overhang. Its charm is somewhat marred by the overabundance of shops. The massive building with a slender oriel projecting from the roof is the town hall (1579).

Nearby runs the picturesque Kalandgasse with the **Lateinschule** (school of Latin; 1602), a former college whose decorated façade is inscribed with

Herrenhäuser Gardens, a fine expression of Baroque sentiments.

Biblical quotes. Just a few steps further on is the **Stadtkirche** (city church), a Gothic building with Baroque additions. Every day at 7.30 a.m. and 6.30 p.m., the town bugler climbs its 235 steps to sound his horn. South of the old town, in the **Französischer Gärten** (French gar-

den), you find a very informative museum on beekeeping, honey being a major product of the Lüneburg Heath.

One of Celle's main attractions is the princes' elegant white Schloß, surrounded by a moat with swans. The state rooms are furnished in Italian

Honey on display.

Green Country

Baroque, very playful and a bit incongruous in this part of Germany, where the population is proverbially reserved and unplayful. Do not miss the beautiful 15th-century chapel with ogive vaulting and Renaissance decor, and try to get a look at the theater (1674), the oldest of its kind in Germany, and still used for performances of the classics.

North of Celle begins the vast and strangely enchanting **Lüneburger Heide** (Lüneburg heath), where grassy prairies full of sheep alternate with marshy ponds, low valley and forests rich in game. Grand and somber during most of the year, it lays on a bit of color in August and September when the heather is in bloom and the juniper plants are in leaf. It is a popular venue for holidays on a farm, since it is ideal for hiking, cycling and horse-riding – the well-known Hanoverian horses are bred here. The Heath includes several nature reserves of which the bird sanctuary just north of Walsrode, the

A peaceful farm in
Lüneburg Heath where the
Germans officially
surrendered at the end of
World War JJ.

Lüneburg until 1980; since then the **Deutsches Salz-museum** (German salt museum) has been built at the spot where the last saline pit was.

A legacy from that prosperous time is the big **Rathaus** (13–16th century), whose sumptuous interior should not be missed; the Gothic Fürstensaal is decorated with lamps made from stags' antlers, and the Große Ratsstube (council chamber) of c.1566 is a Renaissance masterpiece paneled and adorned with intricate wood sculptures by Albert von Soest. The large clock and belfry tower has Meißen porcelain bells which ring out the hours.

The city's pedestrianized center has many fine old red-brick buildings; and the nearby **Wasserviertel** (water quarter) by the river is delightfully picturesque with, among other things, a half-timbered millhouse, a gabled Renaissance brewery and an 18th-century crane. Continue southward along the river and take a look at the 14th-century

Vogelpark Walsrode, is the most fascinating. Some 900 species from all over the world live here in relative freedom, ostriches and parrots, cranes and flamingoes and many tropical birds (open mid-March to October).

At the northern end of the Heath, about 56 miles (90 km) north of Celle, lies the very handsome old city of **Lüneburg**, which grew rich from its salt deposits in the Middle Ages. It sold salt to the Baltic cities and Scandinavia; as salt in those times was the only means of preserving food, it was almost worth its weight in gold. Salt was mined at

brick **Johanniskirche** with a massive leaning spire. Inside are an organ case (1715) on which J.S. Bach played, splendid chandeliers and a marvelous high altar (1430–85).

Delightful Towns

South of Hanover, at least two towns are worth a visit, Goslar and Hameln, both full of medieval and Renaissance features. On the way to Goslar, make a detour from the autobahn to **Hildesheim**, capital of Romanesque art in Germany. The cathedral is a reconstruction of the 11th-century basilica. The interior contains several magnificent works of art: an immense 11th-century chandelier, a rare carved font of the 13th century and a bronze column depicting the "Life of Christ" (11th century). The impressive two-storey Romanesque cloister lies at the east end of the cathedral; and the bronze west doors, examples of primitive Romanesque sculpture, depict scenes from the Old and New Testaments.

Some regard **Goslar** as the loveliest old town in North Germany. It was the favorite residence of the Salian emperors (1024–1125) and a former Free Imperial City, and owes its architectural glories to its prosperity as a center of lead and silver mining in the Middle Ages. It began to decline after 1550 because of religious feuds; however, some of those old mines are still worked today (e.g. the Ramelsberg lead and

zinc mines), and the town itself looks well-to-do and very *gemütlich* (cozy).

Goslar's intimate charm rests on the variety of buildings of different periods and styles, all huddled together in an area of narrow streets, much of it closed to traffic. The façades are mainly of black and white half-timbering or plain stone. At the center of the picturesque **Marktplatz** stands a fountain with two bronze basins (1230). The old town hall with an arcaded gallery is famous for its Huldigungssaal (chamber of homage), a small room painted with gorgeous frescoes by an unknown artist around 1510. Along the walls are effigies of Roman emperors and Sibyls in Renaissance costume. A display case presents the *Goslar Gospel*, a rare 1230 manuscript. Also facing the market square is the Gothic **Kaiserworth** (1494; now a hotel) with Baroque statues of emperors beneath canopies. Northwest of the market past the Rathaus is the **Schuhhof** (shoe courtyard), a square entirely surrounded by timber-fronted houses. West of the Marktplatz past the Marktkirche is the immense pointed roof of the house called the **Brusttuch** (the shawl), dating from 1526. A rich mine owner had it decorated, in accordance with Renaissance taste, with a host of mythological, Biblical and buffoon motifs.

Further down the Bergstraße you encounter the **Siemenshaus** (1693), built by an ancestor of the famous Berlin industrialists. It is a striking half-timbered house with a beautiful entrance hall paved with small tiles. The most important of Goslar's churches is the Romanesque **Neuwerk Kirche**, alone in a garden, with a heavily ribbed pointed vaulting and on the organ loft balustrade six elegant Gothic low reliefs.

Rats!

About 28 miles (45 km) southwest of Hanover lies the pretty town of **Hameln** (Hamelin), well-known for the legendary Pied Piper and graced by some of the best examples of the regional architectural style called "Weser Renaissance" of the late 16th, early 17th century. Most of the town center is traffic-free. At the **Marktplatz** stands the **Hochzeitshaus** (marriage house; 1610–17) with three elegant gables. It formerly acted as a reception building for burghers' weddings. The large Rattenfängerhaus (ratcatcher's house; 1603) at the eastern boundary of the Altstadt has a façade made up of sculptured stonework decorated with carved busts and masks. This is probably the most impressive example of Weser Renaissance style, which is characterized by ram's horn scrollwork, forward wings and pinnacles on the gables.

There is no getting away from the Pied Piper, whom the Germans call the "ratcatcher of Hameln". The souvenir shops sell sweets and toys in rat shape, and the restaurant in the historical **Rattenfängerhaus** serves a dish of "rat tails", really pork fillets flambéed with Calvados. The famous legend – told by Goethe and Browning and the Brothers Grimm – is about a piper in motley who in 1284 enticed the town's rats to a watery death in the Weser, then lured away all the children when he was not given his promised reward. This is said to have happened exactly on 26 June in the Bungelosengasse, where to this day an unwritten rule forbids music of any kind to be played. Every summer Sunday at noon a dramatized performance of the legend is given in front of the Marriage House. The historical truth behind this motif seems to be that during the 13–14th century young people were often brutally abducted and deported to colonize areas in the east.

Surrounding Seas

A completely different type of legend and truth, namely the facts and fiction of piracy, suffuses the clear, bracing air of the East Frisian coast. From Hanover drive via Bremen in the direction of the town of Norden. **East Frisia** (Ostfriesland), with rich and heavy soil and large tracts of moors, has a sinister charm on overcast days when the wind sighs in the bent trees and every gray moving form, be it man or beast or something in between, looks strangely indistinct and mysterious. No wonder that German crime writers like to set their stories in this region, where people are proverbially taciturn, brooding, a bit backward. Historically, this part of Germany maintained its independent, feudal status almost intact right to the end of the 18th century. The local rulers were called *Häuptlinge* (chieftains), and quite a number of East Frisian families can trace their ancestors right back to the 12th and 13th centuries. The East Frisians – like their neighbors, the Dutch, whom they in many ways resemble – drink a lot of strong tea and Korn, live in low-lying brick houses which are often thatched, and have their own dark and sonorous dialect which derives from Anglo-Saxon.

The major towns are **Emden**, formerly an important naval base and now much industrialized, and **Aurich** on the Ems-Jade-Canal, which connects Emden (where during the 16th century more ships put ashore than in the whole of England) and Wilhelmshaven and is the unofficial border between East Frisia and the rest of the world. **Norden** with its partly Romanesque Ludgerikirche containing a famous 17th-century organ by Arp Schnitger and with the stately Schöningh mansion (1576), is the main gateway to the seven inhabited East Frisian islands, all popular in summer, all reachable by ferry, and some with very odd names. **Spiekeroog** has the highest dunes (245 feet [75 meters]) and an old church with souvenirs from the Spanish Armada of 1588, while **Juist** and **Langeoog** have bird sanctuaries. Take the ferry from the little fishing harbor of Norddeich, 2.5 miles (4 km) north of Norden, to **Norderney**, the most

Weser Renaissance architecture, typical of the pretty town of Hameln.

developed island and the second oldest seaside resort in Germany (1797). The history and folklore of the islands can be studied in the small **Fischerhaus** museum, and the town offers lots of amenities like concerts, a nine-hole golf-course, horse-riding and a heated seawater pool. The hotels and other buildings – there is a casino, but it is not smart – are grouped together at the west end, the rest of the island consisting of a 7-mile (12-km) stretch of rolling dunes mostly covered with scrub or wild grass. On the beaches close to town you can hire canopied wicker beach chairs, a sensible private changing-room-cum-armchair and a standard feature of the well-organized German bathing ritual found all along the country's seaboard.

Hamburg

Hamburg, Germany's leading port and its second largest city (after Berlin), lies on the Elbe 60 miles (100 km) inland from the open sea and is a region in its own right. In the "Free and Hanseatic City", as it has been calling itself since 1806, water is much in evidence: not only are there miles upon miles of quays and canals around the harbor, but the center itself is dominated by the wide expanse of the lovely Alster lake. Whether in summer or in winter's twilight months, the lake adds a sheen and shimmer to the air and the buildings.

It may not be a city to fall easily in love with, but it is much admired, not least by its own people who are indeed very proud of it. Life here is graceful and civilized, the Hamburgers themselves being a reserved and prudent lot, heirs to a great mercantile seafaring tradition, strongly

The flag of Hamburg with its white seal.

On a promenade, a treasured leisure activity.

liberal, cosmopolitan and anglophile; like the English, they pronounce "st" and "sp" as a diphthong, and according to an old saying, "When it rains in London, Hamburgers put up their umbrellas." Likewise, their tolerance and understatement links in with British traits, and their fashion shows subdued good taste, nothing too flashy.

Unlike other German cities of comparable size, there are not many buildings of distinction, mainly because Hamburg never was a major center of the Church or aristocracy, so medieval palaces and mighty churches are non-existent. The downtown business area is in local red brick and not beautiful, but then again there are almost no ugly concrete blocks and boxes like in other cities, and no skyscrapers mar the skyline. Central Hamburg is very spacious and the sights are often rather far apart. Traffic not being too heavy, you could visit the main spots by car or use the *U-Bahn* (underground); and boat cruises provide a charming introduction to the bustle and beauty of Hamburg as well.

At any time of year there is a host of locally organized fairs and festivals. The big traditional celebrations are the *Hafengeburtstag* (port anniversary) on 10 May, and three times a year in spring, summer and autumn there is a huge funfair called the *Dom*. In June or July the *Stuttgarter Weindorf*, a wine festival, is held in the Rathaus square, and various musical festivals and cultural activities are organized during the summer.

Turning Back the Clock

Already a Saxon settlement in the 7th century, in 831 Hamburg was raised to a bishopric and registered as a port in 1189. It soon afterwards joined the Hanseatic League and in the 14th century was Lübeck's main subsidiary port, responsible for North Sea trade. From 1460 to 1806 its patrician government was under Danish suzerainty. Germany's first stock exchange was founded here in 1558, and in 1768 Denmark acknowledged its position as a Free Imperial City. In the late 18th century Hamburg forged trading links with the young United States, and in the 19th

The Dom fun-fair.

century trade with the Americas brought fantastic boom and growth. The Great Fire of 1842 destroyed a quarter of the city, which was quickly rebuilt on a much larger scale; the grand old brick warehouses along the quays still bear witness to this tremendous upsurge.

1847 saw the foundation of the Hamburg-Amerika-Linie (today Hapag-Lloyd), which up to the First World War was the world's greatest steamship company. After 1933 Hamburg was less welcoming to the Nazis than any other big German city, and Hitler staged no major rallies here. So it is ironic as well as tragic that it was very heavily bombed in 1943 by the RAF. After the war much was quickly and intelligently rebuilt. During the last decade, the city has suffered from the general decline in ship-building and the shifting focus of German industry and business to the south. But it still is Europe's fourth largest port, has more consulates (80) than any other European town, more bridges than any other metropolis – 2,195 compared with Venice's 400 – and much high-tech industry, especially in aeronautics. Germany's three leading weeklies, *Stern*, *Die Zeit* and *Der Spiegel*, are published here.

A Good Beginning

The **Rathaus**, as usual, provides a good starting point for a tour of the city. With its long regular façade and high tower,

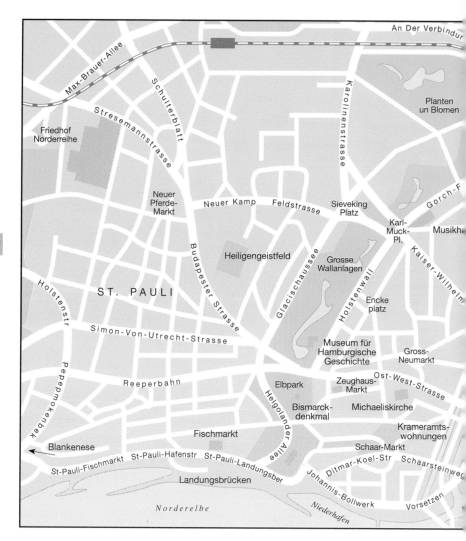

the neo-Renaissance building is a typical expression of civic pride. Like most of this quarter, it rests on long timber posts (4,000 in this case) driven deep into the marshy soil. This is Hamburg's main shopping area. Across the town hall square lie six big new shopping arcades, and the Hanseviertel beyond is a gourmet's dream where you can have a snack of oysters, lobsters and champagne without even sitting down. East

of the Rathaus rise the spires of **St Petri** with its tall 14th-century tower, and of **St Jacobi**, a fine northern late Gothic hall church. Both are close to the broad shop-lined Mönckebergstraße leading to the *Hauptbahnhof* (main railway station).

Just south of the station is one of Hamburg's three major museums, the **Museum für Kunst und Gewerbe** (decorative arts and crafts). Among its treas-

Hamburg

ures are remarkable pieces of medieval statuary, sumptuous Renaissance furniture, precious clocks from northern Germany and a comprehensive collection of Jugendstil (Art Nouveau) objects. Specialists will find much of interest in the Chinese, Japanese and Islamic art sections.

North of the station, the **Kunsthalle** has one of the finest painting collections in Germany, from the 14th century to modern times. The *Grabower Altar* (1379) by Master Bertram for St Petri is perhaps the greatest example of North German primitive painting. Dutch masters of the 17th century are well represented (an early Rembrandt, several Ruysdaels and Avercamps) as are German painters of the 19th century, with impressive works by C.D. Friedrich and the portraitist P.O. Runge, a Hamburger by adoption. Some well-known works by French

Enjoying a drink outdoors.

Impressionists are exhibited (Manet's *Nana*, apples by Cézanne), and works by the *Brücke* group and the *Blaue Reiter* form an outstanding display.

Nearby is the elegant **Jungfernstieg** (ladies' promenade), the southern termination of the **Alster**. This lake, a favorite venue for local sailing and windsurfing enthusiasts, is really a tributary of the Elbe; two bridges divide it into an inner and outer section, the **Binnenalster** and **Außenalster**. From the **Alsterpavillon**, a charming lakeside café and rendezvous spot since 1799, you have a grand view over the Binnenalster, surrounded by 19th-century office blocks. At the quayside, boats leave on tours around the Außenalster, and this is the most enjoyable way to

take in the harmonious city silhouette pierced by the spires of Hamburg's five major Protestant churches and of the Rathaus. The entire shoreline is a vast, tree-lined park with splendid 19th-century villas half hidden behind rhododendron and rose bushes; there is a 4.5-mile (7.5-km) path along the water, much used by joggers. Beyond the two bridges on the west shore you pass the elegant residential area of **Pöseldorf** with chic boutiques and art galleries. As the basin narrows to the river at Harvestehude, you see some of the city's finest mansions, neo-Classical and Jugendstil, gleaming white with immaculate gardens coming right down to the weeping willows at the water's edge.

East of the central city, beyond the

View over the inner Alster to the Rathaus and the Nikolaikirchturm from Lombardsbrücke.

former ramparts, lies the huge **Planten un Blomen** (Low German for "plants and flowers") flower-garden and its southern continuation, the Botanical Gardens (giant Amazonian water-lilies). At the southern tip of this parkland stands the **Museum für Hamburgische Geschichte** (local history museum), stronger on technical and industrial than on cultural exhibits. It has models, paintings and photos of old Hamburg and the port, and can help North American visitors trace their family's history through manifest records which date from 1850 to 1914.

Here you are already in **St Pauli**, Hamburg's famous red-light district. In fact, most of it consists of respectable if rather run-down working class

Nature, treasured by the German spirit, is prevalent even in the cities.

Bierhaus on the Reeperbahn a section famous for its nightlife.

neighborhoods, while the area of sex bars, night shows, striptease joints and rough pubs is concentrated around the **Reeperbahn** and **Große Freiheit**. In recent years, partly under the impact of the Aids scare, business has become more subdued, and the area, though still garish and vulgar-looking, has moved slightly up-market, with smart restaurants creeping in.

some Baroque church of **St Michaelis**, one of Hamburg's best-known landmarks, because it was here that the great ocean liners tied up, in the days when they still ploughed the waters of the seven seas. From the church platform (open daily) you get a fine view of town and port. Right behind St Michaelis are the charming **Krameramts-wohnungen**, built in 1620-76 for the widows of the shopkeepers' guild and typical of early Hamburg courtyard resi-

Gateway to the Seven Seas

Near the quayside rises the steeple of the hand-

Speicherstadt in Hamburg.

dences. The quaint brick-and-timber buildings now house bistros, boutiques and art galleries.

Come early for the St Pauli **Fischmarkt** (fish market) held every Sunday from 6 to 10 a.m. just below St Michaelis at the *Landungsbrücken* (landing-stages); it sells not only freshly-caught fish, but also fruit and vegetables and all kinds of trinkets to the milling crowds of late-night revelers, tourists and Hamburg housewives. Take a boat here for a *Hafenrundfahrt* (port cruise), which speeds along massive supertankers and offers a glimpse of the inner workings of the busy port. The eastern part of the cruise gives an idea of what it must have been like before the fire of 1842. Nicely restored gabled ware-

houses front the curving banks of the Nikolaifleet canal, parallel to the narrow Deichstraße lined with prosperous-looking 17th-century merchants' houses, many of them now used as restaurants serving traditional food. Near the eastern end of the harbor is the **Speicherstadt** (city of warehouses), a massive ensemble of gabled red-brick storage buildings. They were erected in the 1880s during the boom in overseas trade and are still used for storing tobacco, silks, spices and more mundane goods. West of St Pauli, the beautiful **Elbchaussee** avenue lined with luxurious villas and fine restaurants runs on for miles through several of Hamburg's posh suburbs. The **Altona Museum**, devoted to North German history and

A work of art from the Altona Museum.

where a riverside café, the **Schulauer Fährhaus**, puts on a nostalgic spectacle: the colors of passing ships are saluted in accordance with maritime practice and the national anthem of the ship's country of origin is played. Wedel also boasts the world's only museum of miniature ships in a bottle, the **Buddelschiff-Museum**.

From Blankenese you can take the ferry to the other shore for an excursion through a countryside as flat as it is pleasing, the **Altes Land** (old country). It is Hamburg's orchard, in fact Europe's largest homogenous fruit-growing region, and visitors come especially in May to enjoy a sea of pink and white blossoms. It is a prosperous area, yet the tiny villages here exude a rural, peace-

culture, has a fascinating collection of models of traditional farmhouses, an array of very fine 18–19th-century figure-heads, and a fully restored rural cottage of 1745, now the museum restaurant. Past Altona you come to the landscaped Jenisch Park with the white neo-Classical **Villa Jenisch** (1831), open to visitors and showing beautiful interiors from the late Renaissance to early Jugendstil. Next to it, the **Ernst-Barlach-Haus** celebrates the great modern sculptor and draughtsman whose expressive works grace many squares, malls, parks and churches in northern Germany.

The former fishing village of **Blankenese** is now a fashionable suburb with steep alleys and well-appointed villas on the hillside. Drive on to **Wedel**

Colorful German flowers.

The prominent Holstentor, a reddish twin-towered gateway is a landmark in Lübeck.

ful, uncommercial atmosphere. Black-and-white half-timbered farmhouses dot the landscape. The small parish of **Jork** is famous for its many thatched houses, and often graced by carved doorways showing rural scenes and floral ornaments.

Schleswig-Holstein

The most northerly German *Land*, made up of the two former dukedoms of Schleswig and Holstein and bordering on Denmark, was until recently outside the mainstream of German cultural and political developments. It has, however, much to offer the discerning visitor: bronze-age burial sites, clean-limbed little palaces surrounded by water and woods, one of the busiest shipyards in the country, sandy beaches and fashionable resorts, a sprinkling of literary fame and delicious fresh seafood.

Most of the countryside is exceedingly flat; only in the southeast between Lübeck and Kiel does one encounter rolling hills and small dark blue lakes, which are a bit cold for swimming but ideal for sailing. The eastern coastline looking towards the Baltic is characterized by numerous deep bays and estuaries, while on the North Sea side the boundary between land and sea is forever shifting.

For centuries wind and waves have steadily been eroding the shoreline, constantly changing the shape of the many small islands. Whole villages have disappeared during a storm, and even today the coastal population has to keep a sharp eye on the greedy sea. Inland it is much more tranquil where sheep graze and black-and-white Holstein cows munch their way through life. Fishermen and sailors are worried, as year by year their catch becomes smaller and the good fishing grounds recede further northwest from the North Sea far into the Atlantic.

Before the arrival of Charlemagne's armies in the region, Saxon tribes had settled here from around AD 350 onward. In 449 many of the Angles, Saxons and Jutes under Hengist and Horsa sailed for Britain (for unknown reasons), where they were not welcome. Slav tribes from the east then emigrated, into the much depopulated country. Early in the 9th century Charlemagne subjugated the Saxons, drove the Slavs back to the northeast and repelled the Jutes (who became first the Vikings and then the Danes) beyond the river Schlei. He consolidated and fortified his new territory, building long earthworks and citadels. Christian missionaries began to work from Hammaburg (to become Hamburg much later) and Meldorf, but it took centuries before the recalcitrant natives gave up their pagan gods and rituals for Christian ones.

The Danes were not happy with the new territorial division, made forays to the south and were repelled again and again. Only in 1460 was a satisfactory solution found by joining the areas under German and Danish influence and establishing a kind of feudal federation under the King of Denmark. Under the influence of the nationalist ideals proclaimed by theorists of the Romantic movement, the inhabitants of more southerly Holstein began to find their Danish overlord an imposition, and fought a few unsuccessful battles. Then Prussia came to their aid, defeated Denmark and turned Schleswig-Holstein into a Prussian province under the nominal rule of the old regional nobility (1864). In 1937 Lübeck lost its position and privileges as a free Hanse city. The latest redrawing of the political map in 1960 involved a shift of the frontier-line which left 20,000 Germans on Danish soil and some 60,000 Danes living and working on German territory.

Town crier cum tour guide!

Lovely Lübeck

In 1159, two years after a great fire that destroyed the original settlement founded in 1145, Henry the Lion began to rebuild the town of **Lübeck**. Less than a hundred years later it formed with Bremen and Wismar a trading corporation which became the nucleus of the Hanseatic League or Hanse. This company of merchant adventurers during its heyday comprised a network of some 200 cities and towns spread over the whole of Northern Europe, ruled the Baltic and monopolized its lucrative trade in timber, amber, furs and salt fish. Lübeck's merchants became very prosperous and graced the town with magnificent buildings, some of which survived wartime bombing and have been lovingly renovated. The city's oval-shaped medieval center lies between two arms of the river Trave, just above its estuary on the Baltic.

After Lübeck became a Free Imperial City in 1226, it was ruled by its own merchants as one of Germany's earliest self-governing towns. Of its mighty merchant families few survive. Still the city has kept something of the "Hanseatic spirit" cultivated by the patrician families, and a certain natural grace and good manners, an atmosphere of culture and self-confident good taste similar to that apparent in Hamburg.

A good entry point is the **Holstentor** (1477), a reddish twin-towered gateway

The old gabled houses and ships are reminders of Lübeck's medieval past.

and the city's landmark, now housing a historical museum. As you cross the river, note the fine gabled warehouses (16–17th century). Keep to the right and pass the Gothic Petrikirche, and about 650 feet (200 meters) further down in the narrow street called **Kolk** you find the remarkable **puppet museum and marionette theater** (shows daily), which houses the largest puppet collection in Germany. Continue in this direction and reach the **cathedral** (first built in 1173), a Romanesque structure with a Gothic chapel added later. Among its treasures are a Renaissance pulpit, a huge triumphal cross of 1477 and a mid-15th-century baptismal font.

The first remarkable building in the western half of the old city is the **Rathaus** (town hall; first erected in 1250) of dark glazed brickwork with Gothic blind arcades and Renaissance additions; the council chamber with portraits of Lübeck patricians is open to public. Across the road on Breite Straße stands the famous **Niederegger** marzipan store. Beside the Rathaus is the lofty twin-spired **Marienkirche** (1250–1440), said to be Germany's oldest Gothic church built in brick and with the world's highest brick nave; it became the model for all the main churches along the Baltic seaboard. During renovation work the original Gothic frescoes were rediscovered under whitewashing and Baroque additions; they have been refurbished since, and the interior with its fine ribbed vaulting again looks much as it did when first built. Note also a carved and gilded altarpiece made in Antwerp in 1518, and a huge mechanical clock with figures parading at noon.

Opposite the Marienkirche stands the **Buddenbrookhaus** (only the façade is original), the stately mansion where the Mann family lived in 1841–91 and which Thomas Mann immortalized in his first highly successful novel *Buddenbrooks*, the saga of the slow decline of a Lübeck merchant dynasty in the 19th century. It is one of the best-loved of his books; unfortunately its famous ironic style does not translate well. A collection of memorabilia of the Mann family can be viewed at the **Drägerhaus** in the Königsstraße; its neighbor, likewise a patrician house of great elegance, is the **Behnhaus** with Expressionist paintings by Kirchner, Munch and others. Regain the Breite Straße and view the **Jakobikirche**, traditionally the mariners' church, with splendidly carved 16–17th century organ lofts. A bit further west is the **Haus der Fischergesellschaft** (the fishermen's guildhall), a tall step-gabled Renaissance mansion and long-established restaurant full of nautical paraphernalia. Nearby is the **Heilig-Geist-Hospital** (hospice of the holy spirit), built c.1280 and for centuries used as an old people's home (a few pensioners are still housed here). Its vaulted Gothic chapel with 14–15th-century wall-paintings and altar screen (much restored) is impressive, as are the huge hall at the back, the cellars with two fine restaurants and the beautiful little garden.

Lake District

From Lübeck head north, and 20 minutes later the usually flat countryside begins to roll. This is the **Holsteinische Schweiz** (Holstein Switzerland), with lakes surrounded by hillocks and boskets and winding country lanes splendid for cycling. You will find no jagged peaks or cuckoo-clocks here, but at least one remarkable cheese, namely Germany's oldest, in continual production for 500 years around the village of **Wiltstedt** in the southwest.

Eutin lies in the heart of the lake-dotted region, a well-mannered and well-scrubbed little town known affectionately as the "Weimar of the North". It gained this reputation in the last quarter of the 18th century, when its prince-bishops gathered together a fine group of regional artists, architects and writers. The town is the birthplace of the

Sunset over the Water Castle at Glucksburg.

Romantic composer Carl Maria von Weber, and both the librarian Johann Heinrich Voß, famous for his melliflu-ous translations of Homer's *Odyssee* and *Iliad*, and the minor poet Leopold von Stolberg lived and worked here – each of them today honored with a little mu-seum. Eutin still is an active promoter of the arts. The neo-Classical Altstadt con-tains the **Witwenpalais** (widows' pal-ace) of 1786, a charming building to which the widow of the late ruler used to be moved to have her out of the way and not meddling in the family affairs of the new duke. The red-brick basilica of **St Michael** (13th century) is also worth a look. The stunning water-girt *Schloß* (pal-ace) surrounded by landscaped gardens was constructed in the 18th century on the site of a medieval castle; it contains some notable porcelains and tapestries as well as many portraits by Johann H.E. Tischbein (1751–1829), which give an idea of the extensive family connec-tions of the Gottorf dynasty. One of the Gottorf scions caught the eye of the young Catherine the Great, who quickly married him and translated him to Rus-sia, where he became Czar Peter III.

The small town of **Plön** makes a good starting point for a *Fünf-Seen-Fahrt*, a cruise of five lakes which offers tran-quil vistas of wooded hills, green pas-tures and lots of waterfowl. On a terrace towering above the town stands the former residence of the local dukes; built on the site of a 12th-century castle, it was enlarged in 1636 to form the present

Kiel Canal, the world's busiest waterway.

high, two-winged *Schloß* with Renaissance roof lanterns. Since the mid-19th century it has been used for educational purposes, first for navy cadets, then for an elite of Nazi youth and latterly as an upper-class boarding-school. Take in the wide vista across the Plöner See – the large island is called **Olsburg** and was the site of a Slav refuge keep, destroyed in 1139 – and go for a walk to the tip of the **Prinzeninsel** (princes' island), where an open-air restaurant serves simple, nourishing dishes.

Capital City

Some say that **Kiel**, the *region*'s capital, rose from the war's rubble and debris "like a phoenix". If that was true, then the bird's plumage is of a rather modern make, for few notable buildings have since been rebuilt. The bright brickwork of modern houses and office blocks somehow intensifies the chilly winds that perennially blow through the city. The **Nikolaikirche** at the modernized Alter Markt (old market) dates from the 13th century and has neo-Gothic facing, while the **town hall** (1907–11) is a good example of German Art Nouveau. Kiel used to be Germany's leading naval base – therefore the very heavy bombing – and is still an important shipping center with big shipyards. Linking the North Sea and the Baltic, the Kiel Canal (60 miles [99 km] long) is the world's busiest waterway with more than 50,000

Statue in the main square, Schleswig.

Northwest of Kiel lies the appealing old maritime city of **Schleswig** on a fjord full of sailing boats. The oldest city in Schleswig-Holstein – it received its charter c.1200 – it was an international trading post long before the rise of Lübeck and the Hanse. Graced by dozens of solid burghers' houses of the 17th to 19th century, Schleswig's main religious building is the high-towered cathedral **St Petrim** (12–15th century) with a richly painted cloister and the superbly carved Bornesholmer Altar (1521) by Hans Brüggemann. The city's chief distinction is the majestic white water-castle **Schloß Gottorf** (16–18th century), main residence of the dukes of Schleswig since 1268 and the major *Land* museum since 1948. The Schloß boasts a magnificent Renaissance chapel and a sumptuous Gothic hall with painted ceiling. The museum is definitely worth a visit, if only for the splendid Nydam boat of c. AD 300, a 70-foot (21-meter) oaken rowing boat found in 1863 in the marshes; and for a number of gruesome "moor corpses", 2,000-year-old skeletons of people condemned to death. Some of the condemned were killed and deposited in the moor so that their souls would not return to haunt the living; others seem just to have been bound and blindfolded and deposited in the marshes to die a slow death.

ships a year. Southwest of the city, the **Freilichtmuseum Molfsee** is one of the country's best open-air museums with some 30 old farmhouses, windmills, watermills and a vicarage of 1569; watch carvers, bakers, potters and other costumed craftsmen work with traditional tools and techniques. Kiel's chief pride is the **Förde**, the long bay which opens into the Baltic. This is the venue for the annual Kieler Woche, the international regatta of sailing boats and yachts. It is a spectacle as graceful as it is exciting, and one of the best observation spots is **Laboe** at the tip of the fjord. There you also find a sombre, elegant naval war memorial, a tall dark-brick tower shaped like a ship's stern, and a museum of modern German naval history.

The Northernmost Point

A two-hour drive takes you to **Sylt**, the

largest and most fashionable of the North Frisian islands on the west coast of Schleswig. A narrow strip of land, 25 miles (40 km) long, it is linked to the mainland by a causeway which cars have to cross atop a train shuttle. Windy and invigorating, just by standing in the dunes and looking out to the sea one feels much healthier already. The eastern coastline is more sheltered and varied, while the western one, exposed to the North Sea, offers one unbroken line of sandy beach, backed by high, cliff-like dunes.

In the 1960s Sylt became the haunt of film-stars and rich playboys and playgirls, and was nicknamed "St Tropez of the North". Life has quietened down a bit since then, but the island in places has a glitzy look with many antique shops and boutiques selling top-of-the-range fashion.

Of the resorts, **Westerland** is the biggest, but most of the politicians, editors, bankers and tycoons who come seeking privacy prefer to live around smart **Kampen** with its modern thatched villas and cottages screened off by high hedges and pine trees. **Keitum**, the show-piece village, has several art galleries and a museum housed in an old farmhouse with tiny rooms and low ceilings. With their sophisticated clientele, the markets and restaurants offer a great variety of superb fish. Look for a local rarity, the grainy black caviare produced by sturgeon caught in the Eider, the river separating Schleswig and Holstein.

The drive south from Sylt to Hamburg through fertile farming land can be very beautiful; right and left large farmhouses with roofs almost touching the ground stand sheltered by high tress, lines of willow mark the course of irrigation channels, and overhead the wind whirls clouds into bizarre shapes, with ever-changing patterns of light. There are several towns deserving a quick visit. Wind-swept **Husum**, with the largest market square in Germany, is the hometown of Theodor Storm (1817–88), a writer who made use of regional culture and experience to produce novels of great sense and sensibility.

In **Meldorf** you find the so-called "cathedral" – it never was a bishopric – of the second half of the 13th century, the most important brick church on the west coast. It was used as a town hall in the days when the Dithmarschen region was ruled by a council of 48 families as a curious kind of semi-democratic republic of landowners.

For hundreds of years this part of the country was independent of any overlord, and the "republic" was defeated only in 1559 by the combined armies of the king of Denmark and the dukes of Gottorf. Last stop before Hamburg is **Itzehoe** with an old town center rebuilt after the Thirty Years' War. Right in the middle of the square stands a mysterious bronze-age burial mound; it is dubbed a "Germanic grave" rather carelessly, for we know next to nothing about the human prehistory of these northern regions.

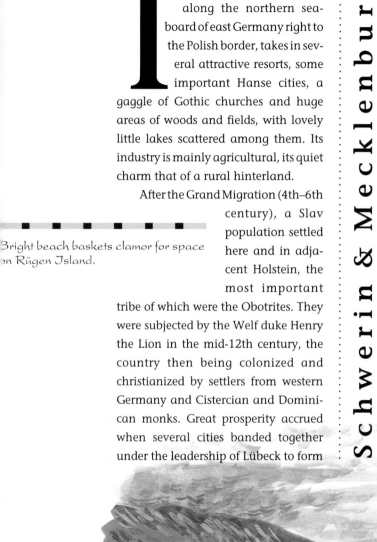

This region, stretching all along the northern seaboard of east Germany right to the Polish border, takes in several attractive resorts, some important Hanse cities, a gaggle of Gothic churches and huge areas of woods and fields, with lovely little lakes scattered among them. Its industry is mainly agricultural, its quiet charm that of a rural hinterland.

After the Grand Migration (4th–6th century), a Slav population settled here and in adjacent Holstein, the most important tribe of which were the Obotrites. They were subjected by the Welf duke Henry the Lion in the mid-12th century, the country then being colonized and christianized by settlers from western Germany and Cistercian and Dominican monks. Great prosperity accrued when several cities banded together under the leadership of Lübeck to form

Bright beach baskets clamor for space on Rügen Island.

371

Schwerin & Mecklenburg

Thatched house and cart in Freilicht Museum.

the Hanseatic League, and many of the cultural and architectural high points of the region date from the heyday of the Hanse, namely the 13th to 15th century. At the end of the Thirty Years' War (1648) the northern seaboard became Swedish until 1815, when it fell to Prussia.

Its natural orientation towards Lübeck and the Scandinavian countries has remained alive to this day in the form of trade and tourism. In terms of mentality, a clear distinction exists between the more outward-looking towns and seafaring folk of the coastal areas and the rather conservative attitude of the farming communities living inland.

Mecklenburg's traditional fare reflects the poverty of the rural popula-

tion and is made up of such basic dishes as fried black pudding and *Himmel und Ärd* (heaven and earth), a concoction of boiled potatoes and pears or apples with bacon, eaten around harvest time.

The Baltic Sea and the inland lakes still provide a wide range of seafood, which is prepared in heavy, no-frills style. The people here speak *Pommernplatt* (Pomeranian Low German), which is very similar to the dialect around Hamburg; its most conspicuous feature is the pronunciation of "st" and "sp" as a diphthong and not as "scht" and "schp". Another thing they have in common with their western neighbors is a fondness for so-called Prince Henry caps, dark blue and with a high border.

A French Dream

Coming from the west, your first place of some importance is the town of **Schwerin**, capital of the region and attractively situated on a peninsula surrounded by two large pieces of water with villas and parks along the waterside. The main attraction is the **Schloß** (1843-57) on a tiny island, occupying the site of a pre-12th-century Slav castle. Its main inspiration was the château of Chambord in the Loire Valley near Orléans, but various architects had a hand in it, and the whole building is an amusing mixture of Gothic, Renaissance and Baroque elements, without any of the serenity, elegance and graceful proportions of its French model. A number of sumptuously decorated rooms can be visited – the former palace dining room has been converted into a café with concerts given daily – as well as a museum of prehistory and of Mecklenburgian paintings. The extensive grounds include rare trees, a grotto and an orangery, and the Schloßgärten south of the island is decorated with a couple of moss-covered statues of military and mythological character.

The square opposite the Schloß, a former army parade ground, is surrounded by some surprisingly grand buildings: the official residence of the region's minister-president, the State Theater and the State Museum. The latter is worth a visit because of its huge collection of prints and paintings mainly by Dutch and Flemish artists, works often sleep-inducing on account of their sheer pleasantness.

A short walk takes you to the town center, where the market square is fringed with rather plain 17th-century burghers' houses. The town hall's neo-Gothic façade hides four half-timbered houses, two dating from 1351, the others of more recent date. They look onto an intimate, leafy square with market stalls and 18th-century buildings. The restoration of Schwerin's historical structures has so far been confined to those in the immediate vicinity of the **Marktplatz**; should you venture further afield, the gloomy, neglected rows of "normal" houses will give you an authentic impression of how depressing – both spiritually and visually – a picture the towns during the life of the former GDR presented.

The important Slav settlement of Schwerin was conquered by Henry the Lion in 1160, and he conferred a charter to the German enclave around the central market and made the town a bishopric. The **Mariendom** (cathedral) dates from 1327 to 1416 and is a huge Gothic edifice with interesting stone and brass tablets and frescoes (14th century). During the 16th and 17th centuries the town was the cultural and intellectual center of the whole Mecklenburg region; in 1815 it became the seat of the grand dukes of Mecklenburg (by the grace of the king of Prussia), and from this period date many of its finest neo-Classical buildings, often the work of

Schloß Schwerin.

the architect Georg Demmler, like the theater and the museum.

The city of **Wismar**, north of Schwerin, was an important member of the Hanse, which it joined in 1266; today it is the second largest eastern German port, after Rostock. The clear lay-

out of the old town center dates from 1226–29; the late Gothic brick **Marienkirche** is remarkable mainly because it is the repository of a great many architectural fragments from demolished churches and monasteries. The wide market square is graced by the

A street scene in old Schwerin.

Alter Schwede (old Swede), a town house with a decorative gable (1380), while next to the massive ruins of the **Georgenkirche** (15th century) you will find the **Fürstenhof**, a Renaissance building with finely decorated windows and portals.

On the road to Rostock you pass two resorts of some renown. **Bad Doberan**

boasts the earliest horse-racing track on the continent (1807), now under conservation order. Nearby is **Heiligendamm**, a quiet little town with some seemingly oversized villas and public buildings from the 19th century, vestiges of its glory as Germany's first seaside resort, the brainchild of Duke Ferdinand Franz I of Mecklenburg in 1793. One of the first to suggest that the seaside was more than a meeting-point of land and sea and the province of rough seafaring folk and that it had invigorating qualities, was the mathematician and essayist G.F. Lichtenberg (1742–99), who had been inspired by the English fashion of dipping into the sea from bathing machines. Appropriately enough, Heiligendamm's solid little summer

Pleasure boats in the harbor of Warnemünde.

houses are called "cottages" and, built in the early 19th century, contribute much charm to the peaceful little resort.

Stalking Rostock

Rostock, the old Hanseatic town, was the center of shipbuilding in the former GDR, and as you approach the city, the silhouette provides a striking contrast where the mighty towers and roofs of Gothic churches rise against a background of miles upon miles of curiously angled modern cranes.

Situated at the mouth of the Warnow a few miles inland from the estuary, Rostock was colonized in the 12th century mainly by settlers from Westphalia, Lower Saxony and the Rhineland. It was a founding member of the Hanse and soon grew to become one of the largest towns in Germany. On its markets Russian furs, Flemish cloth and French wines were sold, while its ships mainly plied the Scandinavian trade-routes. With the demise of the Hanse, the general impoverishment after the Thirty Years' War and the conservative rule of the Mecklenburg princes, the city fell on hard times and lost out to the more enterprising trading centers of Lübeck and Bremen. Bombing raids in 1944 destroyed some 40 percent of the built-up area, followed by further demolition work after the war to make way for mass housing.

Lucky the visitor who arrives in Rostock when the sun is out and there is no wind blowing – a rare coincidence. Much of the center has been rebuilt either with copies of 15th- and 16th-century houses or with rather inspired modern versions of traditional vernacular architecture. The streets, however, have incautiously been planned so wide that they do not give any protection against the chilly winds blowing in from the Baltic; here the Rostock *Doppelkümmel* (schnapps) comes in handy.

A good starting-point for a tour of the city is the **Kröpeliner Tor**, a gate-tower of the 14th century with a museum of local history tucked inside. Going down the pedestrian mall you pass one of the most successful modern buildings interpreting the typical Gothic style of the region, the **Fünfgiebelhaus** (house of five gables) of 1983–86, its façade with a strong upward surge and decorated with several remarkable bits of modern sculpture. At the end of the Kröpeliner Straße lies the old market square, now full of traffic. It is surrounded by some cheerful rebuilt 15th/19th-century town houses focusing on the **Rathaus** with an arcaded Baroque front and a Gothic screen wall peeping over its roof. Turn right in front of the town hall and have a look at the Steintor, the best preserved of the three remaining city gates.

North of the Kröpeliner Straße you find more examples of the architectural renaissance of the 1980s, when the town planners found happy inspiration from traditional building styles and conservationists. To the south there is a dreamy, leafy square in front of the 19th-century university building. No trace remains of its predecessor, the first university in northern Germany, founded in 1419 by Rostock's proud and prosperous merchants. The Gothic **Marienkirche** counts among its treasures a beautiful 13th-century decorated font and bronze cover, while the **Heilig-Kreuz-Kirche** is full of late Gothic furnishings.

Small Town Beauty

While Rostock is good for sightseeing, **Warnemünde** is ideal to spend the evening and stay the night. The small town has many pleasant if not particularly ancient buildings and a tiny church in the marketplace surrounded by elegant shops selling jewelry, fashion,

The Rathaus in Stralsund.

cosmetics and books – a mixture typical of a spa for the well-heeled. If you ignore the nondescript outskirts, you feel almost transported to a smallish smart resort somewhere in the more fashionable west. This sophisticated handling of taste and services, a thing still rare in eastern Germany, is mainly due to the close links with towns along the western Baltic seaboard like Lübeck and Eutin, from where tourists and holiday-makers have been coming to Warnemünde since long before reunification.

The town has a long sandy beach – the median water temperature of the Baltic during the summer season (end of May to end September) is 59°F to 64°F (15°C to 18°C) – and a little fishing harbor with a long pier. Here along the

quay and facing the sturdy fishing boats, are many cafés, *Kneipen* (pubs) and restaurants, some big and brassy, others cozy and colorful, with dark paneling and decorated with nautical paraphernalia. In the evening the quay becomes a lively promenade where you can dine alfresco, sampling the best of the morning's catch. Afterwards take a constitutional to the lighthouse at the end of the pier where anglers congregate; and throw a glimpse at the curious café **Teepott** (teapot, naturally), a smaller version of the Berlin Kongreßhalle nicknamed the "pregnant oyster".

East of Warnemünde lies the enchanting nature reserve of **Darß and Zingst**, a famous resting place for migrating birds with lovely wild woods

The coat of arms is a proud reminder of Stralsund's history.

made for walking. For a while the road runs alongside a dike, and beyond it is a long stretch of dunes and beach. You pass through **Ahrenshoop**, formerly an artists' colony and later a well-guarded resort for the high and mighty of the former GDR. It is full of graceful villas with thatched roofs, often hidden behind trees and shrubs. The end of the beach is marked by steep chalk cliffs.

Stralsund

Architecturally speaking, **Stralsund** is the pearl of the coastal towns. Together with Lübeck, Rostock and Wismar, it was a founding member of the Hanse and developed into the commercial

center of western Pomerania. The Peace of Stralsund (1370) between Denmark and the Hanse gave the merchants' association virtually a trading monopoly in the Baltic. The town was Swedish from 1648 to 1815, and in 1720 became the capital of Swedish-Pomerania.

Favorite son is the dare-devil Lieutenant von Schill (1759–1805), who with a small band of men rashly took up arms against Napoleon, fell into the hands of the French, was shot and decapitated. For several years his head was kept preserved in a jar before it was accorded a patriotic burial. Another remarkable son of Stralsund was the zoologist Hermann Burmeister, who in the mid-19th century founded a museum of natural history in Buenos Aires.

Stralsund is beautifully situated between two lakes and the Strela Sound, with parks and weeping willows and swans. It not only consists – as many old towns do – of a spruced-up center, but also has much interesting architecture of great variety and individuality in the surrounding area.

Among its sights, pride of place goes to the magnificent **Rathaus**, now arcaded but originally consisting of two emporiums. A very pretty passageway runs between them, with decorated pillars, a gallery on the first floor and a bust of King Gustavus Adolphus of Sweden, defender of Protestantism in the Thirty Years' War. The north front of the town hall shows a marvelous screen wall, perhaps the most beautiful of its kind, decorated with pointed gables and filigreed stars within circles, an ingenious adaptation of the more common rosette of Gothic architecture.

Among Stralsund's churches, the most notable is the Gothic **Nicolaikirche**, richly furnished and with a south tower with an intricately constructed roof. The former **Katharinenkloster** (St Catherine's monastery) now houses a splendid maritime museum with huge tanks full of exotic fishes, models of every kind of fishing boat and display cases with fishing gear and stuffed sea creatures; it is cleverly organized and fascinating not only for children.

Nearby are the sombre ruins of the **Johanniskloster**, fronted by a very charming little square surrounded by half-timbered houses with very low rooflines and lace-curtained windows, with an old rowan tree in the middle and cats sunning themselves.

Island Getaway

Northeast of Stralsund looms the irregular shape of **Rügen**, Germany's largest island and since 1936 connected with the mainland by a 1.5-mile-long (2.5 km) causeway. Since the beginning of this century it has been a favorite holiday resort and is full of vintage summer houses exuding an air of prosperity and the genteel pleasures of the seaside. This atmosphere is most pervasive in the towns of Binz and Putbus, while Saßnitz is chiefly known as an embarkation point for ferries to Denmark and Sweden. **Putbus** is also a prime example of the planned and regular towns laid out in the mid-19th century according to classical precepts. The oldest village on the island is **Garz**, built on the site of a Slav castle, and has remains of a pagan sanctuary and a royal residence. Its streets are lined with attractive craftsmen's and landowners' houses built after 1745.

Rügen's main attractions are its varied landscape and sandy beaches. Take a walk straight across the island (about 9 miles [15km]) to get the flavor of its bracing sea air, its woodlands and pastures, its hamlets with thatched cottages and trained rose bushes. Or find the path running from Baabe to Binz along steep chalk cliffs and through a patch of ancient forest. The most stunning cliffs are at Stubbenkammer (380 feet [117 meters]), where the pirate Klaus Störtebeker in the 14th century is said to have hidden his loot in the caves which pit the hillside; and at the promontory of Kap Arkona with remnants of an important Slav castle and sanctuary captured and destroyed by the Danes in 1168. The chalky precipices, where the primeval forest runs to the edge of the sea were a favorite subject of C.D. Friedrich (1774–1840), the most interesting and modern of German Romantic painters.

The outline of Rügen is constantly and almost imperceptively changing due to the currents of wind and water; some of the shallow, elongated beachheads get longer while others may soon completely disappear. **Hiddensee**, a small island to the west, would have joined Rügen by now but for the efforts of the GDR's army corps of engineers. Before the last war it was an exclusive summer resort, where rich Berliners built their villas and cottages and members of Germany's cultural and political elite would sojourn. Later privileged members of the GDR elite took their holidays here. The great dramatist and novelist Gerhart Hauptmann (1862–1946) lived here for many years and is buried in the cemetery at Kloster.

South of Rügen lies **Greifswald**, once a famous university town but now rather a cultural backwater. It was founded by Cistercians who, so legend has it, were led to the spot by a *Greif* (griffin). The town joined the Hanseatic League in 1278 and became very prosperous. In the Humanist tradition of the times, its rich burghers bestowed a university upon it (1456). It counts among its famous alumni the Humanist Ulrich von Hutten, a friend of Luther's, and the patriotic poet E.M. Arndt (1769–1860).

The university building of the mid-18th century is an unusually ornate Baroque work, designed by a Bavarian architect from Augsburg; its storerooms are filled with remarkable works of art, shown during special exhibitions. The **Marienkirche** (begun in 1280) boasts a richly carved pulpit and the painting of a huge whale.

The town houses have a prim and rather severe look; two impressive late Gothic ones face the main square while other houses and warehouses of later date can be found in the Kuhstraße, Baderstraße and Steinbeckerstraße. The picturesque ruins of the monastery at Eldena in the eastern outskirts of Greifswald were the subject of a famous painting by C.D. Friedrich, who was born in the town into a large craftsman's family.

Further east lies the island of Usedom, almost closing off the wide Bay of Stettin (Szczecin) with the town of Peenemünde. It was here in a huge compound surrounded by forests that a team of German engineers under Wernher von Braun – later to head the US space program – developed and launched the supersonic flying rocket V2, the prototype of all guided missiles, which caused terror and destruction in southeast England in 1944.

H

istorically, the Germans have been known as great eaters and drinkers, less concerned with quality than with quantity – the more the better. German food was held to be stodgy, its cuisine uninspired, table manners rough, the enjoyment of wine and beer spoiled by subsequent drunkenness. The situation has changed fundamentally since the 1960s, for various reasons: widespread affluence, labor-saving devices, interest in foreign foods both through travel and the influx of foreign workers and establishment of restaurants catering to their tastes, and latterly a concern with health and purity. At present, German cuisine can be characterized by two trends. On the one hand, the *Neue deutsche Küche*, a variant of cuisine nouvelle, follows a preference for lighter cooking, smaller helpings, fresh ingredients,

Cuisine

383

Fresh German produce on display.

Bread

Bread has a history which dates back to the Middle Ages

Brown or black or white, crusty, fragrant and crunchy – German bread is one of the humble glories of German food. The loaves come in all shapes and sizes and with as many names as subtle differences in texture and flavoring. There are ones with high crowns and low crowns, others shaped rectangular like boxes or round like wheels; some have a coarse or lumpy texture, others are light and airy, some taste nutty, some wet and yeasty, and there are also ones with an oily or fruity aftertaste.

The first commercial bakeries in Germany we know of were set up in the 10th century, contemporaneous with the establishment of fortified cities. For the 12th and 13th centuries some 20 varieties of bread are documented; today there are some 200. During the Middle Ages, banquet tables were sometimes covered with a huge pizza-like sheet of bread, from which the guests would tear off chunks to go with the soup and meat dishes.

Especially in small towns and villages, bakers usually open at 7 a.m. after finishing all the necessary preliminaries like mixing the dough and letting it rise, heating the electric ovens and tidying themselves up with a clean apron and a freshly starched little cap. For breakfast, Germans prefer rolls to sliced bread; the more fancy ones are sprinkled with coarse salt, cumin or poppy-seed. Rolls are generally called *Brötchen*, but in Hamburg they are *Rundstücke*, in Berlin *Schrippen* and in Munich *Semmeln*.

The basic outlines of bread-making is that you mix flour with water and knead that into a dough. To let it rise, you add either sourdough to get rye bread, or bakers' yeast to get white bread. While the dough is baked in the oven, alcohol evaporates and carbon dioxide is generated, which has the important function of making the dough lighter.

The famous pumpernickel, a speciality of Westphalia, is dark brown or almost black and has a mild bitter-sweet taste; it is made of coarse rye meal and baked at very low temperatures for a relatively long time. Rye bread is more popular in north and northwest Germany, and white bread – the whiter, the better – you will find more in the south.

decorative arrangement on the plate and the use of exotic vegetables and seasoning. Simultaneously there is a movement inspired by ecological considerations and an interest in local traditions. This shows up as a revival of traditional recipes using natural prod-

ucts (preferably organically grown) in a simple, hearty and savory manner.

Gastronomically speaking, Germany can be divided into three main regions. Along the seaboard, salt-water fish dominates the menu. In its traditional form, it is most often treated like

A well-known chic restaurant in Munich.

meat, namely fried and served with potatoes, vegetables and lashings of white sauce. The landlocked areas of northern Germany offer a great variety of smoked meats, served either hot or cold; and far more fresh vegetables are consumed here than in the south. The Rhine Valley and Westphalia have their own traditions: the Rhine with its many types of rolls and bread, cakes, fritters and biscuits which are to be seen in every bakery, and Westphalia with its hams. Southern Germany offers rather fat food, in particular a wide range of sausages and pork butchers' meats. Potatoes are sometimes replaced by dumplings called *Klöße* or *Knödel* filled with croutons or plums, and *Spätzle*, a kind of freshly made noodle.

Breakfast, whether at home or in a hotel, usually is a bigger affair than what is known abroad as a "Continental breakfast". It is expected to give you a good start for the day. In hotels, a buffet breakfast will often include a selection of bread and rolls, cheeses, sausages, slices of smoked meat, eggs, yogurt, cereals, stewed and fresh fruits and preserves. The main meal can be either lunch or supper, depending at what time the whole family manages to get together. In rural areas people tend to go to bed early, and you should make sure that you have a bed and a meal by 9 p.m.

Restaurants are usually closed for the afternoon or else offer a very limited choice of hot food. Game dishes are

Classic German cold meats and sausages.

quite common during the hunting season, with deer, leg of venison, pheasant and larded hare being the most popular, while the gobbling turkey is as yet a rather exotic item. Catholics tend to keep the rule of having fish on Friday; it is still eaten in families with two forks, a custom dating from the time before the invention of stainless-steel knives. In the family, the one who finishes first is called the *Kaiser* (emperor), the last the *Bettelmann* (beggar), to encourage children to eat up quickly.

Around Christmas time, it is traditional to have goose, the days between St Martin's (11 November) and Christmas Eve being favorite occasions for dinner invitations, when old-fashioned food is served and parlor games are played. The goose, for some inscrutable reason, is traditionally associated with St Martin.

Regional Food

Most of the regions and even the localities in Germany lay claim to some special dish or method of preparation. The more you ask about this, the more detailed and varied do such claims become. It is, however, often difficult to find a restaurant that does traditional dishes according to family recipes. The following breakdown by regions give a rough idea about the variety on offer; should you spot any of these dishes on the menu, give them a try.

Roasting on a spit.

Bavaria

Here you are offered basically a heavy peasant cuisine, well-seasoned and quite varied. Sausages of all kinds are popular, and pride of place goes to the boiled *Weißwürste* of Munich, made of minced veal, various herbs and grated lemon peel, and because of their volatile freshness not to be eaten after midday; and the spicy, charcoal grilled *Bratwürste* of Nürnberg and Regensburg. Try also *Schweinshaxn* (roasted knuckle of pork) and *Leberkäse*, a kind of meatloaf. *Semmelknödel* (dumplings made from stale bread) are often served instead of potatoes, while *Leberknödel* (liver dumplings) find their way into soups. For afternoon coffee have a *Dampfnudel*, a huge yeast dumpling containing plums and served hot with vanilla sauce. White radishes and pretzels are a popular nibble with a glass of beer. Bamberg's speciality is carp cooked in beer. Franconia, being a wine area, tends to have lighter cooking, but also has some notable beers like the curious smoked beer of Bamberg and the strong Kulmbach ale.

Baden-Württemberg

The western part of the *region*, influenced by neighboring France, has light and sophisticated cooking; game and snails, smoked meats and sauerkraut are delicious. The famous *Schwarzwälder*

Kirschtorte (Black Forest cherry gâteau) hails from here as does a variety of excellent local fruit brandies.

Swabia's cuisine includes the delicate *Maultaschen* (mouth pockets), a kind of spinach-filled ravioli eaten either in soup or fried in butter and onion, and *Zwiebelbraten*, beef in onion sauce. This is the home of the *Spätzle*, a kind of pasta made of flour, eggs, salt and water, then grated and boiled. It is usually served with meat and vegetables and should preferably be *hausgemacht* (home-made).

Berlin

Its greatest contribution to neo-German cuisine is the *Currywurst*, a grilled sausage covered with blood-red ketchup and sprinkled with curry powder. It is one of the rare culinary inventions which can be precisely dated: it was first sold on 4 September 1948 at the food stall of a woman called Herta Heuwer.

Another very basic and popular dish that originated in Berlin is *Eisbein*, knuckle of pork served with sauerkraut and pea-pudding or mashed potatoes. In Berlin a hamburger is called a *Bulette*, and the ubiquitous *Kasseler Rippspeer* (smoked pork rib) does not come from Kassel at all, but was invented by the Berlin butcher Cassel. As for drinks, the typical *Berliner Weiße mit Schuß* is a pale wheaten beer with a dash of raspberry or woodruff syrup which turns it red or green.

Brandenburg

The region has few truly local dishes. Leg of lamb with beans has become something of a speciality in the region between Berlin and the Polish border since the agricultural reformer Thaer introduced sheep to the area in the 19th century. Dutch textile workers from the Lower Rhine, coming as colonists to the swampy Spree lowlands in the 16th century, first grew cucumbers there, and pickled gherkins are still used as a favorite pick-me-up against a hangover. The same Dutch introduced Brandenburgers to the delights of brandy, whereas hop-growing is mentioned near Berlin as early as 1291, and a tax on beer provided the elector Johann Cicero with his first regular income from tax (1488).

Bremen and Hamburg

In both these cities and all over Schleswig and Friesland, the smoked or grilled eel is excellent; eel cooked in a creamy dill sauce, *Aal grün*, makes a delicate green-and-white dish, and the *Hamburger Aalsuppe* is sweet and tasty. *Labskaus*, a hearty, historic sailors' hash, is made of pickled corned beef, herring, potato, beetroot, with a fried egg on top. Named after a Hamburg suburb, *Finkenwerder Scholle* is a tender, plate-sized plaice sautéed to a golden hue. One of Bremen's specialities is *Kükenragout*, a delicious stew of chicken, veal, sweetbreads and clams, worked in a white sauce. For dessert, order *Rote Grütt*, a cool berry pudding, or *Fliederbeersuppe*, cold, mouth-watering elderberry soup served with apple slices and delicate miniature dumplings.

Hesse

Here again, there is a dearth of typical local cuisine. The Frankfurt sausages, made with smoked pork and spices and always served in pairs, have a history going back to the 14th century. The bleak, isolated Schwalm region is said to produce the best sauerkraut, which is often served with pork ribs. In his autobiography, Goethe talks fondly of *Grüne Sauce*, a green sauce made of eggs, sour cream and nine different herbs and served with boiled beef. One of the few places where wild boars appears on the menu is the region around Kassel.

Mecklenburg-Vorpommern

All along the Baltic shore you find seafood restaurants serving simple, traditional fare. Culinary standards under the Socialist regime not having been particularly high, the variety of fish and its preparation is quite limited. *Butt* or *Flunder* (flounder) is very common, as is *Hecht* (pike) caught in the Baltic; this is exceptional, because pike normally is a freshwater fish. Further inland, the Mecklenburg lakes provide a greater variety of fish. In the traditionally-minded farming areas two time-honored peasant dishes can occasionally be found: *Enteneintopf* (duck stew with cauliflower, leeks, celery and turnips) and *Kalbsbrust mit Stachelbeeren* (breast of veal with gooseberries). In the old days before the invention of the steel nib, geese also came in handy as suppliers of quills and of down for feather beds. *Doppelkümmel* from Rostock is a fine clear spirit similar to gin, but flavored with cumin and caraway seeds instead of juniper berries.

Lower Saxony

The fish dishes here are much the same as in Schleswig-Holstein and Hamburg. In the small seaports of East Frisia you can buy fresh fish straight after the catch, and home-smoked eel and sprats at cottages with a sign saying *Räucheraal*. A delicious nibble with a glass of beer is *Krabbenbrot*, buttered slices of brown rye bread, liberally spread with tiny boiled prawns. *Grünkohl mit Pinkel* is assorted meats with stewed cabbage picked after the first frost. In the Lüneburg Heath area, the sheep which feed on juniper and heather produce a tender, fragrant mutton, served as a roast and then called *Heidschnuckenbraten*; it is mostly served with string beans and cranberries, and is quite expensive. Strong tea is drunk everywhere, and in the coastal regions it is really authentic if sweetened with

Cakes are inevitably on the German menu.

large lumps of candy sugar called *Kluntjes*. The favorite alcoholic drink besides beer is *Korn* (the word for "cereal", but in this case to mean schnapps).

North-Rhine Westphalia

Westphalia is noted for its smoked meats, especially ham, which is smoked over juniper and resin-free wood. *Pumpernickel*, now a generic term for black rye bread, originated in this region; its slight sweetness provides a nice balance for the fragrant hams and moderately spicy *Leberwurst* (liver sausage). Cologne's *Halve Hahn* is not half a chicken, but cheese with mustard on a rye roll, and its *Kölsche Kaviar* is simply black pud-

ding with rye bread. No wine is grown north of Bonn, but there are some remarkable beers like the clear, highly fermented *Kölsch* of Cologne, the dark, sweetish *Altbier* of Düsseldorf and many lager and Pilsener-type beers of Dortmund, Europe's leading beer town in terms of output.

Rhineland-Palatinate

Best-known among the few traditional dishes is a snack called *Handkäs mit Musik* (hand cheese with music): a soft, ripe, odorous local cheese, marinated for two or three hours in vinegar and oil, sprinkled with caraway seeds and served with chopped onions and fresh bread and butter. In the Hunsrück mountains there is a traditional dish called *Festessen*, literally a feast, but actually more a simple peasant's meal which consists of ham, sauerkraut, pea-pudding, potatoes and freshly grated horseradish. The region produces a lot of wine, some of which is excellent.

Saxony

While Frisians are known as inveterate tea-drinkers, the Saxons have a great reputation for coffee-drinking, which was hard to indulge in during the former Socialist regime. This goes well with their penchant for cream cakes and all kinds of pastries. Somewhat like the Scots, they pride themselves on the large number of brilliant minds that have come from this area of the river Elbe; to them, Prussians (i.e. Berliners) are mere upstarts, with a rasping intonation good for barking military commands, but quite ludicrous for polite conversation. Germany's first coffeehouse was established in Hamburg in 1668, but Leipzig's **Kaffeebaum** is almost as old (1694) and still in business. Coffee, regarded as intoxicating, was a popular drink from its early days. To the authorities, the conviviality of coffeehouses seemed to breed sinister and conspirational activities, which is why they were often shut down on military orders. When Napoleon sealed off the western coast of Europe against military intervention and foreign imports, the Saxons were deprived of their favorite beverage and had to make do with roasted chicory.

German traditional Christmas fare includes a *Weihnachtsstollen* (Christmas fruit loaf) which is produced in many parts of the country, but the best ones – light and moist – come from Saxony, either from Dresden or Leipzig, depending on which school of gourmandise you subscribe to. *Pflaumenkuchen* (plum cake) is another speciality of Dresden.

Saxons love dumplings and even serve them with *Karpfen sächsisch*, a quite delicious dish of carp which is first sautéed and then braised. *Leipziger Allerlei* is a vegetable hotchpotch of tenderly cooked peas, carrots, maize and cauliflower. Leipzig once produced well-known beers, and this has remained the most common alcoholic drink in Saxony, although the quality has much declined. Saxon wine has always been something of a curiosity. The first vines are said to have been introduced by a bishop from Meißen around the year 1080. Luther mentions Saxon wine with approval. In the 1880s, the phylloxera plague killed the Saxon vines almost completely, and replanting was only started in the early 20th century by Carl Pfeiffer, a vintner from Oppenheim in Rhinehesse. The main wine-growing region is still around Meißen.

Saxony-Anhalt

The central part of the region, especially around Magdeburg, has fertile soil and

The well-known open-air market,
Vilktualienmarkt, sells fresh produce
in the middle of the city.

is a big producer of vegetables. The town of Salzwedel north of Magdeburg is well-known for its succulent hams and sausages, and is the birthplace of the famous *Baumkuchen* (tree cake), a pastry of multi-layered cake with a thick covering of chocolate. The cake is built up on a long revolving rod and its shape somewhat resembles several tiny Christmas trees stacked on top of each other. *Kartoffelpuffer* (pancakes of fresh, grated potatoes) with raspberries is also popular here. The area around the rivers Saale and Unstrut is Germany's northernmost wine-growing region; the earliest regulations concerning wine production date from 1588. These dry wines, low in acidity, taste a bit like those from Franconia.

Schleswig-Holstein

This water-bounded region has a great variety of seafood, which is usually prepared in a solid but unimaginative manner. For both good traditional and lighter modern cooking the more up-market restaurants are a save bet. Lübeck does a fine *Schellfisch-Auflauf* (haddock soufflé) and an interesting *Bücklingsuppe*, a soup with buckling (smoked herring). The small river Eider is inhabited by sturgeon which produce a gritty black caviar. Lübeck is famous for its nutty-tasting marzipan which is pure white, while the type called *Königsberger Marzipan* has a burnt look and is slightly stronger.

Thuringia

Foodwise this region is primarily known for its charcoal grilled sausages and its dumplings made from raw potatoes and therefore called *grüne Klöße* (green dumplings); they accompany a roast joint and lashings of gravy. Each and every village has its own particular version, and you will find them on every menu.

Wine

Germany produces much wine, about 80 percent of which is white. The best white varieties use the light and fruity Riesling and Sylvaner grapes, while

The popular barbeque.

among the reds the fresh Trollinger and velvety Spätburgunder are particularly good. Wine is rather pricey and is drunk in small quantities and served in a large glass (*Viertel*) or a smaller one (*Achtel*, i.e. one-eighth of a liter). Each of the main wine-growing regions has its own distinctive character.

Ahr (south of Bonn): vigorous, powerful red wines and steely, fresh white ones.

Mosel-Saar-Ruwer (southwest of Koblenz): racy, piquant wines with elegant fruit and fragrant bouquet.

Middle Rhine (north of Koblenz): hearty, full-bodied wines with a pronounced fruity acidity, from steeply-terraced clayish slate soils.

Rheingau (north bank of the Rhine around Rüdesheim): the full and dry white wines, primarily Riesling, are among the best in Germany.

Nahe (along the river Nahe southwest of Bingen): fruity and flavorful wines, slightly fragrant.

Rhinehesse (south of the great bend of the Rhine at Mainz): hearty, refreshing white wines and mild, velvety red ones.

Rheinpfalz (south of Rhinehesse): fruity and high in alcoholic content.

Franconia (mostly grown in the Main valley near Würzburg): dry and strong wines.

Württemberg: light, very fruity wines from the Stuttgart/Heilbronn area.

Baden: fragrant white wines, mostly dry, some sweeter, and velvety to fiery

Frankenwein, a classic German white wine.

excellent reds.

Since 1971, wines are graded by quality. *Deutscher Tafelwein* is ordinary blended table wine; *Qualitätswein b.A.* is quality wine from specified regions; *Qualitätswein mit Prädikat* is quality wine with special attributes. The latter is again subdivided according to the timing and manner of the grape-picking. *Spätlese* is from late-picked grapes which give full flavor, while *Auslese* is made from grapes that have been picked separately to produce a rich, well-rounded, noble bouquet.

Wine labels are strictly regulated and give the year of vintage, the vineyard, the variety of grape, harvesting (e.g. *Auslese, Spätlese*), the region of production, the quality control number and details of the wine merchant. *Erzeugerabfüllung* means that the wine has been produced and bottled on the estate.

Many growers and growers' cooperatives welcome visitors. For details about wine-tasting sessions, wine seminars and wine educational trails, contact the tourist office of the region, the region or the specific village you want to visit.

Beer

With an average consumption of 143 liters per head, the Germans are the world's heaviest beer drinkers, after the Belgians. The habit started early: according to the Roman historian Tacitus' *Germania* (AD 1st century), the German tribes brewed some potage made of barley, wheat, cranberries and fragrant leaves.

It played a prominent part in Nordic sagas, and the Germanic peoples' highest god, Odin, was also regarded as the supreme beer brewer. For a long time brewing was a household activity, but developed into an industry in the 11th century. Some of the oldest breweries still in existence are based in Munich: the Augustiner brewery was founded in 1328, Löwenbräu in 1383 and Spaten in 1397.

In the 16th century, the brewers invented their own patron, Gambrinus. He was a legendary or historical person and has been variously identified with a king of Brabant and the Burgundy prince Jan Primus. In 1516 the Bavarian duke William IV promulgated the famous *Reinheitsgebot* to guarantee unadulterated beer: only bitter hops, sweet malt and water were allowed to be used in its production.

Beer is made from barley, which is soaked and allowed almost to germinate, then baked to form brewer's malt. This is added to the hops, which give it flavor and aroma, and then fermented. The maltier the beer, the darker it is and the sweeter it tastes. There is much variety in the deceptive beer.

Vollbier is what you get when you order *"ein Bier, bitte"*, and is 4 percent proof, while *Export* is 5 percent and *Bockbier* 6 percent proof. *Pils* or *Pilsener*

Beer is served in huge liter mugs.

contains more hops and is recognizable by its clarity and slight bitterness. Around Bamberg you will find *Rauchbier* with a distinctive smoky aroma. In Berlin, the pale wheaten beer known as *Berliner Weiße* was first brewed by Huguenots in 1741. Germans like their beer moderately cool and with a frothy, thick, creamy "head", which takes about five minutes to draw.

There is a fascinating museum devoted exclusively to beer in Einbeck, a picturesque town north of Göttingen in Lower Saxony with many half-timbered houses around the cobbled Marktplatz. In the Middle Ages the town had no less than 700 breweries; and although only one remains, it still produces a well-known and potent brew.

A visit to Germany does not have to be a succession of dawn-to-dusk raids on museums and castles, Baroque churches and Rococo palaces, medieval town houses, stately gardens, memorials to the famous and half-timbered villages. For those who prefer the 'musts' in small portions and occasionally feel the itch to vary their diet, there is a lighter side to getting acquainted with the country and its people.

Kayaking on the meandering Wiesent River.

Sports

The Germans are said to have a love affair with nature; and indeed they have found so many ways of making her easily accessible that visitors from abroad will have no difficulty in joining this relationship. Moving through Germany's landscape by various means is one of the most relaxing, entertaining and enlightening ways of travel and a superb test to see whether the limpid mountain lakes, huge tracts of darkly brooding

At one with nature in the Englischer Gärten.

forest, wind-swept marshes, meandering rivers, roadside taverns overgrown with ivy and farmhouses with window-boxes of blazing geraniums do cast the spell promised by travel writers and agents.

"Green" issues and a serious concern about ecological matters play an important part in the renewed interest many Germans take in their country, its beauty, history and identity. Curiosity about roots, whether those of the family or of trees, has boosted the number of Germans who spend their holidays within the country, exploring parts of the long-lost eastern provinces and savoring the quiet charms of village lifestyle beyond the beaten paths. This is not to say that the number of those

who, instead of spending 3 weeks in the hinterland of Berlin, Bielefeld or Bamberg, prefer to take wing and land in Bali, Benidorm or the Bahamas, has seriously diminished.

There are hundreds of sign-posted hiking trails, and from excellent maps, often available only at the local tourist office, you can select your own menu in terms of length, number of sights and grades of difficulty. Good ideas are to walk along the bank of some large river like the Rhine, Moselle, Weser or Elbe and return by boat; to traverse the mountain ridges of Thuringia along the Rennsteig trail, with the fairy-tale village of Friedrichsroda as a base; or to explore the Lüneburg Heath with its numerous lakes and streams, mysteri-

Walking in the forest is the simplest and one of the most pleasurable pastimes.

ous megaliths and the "world's largest bird park" near Walsrode.

Cycling is much facilitated for visitors by a system that lets you rent a bike at a railway station and return it at another one of your choice. A new idea to close scenic motor roads on certain days of the year to all traffic except bicycles has been instituted in various parts of the country and has become very popular (not least with party politicians in need of votes).

For a day or two the usual hum of motor traffic is replaced by an eery stillness as flocks of cyclists pedal along smooth tarmac, with refreshment stalls beckoning with great frequency. In the foothills of the Alps, strenuous mountain-biking can easily be combined with a refreshing swim in some clear if chilly lake.

Caravaning and camping are also leisurely ways of surveying different regions and discovering their special character, the typical shape of houses, the local manner of preparing food, the general appearance and talk of the inhabitants. Most of the camping sites are well-appointed, and fellow travelers tend to be particularly helpful and friendly if you come from a country other than east European. Holidays on a farm have become quite popular in recent years, especially with large families. A working farm is a world of its own and for kids from the city a splendid way of making acquaintances with farm animals like geese, chickens, pigs and cows,

Trout fishing in the Pegnitz River.

a dip in the local pond or stream, today everybody can enjoy such exercises for a small entrance fee. Golf, on the other hand, has not really caught on in Germany yet. Many still regard it as a rather boring, slow-moving activity of self-indulgent businessmen and retired tycoons, an image that clubs reinforce by membership restrictions and steep fees.

In summer, during the long school holidays, some beaches along the Baltic and North Sea can get rather crowded, with toddlers stumbling you, spilling their icecream and beaming a beatific smile. While the kids build sand castles complete with moat and ramparts, fly kites and play ball, the more seriously-minded adults sprawl in their "beach

with horses and ponies and hunting dogs and with all the creepy-crawlies of cellar and loft, orchards and stables. Angling is being promoted especially for nerve-racked businessmen as another relaxation in rural surroundings. So when you are driving through some remote area and suddenly see a couple of huge colorful umbrellas propped up next to the river-bank, you will know what is happening there.

Tennis courts and swimming pools open to the public are never far away. In the late sixties large and small communities vied with each other to build indoor and outdoor sports centers. So whereas in earlier days tennis was an elegant pastime of the wealthy and well-connected, and swimming simply meant

Swimming in the mineral bath
in Bad Tölz.

Golf has yet to catch on as a favored activity.

askets" (a kind of chair with a canopy
nclosing you on three sides, often of
wickerwork) almost immobile, soaking
n the sun for hours on end.

Watersports like sailing and
windsurfing are becoming more popu-
ar and gear can be rented at many
places, not only at the seaside but also
n lakes and rivers. Rafting and canoe-
ng is widespread in Bavaria.

In winter, an avalanche of skiers
escends on the picturesque villages of
he Alps. In Bavaria, children have spe-
ial ski holidays, and often whole classes
pend a weekend together in the snow,
aught by a ski instructor and watched
ver by their school teacher.

For grown-ups, the daytime pleas-
res of zipping down the slopes are

usually heightened by the anticipation
of après-ski frolics like socializing in a
cozy bar decorated in alpine ambience,
with good food, fresh wine and knowledgeable discussions about pistes,
weather reports, the newest ski gadgets
and fashions.

Besides such outdoor sports and entertainments, there are of course many
opportunities for visitors hard-pressed
for time who want to keep in shape and
energize their system. Major hotels often have a solarium, sauna, whirlpool
and gymnasium or fitness center; and
many small towns have beauty and
health studios for all kinds of exercises
and to tone and tan by artificial means
for those who are afraid of an
unbeauteous pallor.

Berlin city by night.

Nightlife

For evening entertainments, those with an interest in the performing arts will find a surfeit of riches in all the major cities, including the regional capitals. On top of the normal venues, most cities and towns put on annual festivals of art, music and film. To see what is on offer in terms of theater, dance, opera, cinema, jazz, pop, folk and classical music, cabaret, musicals and clubs, the best thing is to buy a listing magazine.

For a glittering night at the opera, everyone dresses up to the nines. The program of the big state-supported theater companies usually veers between highly polished conventional productions and modernistic ones, sure to cause outrage, perhaps even a crowd-pulling scandal. There is also a host of small, often amateur companies of a dynamic, experimental cast, traditionally performing in basements and therefore called "cellar theaters". Musicals, most of which are imported, will normally be in German, offering the chance to informally learn a bit of the language to those who know the original version. Much more challenging in terms of language will be a visit to a cabaret where a constant patter full of colloquialisms and topical allusions keeps the native audience in stitches. The humor tends to be broad, the political barbs witty and harmless and reflecting popular opinion fairly precisely.

Listen to jazz in a *kneipe* (pub), go

The party spirit is boosted by beer.

amusing insights int the costume and man ner of wealthy Ger mans, the minor nobi ity and supporting cast. The managemen abides by rigid rules to prevent impuls gambling; correct dress is black tie o simply suit and tie. Most casinos hav good restaurants attached.

Germans love going out in th evening, indulging themselves a bit b going to the cinema or a play or b dining out; exotic food served in a mild oriental setting is the great favorite, an Chinese, Japanese and Thai eateries d a thriving business. Afterwards on meets up with friends at a café or taver for beer or wine (snacks are often serve here, too) and hold long discussions i

ballroom-dancing in one of the big ho-tels or spend an evening listening to the classical strains performed by an inter-nationally acclaimed orchestra. Discos furnished with all the most recent space-age technology are gathering places for the under-30s. Outside big cities, such *Schuppen* (barns) are frequently found in the middle of nowhere so that how-ever wild and frenzied the goings-on, there will be no neighbors to protest with pitchforks or complain to the po-lice. Should you want to try your luck at the gaming tables, why not head straight for the best? Those at Baden-Baden, Wiesbaden, Hamburg and Konstanz are elegant, fashionable places to be seen, and can afford

Café Møhring on the Kudamm, a popular haunt.

Young people at a "boot party".

hungry East Europeans is putting some variety into the sex industry without diminishing the level of sleaze and violence. Hotel porters and taxi drivers are usually able to offer suggestions where to go (i.e. where they receive commissions, perhaps) and get fleeced; recommendations from friends or acquaintances are much to be preferred, but rarely proffered.

brightly-lit surroundings where the noise of a hundred people merrily chatting and chattering away somehow produces an intimate atmosphere of easy familiarity and warmth.

There is another kind of nightlife which is seldom mentioned in guidebooks, and if you ask for directions you will receive puzzled looks and little help, as though *Nachtleben* referred primarily to the activities of nocturnal animals like foxes, bats and owls. Nightclubs offering sex shows, adult movies and the company of skimpily-dressed hostesses are usually found in the vicinity of railway stations. They are often dreary, sometimes rough, seldom entertaining and generally more pornographic than erotic. Hamburg's Reeperbahn is the only red-light district in Germany with a certain style and atmosphere; it has become more respectable and safe in recent years, with several chic restaurants and bistros in the vicinity providing pleasures of a more genteel nature. The influx of

Besides food, restaurants provide a means for socializing.

TRAVEL TIPS

ACCOMMODATION

Most hotels in Germany are privately owned and family-run. There are a few German and international chains like Steigenberger, Hilton, Holiday Inn and Novotel. Many smaller privately-owned hotels have grouped together for joint publicity and marketing; the Romantik Hotels are mostly in old buildings of character, and Gast im Schloß is an association of charmingly converted castles, not all of them expensive. Standards of service, comfort and cleanliness tend to be high. Room prices are about the same as elsewhere in western Europe. It pays to share a room if you can, because a double room is usually only about 40 percent more expensive than a single one. Nearly all provide a sumptuous buffet breakfast, after which you probably need only a light snack at lunch. It is common practice in the smaller towns and villages to let rooms for a night or longer. Walk around and look for a *Zimmer frei* ("rooms available") sign in the window or ask at the tourist office for a list of addresses. *Gasthof* or *Gasthaus* means a small hotel, and *Fremdenheim* or *Pension* a guesthouse.

Accommodation in eastern Germany is harder to find. Big cities usually have at least one showcase luxury hotel, and others, previously reserved for the Party brass, are fast being privatized. The same applies to former holiday camps for members of social organizations like trade unions and youth federations; these are often sparsely but adequately furnished, although rarely with private baths.

Farmhouse holidays are becoming very popular in Germany and in many ways are the best bargains of all, but of course only if you have your own transport. Regional tourist offices provide lists of such places.

AIR TRAVEL

Domestic flights are numerous and quick be-tween the major cities, but are also expensive. There are a few student fares, but they only apply to those living and studying in Germany. The first and last flights of the day are sometimes slightly cheaper. Advance reservation is recommended. Besides Lufthansa, there are several smaller regional airlines.

For international flights, since there tend to be large price variations between airlines and periods of the year – prices peak between mid-June and early September – it is advisable to have more than one knowledgeable travel agent guide you. Budget travelers usually opt for charter flights, which are much cheaper but have more restrictions too. The cheapest tickets for scheduled flights are APEX, which can save you up to 40 percent on domestic and international flights. They must, however, be bought three to four weeks in advance, have minimum and maximum lengths of stay and cannot be changed once a flight is booked.

Frankfurt is the major gateway to western Germany for flights from overseas, with good onward connections. There is a regular train shuttle both to the city center and the main railway station, as well as a bus shuttle to the Sachsenhausen quarter. Hamburg, Munich, Cologne and Berlin are linked either directly or with connecting flights to most major cities within Europe and the Middle East.

BUSINESS HOURS

There are slight variations in business hours, so if you desperately depend on them, check them out locally.

Banking hours are normally from 8.30 or 9 a.m. to 12.30 or 1 p.m. and from 2.30 to 3.30 or 4 p.m. Over the weekend, only exchange bureaus at big railway stations and at airports are open.

Shops and department stores are generally open in large cities from 8.30 or 9 a.m. to 5.30

p.m. or 6 p.m. Monday through Wednesday, from 9 a.m. to 8.30 p.m. on Thursday and from 9 a.m. to 1 or 2 p.m. on Saturday. On the first Saturday of the month, they remain open until 6 or 6.30 p.m., except from May to September, when they close at 5 p.m. In villages and smaller towns, shops tend to close from 1 to 3 p.m.

Barbers are normally closed all day Monday. Government offices are open to the public from 8 a.m. to noon. On Sunday, only bakers open from 11 a.m. to 3 p.m. Exceptions are allowed for a few food-shops near the main station for the benefit of travelers.

Most museums are closed on Monday. Hours otherwise tend to be from 9 a.m. to 5 p.m. year round, with slightly longer hours in summer. Churches are certain to be open only for Sunday service; for other hours of opening, it is wise to check with the local tourist office.

CAMPING

There are well over 2,000 registered sites, graded officially. Standards tend to be high: even the simpler ones offer a shop, toilets and showers, and you can usually rent a tent and vehicle. Blue signs with a black tent on a white background indicate sites.

Camping purists may find German sites rather too regimented. During the school holiday season between June and September, many sites are nearly always full. Most campsites close in winter, except for those in popular skiing areas.

A full list of sites, with all details, is provided by the Deutscher Camping-Club DCC, Mandlstraße 28, 80802 München 40, tel. (089) 33 40 21; the German National Tourist Office distributes a free brochure and map.

CAR RENTAL

Car rental (*Autovermietung, Mietwagen*) is available at airports and major train stations. In cities, the offices of such well-known companies as Avis, Hertz and Budget are easy to find; smaller local companies often offer better terms. If you book in advance, rates may be slightly lower. With the major firms there are no drop-off charges; you can collect a car at one city and return it to the company's office in another for no additional fee.

CLIMATE

Germany lies within the continental climate zone, and this means that it can be freezing cold in the winter and moderately hot in the summer. Be-

cause of the wind-chill factor, temperatures by the seaside tend to be a bit lower than one would like them. July is the hottest and wettest month. Weather-wise, the best time to travel to Germany is from late May to early October.

CLOTHING

Whatever the season, take both a raincoat and sunglasses with you, because the weather can change in a trice. Even during summer, better bring a sweater, as evenings can be chilly. For trips to the northern seaboard, some windproof clothing is indispensable. Otherwise, casual clothing is fine for most occasions. Germans like to dress up for special events like going to the opera, where long evening dresses and dinner-jackets are still worn, although this is beginning to change.

COACH TRAVEL

Remote areas inaccessible by train can usually be reached by bus from the nearest large town. Long-distance bus services, run by private companies, are often at least as expensive as trains. For intercity connections both within Germany and Europe, Eurolines runs a large fleet of comfortable coaches.

CUSTOMS

Visitors arriving from another EC country may import the following goods without paying customs if they have been bought within the country: 800 cigarettes or 400 cigarillos or 200 cigars or 1kg tobacco; 90 liters of wine, of which no more than 60 liters should be sparkling, or 10 liters of spirits or 110 liters of beer.

If you buy at a duty-free shop, the limit – which applies to both EC members and overseas visitors – on tobacco is 200 cigarettes or 100 cigarillos or 50 cigars or 250g tobacco. For drinks, 2 liters of table wine are allowed plus 1 liter of spirits, strong liqueurs over 22 percent vol. or 2 liters of fortified or sparkling wine or an additional still table wine allowance of 2 liters. The perfume allowance is restricted to 60 ml, for toilette water to 250 ml. Duty-free allowances can be added to the total purchases imported from EC countries. For overseas visitors, gifts, souvenirs and all other goods (except those mentioned above) must not exceed DM115 in value.

There are no restrictions on the amounts of local or foreign currency you can bring into Germany. You are also allowed to bring any personal belongings and equipment as well as reasonable quantities of food for your own consumption.

If in doubt, ask the German National Tourist Office for their leaflet, or go to the red channel inside the customs area.

CYCLING

With a railpass or a ticket, you can rent a bike at over 270 train stations throughout western Germany, and return it to any train station that rents. Bikes can be brought on any train that has a goods wagon (G*epäckwagen*), indicated by a bicycle on the timetable; they are not permitted on fast intercity trains. For further information, including special combined bike/train trip discounts, a brochure "*Fahrrad am Bahnhof*" is available at any train station.

Otherwise, to rent a bicycle, simply look in the phonebook under *Fahrradverleih* for a list of local rental outlets. You are usually expected to leave a deposit.

RV Verlag publishes cycling and walking maps entitled "*Region Concept*"; or contact the Allgemeiner Deutscher Fahrrad-Club, Postfach 10 77 44, 28203 Bremen, Am Dobben 91.

DISABLED TRAVELERS

By and large, Germany is one of the more accessible countries for disabled travelers (*Behinderte* or *Schwerbehinderte*). Trains have a few seats or a compartment reserved for them, and some museums and sights have special access as well. In Berlin, for instance, roughly half of the museums and underground stations have wheelchair facilities. Staff tend to be helpful; tourist offices sometimes have information on accessibility. The international wheelchair icon or a large letter "B" indicates access.

DOCUMENTS

A valid passport is the only requirement to enter Germany. Members of the European Community (EC) only need identity cards.

For US, UK, Canadian, Australian and NZ visitors, visas are not required if they stay no longer than 50 days. Citizens of other countries should inquire at the local German embassy or consulate. Students should have an International Student Identification Card, which entitles them to discounts on museum admissions, public transport, theater and train tickets and other services. Similarly, senior citizens are entitled to many discounts. If you buy a ticket, always try to get a reduction; you may be asked to produce some kind of identification giving your age.

If you think you will stay longer, apply for an extension visa from your local German embassy before departure. When in doubt, contact the *Ausländeramt* (alien authorities) in the nearest large town; addresses are in the phonebook.

DRIVING

Western Germany has an excellent road network of autobahns (motorways), the highest figure in Europe. Highways and secondary roads are clearly signposted. The speed limit in cities and towns is 30 mph (50 kph), and twice that on other roads. Except on some 10 percent of their entire length, autobahns have no speed limit, although it is officially recommended to drive no faster than 80 mph (130 kph). You can be taken to court if you exceed the speed limit by more than 15 mph (25 kph).

Safety belts on front and back seats are compulsory. Maximum permissible blood alcohol content is 0.8 pro mille (about half a bottle of beer). Low-beam headlights are required in darkness, fog, heavy rain and snowfall. Driving with parking lights is strictly prohibited.

In case of breakdown, you must place a warning triangle behind the car. Along the autobahns there are free emergency telephones about every half mile or so, with arrows painted on the posts in between showing the direction to the nearest one. Otherwise, for ambulance, police or any other kind of emergency service, dial 110. ADAC is the main automobile club, operates frequent patrols and will often fix your car for free if the problem is a minor one. They are usually very helpful and efficient, although it helps if you produce the card of an affiliated club.

Overseas visitors will also need an International Driver's Permit, valid for one year, which you can obtain from your local automobile association. The International Insurance Certificate, sometimes called the "green card", is standard auto insurance; get it from an insurance company or rental agency.

In the former GDR, i.e. the *Länder* Saxony, Saxony-Anhalt, Thuringia, Brandenburg and Mecklenburg-Vorpommern, because of genrally inferior roads, speed limits are 60 mph (100 kph) on motorways, 50 mph (80 kph) outside built-up areas and 30 mph (50 kph) in towns, which is also the speed limit 88 yards (80 meters) within a level crossing.

ELECTRICITY

Germany has 220/250-volt, 50-cycle AC. Plugs

are the standard continental two-pin type, for which US and UK appliances need an adaptor.

EMERGENCY HEALTH MATTERS
In the event of an accident, dial 110 for the police, 112 for the fire brigade or 115 for an ambulance, or call the *Rotes Kreuz* (Red Cross) or *Ärztlicher Notdienst* (medical emergency service); telephone numbers are in the phonebook.

Treatment and medication are free for EC nationals and certain other nationalities. All others should ensure that they have adequate health insurance before they leave their home country, as medical fees are high in Germany. *Apotheken* (pharmacies) keep normal opening hours; a list at the window gives the next pharmacy that is open during the night and on weekends.

You should bring your own medication with you, along with a letter from your doctor if you suffer from a particular ailment. Diabetics should contact the Diabetiker-Verband e.V., Hahnbrunnerstraße 46, 67659 Kaiserslautern, tel. (0631) 7 64 88.

FESTIVALS
From spring to late autumn, countless festivities go on all over the country, and wherever you are staying at the moment, there is bound to be some kind of public celebration in the vicinity. For more information, the German National Tourist Office's "*Forthcoming Events*" is a comprehensive annual publication giving dates of trade fairs, art exhibitions, theater and music festivals, sporting events and traditional folklore festivities.

HIKING
Hiking is again becoming very popular, and some of the country's grandest scenery can only be experienced on foot. Make sure you are wearing comfortable, sturdy shoes and have a day-pack for provisions as well as a good map (see "Maps" in this section) and perhaps a first-aid kit for treating scratches and cuts.

There are an estimated 80,000 marked hiking and mountain-walking tracks in the country. Contact the Verband deutscher Gebirgs- und Wandervereine, Hospitalstraße 21B, 7000 Stuttgart 1. The Deutscher Alpenverein, Praterinsel 5, 80538 München 22, owns and operates 252 huts in and around the Alps which are open to all mountaineers.

LOCAL CUSTOMS
Germans tend to be quite formal outside the wine tavern, pub and beer cellar, so it is wise to remember a few conventions. Never use a first name without being invited. Use titles where appropriate, the more the better; so it is "*Herr Doktor Schneider*", not just "*Doktor Schneider*". Only waitresses are addressed as *Fräulein*, unless there is a name attached; otherwise always use *Frau*. When being invited to a German home, it is customary to bring flowers, always an odd number and never roses because they imply intimacy; they should be unwrapped before you present them. Try to be punctual, and thank-you notes are also much appreciated. Always greet the women before the men; shaking hands is getting out of fashion in some quarters, so only grab a hand if it is extended.

A helpful and witty booklet, *These Strange German Ways*, is published by Atlantik-Brücke, Adenauerallee 131, 53113 Bonn 1.

MAPS
Kümmerly und Frey has the whole of Germany in one clear 1:500,000 map, while the ADAC publishes a series in a 1:200,000 scale, detailing minor roads and viewpoints. For the larger German towns, Falk publishes fold-out street plans. Topographical maps, very useful for hiking, in a scale of 1:5,000, are available locally.

MONEY MATTERS
Germany's monetary unit is the Deutsche Mark (DM), referred to simply as *Mark*; it is divided into 100 *Pfennige*.

For changing money, banks and savings banks (*Sparkassen*) give better rates than hotels, travel agencies or currency-exchange shops (*Wechselstuben*). Before leaving home, purchase Travelers' Checks (TC) and arrange to carry some ready cash. You get a better rate if you cash TCs at the issuing bank. Major credit cards like American Express and Diners are in wide use. If you see Eurocard (EC) or Access displayed at an establishment, it means it also accepts Mastercard (MC). Eurocheques are the most popular and the best bet, because they may be cashed practically everywhere.

NEWSPAPERS AND MAGAZINES
Bild is the most popular tabloid, while *Der Spiegel* is the only serious weekly news magazine. *Stern* is still the best photo magazine, even after its reputation was seriously dented by publication of the bogus Hitler Diaries. *Die Zeit* is a middle-of-the-road weekly newspaper with intellectual

ambitions. Among the dailies, the *Frankfurter Allgemeine Zeitung* has the best news and arts coverage, but is right-leaning and a bit pompous; more liberal, if slightly provincial, are the *Frankfurter Rundschau* and the Munich-based *Süddeutsche Zeitung*. None of the newspapers go in for much investigative journalism, which is left to *Der Spiegel* and *Stern*.

Foreign-language newspapers and magazines are widely available at train stations and kiosks in major cities.

POSTAL SERVICES

The *Postamt* (post office) is normally open from 8 a.m. to 6 p.m., on Saturday to 2 p.m. *Poste restante* services are available at the main post office in any town; collect it from the counter marked *Postlagernde Sendungen*, and always bring your passport or identity card. Advise senders to use this German word as well as the international term to avoid confusion. Telegrams can be sent either by calling 1131, or from any post office. For local phone calls, some booths take coins and others phonecards, which you get at the post office and sometimes at newsagents.

For the *Vermittlung* (operator), call 010 (domestic calls) or 0010 (international calls); for directory inquiries, dial 01188 (domestic) or 00118 (international).

When addressing letters, use the zip code; for letters within Germany, it is prefixed by a "W" or an "O", for towns in former West and East Germany respectively; otherwise use the prefix "D".

PUBLIC TRANSPORT

Public transport generally runs from 5 a.m. to 1 a.m. In many cities, an efficient network of bus (*Bus*), tram (*Straßenbahn*) and underground railway (*U-Bahn*) – sometimes connecting with suburbs or a whole region and then called *S-Bahn* – operates as an integrated system, with easy transfer and interchangeable tickets.

Single and multiple tickets are available, as are day, week and month passes. You buy them from vending machines and at ticket counters at the station. A *Tagesnetzkarte* (day card) applies to the integrated network; a *Mehrfahrtenkarte* or *Sammelkarte* (multiple-ride ticket) usually pays for itself by the third ride. Each city has its own variety of ticket schemes, some of them quite intricate and baffling; if in doubt, ask at the information counter at the station. The usual system is to validate the ticket in a little box marked with an "E". On subways you must do this before getting in the car.

RADIO AND TELEVISION

There are two main national channels, ARD and ZDF, and a *Drittes Programm* (Third Program), which features separate regional and educational programs. Satellite TV with its high entertainment content, is fast gaining ground.

The only English-speaking radio channels are the BBC World Service, the British and American Forces stations BFBS and AFN, and Voice of America.

RAIL TRAVEL

Trains are by far the best form of public transport in Germany; there is a good network covering most of the country, and where it seems uneconomical to run trains, *Bahnbusse* (buses managed by the Deutsche Bundesbahn) take over. North-south travel is particularly straightforward. Service is fairly punctual, although on Sunday and during the peak season possible delays have to be taken into account. The two networks, that of the western Deutsche Bundesbahn (DB) and the more primitive old eastern Deutsche Reichsbahn (DR) have not yet been fully integrated; on an indirect route, allow about twice as much time as you would in the west.

Among the several types of trains, InterCity (IC) and EuroCity (EC) are the fastest and most comfortable. Swift service between smaller centers are covered by InterRegio (IR). Further down the scale comes the cumbersome D-Zug, while the very slow E-Zug stops at every village and doghouse.

Trains are rather expensive; often plane or coach are alternatives worth inquiring about. First class costs 50 percent more than second; for longer journeys, return tickets are cheaper than singles.

There is a large variety of special and very special reductions: for people under 26 and over 60, between the ages of 12 and 17 or 18 and 22, for students, families, single parents with children under 18, married couples and many more. Only the more popular ones will be given here; for more information, there is a helpful brochure "*Discover Germany by Rail*", available at tourist offices and railway stations.

The Inter Rail pass entitles travelers under age 26 to one month of unlimited travel in every country in Europe, including Morocco and Turkey. You can only buy the pass in a European country where you have resided for six months. The Eurorail pass gives unlimited travel in West European countries except in the United Kingdom. The Germanrail tourist card and the Eurailpass, which give excellent value, are for non-European residents only, to be purchased before leaving home.

The DB *Touristenkarte* (tourist card) entitles the holder to unlimited travel on all trains and *Bahnbusse*, on buses which ply special scenic routes and the Köln-Düsseldorfer steamers on the Moselle and the Rhine between Cologne and Mainz. The DB *Tourenkarte* (regional rail pass) gives unlimited travel on trains and *Bahnbusse* in all the major holiday spots, but is valid only in specific areas. If you are 60 or over, the Rail Europe Senior Card brings you 30 percent discounts on rail and sea travel in most of western Europe, including Germany. To obtain this card, you must first have a Senior Citizen Railcard (details from any train station).

RIVER CRUISES

Daily scheduled services on the Rhine and Moselle operate from April to the end of October, with the best choice of trips and boats during the peak season (July and August). The Köln-Düsseldorfer (KD) company offers excursions on motorboats, paddle-steamers and hydrofoils. The most popular tour, between Cologne and Mainz, has about 35 stops. You can also cruise the whole (navigable) length of the Rhine from Basle to Amsterdam on boats with full amenities. Regular services also operate on the Main, Danube, Bodensee and the bigger Bavarian lakes. In eastern Germany, the Weiße Flotte cruises the Elbe, Havel, Spree, Oder and Saale and the Baltic Sea.

SPORTS

Watersports: There are more than 30 sailing schools in the north, along the North and Baltic Seas. In the south, sailing on the Bodensee and Bavarian lakes is popular. Contact the Verband deutscher Segelschulen, Varlar 86, 48720 Rosendahl 1. Facilities for water-skiing and windsurfing gear are available only on major lakes and a few places along the sea. Canoeing is big on the Neckar and Lahn and rivers in the Bavarian Forest. In summer, rafting on the fast-flowing Isar is a favorite sport among Müncheners.

For fishing, the Moselle, the Bodensee and other lakes in Bavaria and Mecklenburg are well-stocked; a license, locally available, is required. Common varieties include char, grayling, river and sea trout, carp, pike, pikeperch, rockfish, eel and bream. Contact the Deutscher Anglerverein, Bahnhofstraße 37, 6050 Offenbach.

Winter sports: Some 300 resorts for winter sports are found mainly in the German Alps and the wooded hills of the Harz, Black Forest, Bavarian Forest and Thuringian Forest. *Eisstockschießen* (curling) is a speciality of Upper Bavaria, where it has not yet shed its rustic origins.

On Land: There are tennis courts all over the country, both indoor and outdoor ones; indoor ones cost DM25–35 per play, outdoor ones DM15–25.

Most German golf clubs welcome foreign players. Weekday green fee is usually DM30, on weekends sometimes double. Contact the Deutscher Golfverband, Leberberg 26, 60528 Wiesbaden.

Off Ground: Gliding is a fast-growing sport; there are some 1,000 branches of the Deutscher Aero-Club, Lyoner Straße 16, 6000 Frankfurt/Main 71.

TELEPHONE

For calls to Germany, first dial the international access code, then the country code, then the city code minus the first zero and then the telephone number. Calls to eastern Germany are still a minor hassle because there is a huge shortage of lines; only about 20 percent of eastern Germans have a private phone, and city codes as well as individual numbers are still changing. If in trouble, dial 01188 for inland directory inquiries or inquire at the *Ferngespräche* counter at the post office.

See also "Postal Services".

WEIGHTS AND MEASURES

To convert kilometers to miles, divide the km distance by 8, then multiply the result by 5; for Celsius (°C) to Fahrenheit (°F), multiply °C by 9, divide by 5 and add 32.

1 inch = 24.4 mm	1 mm = 0.039 inch
1 foot = 30.479 cm	1 cm = 0.39 inch
1 yard = 91.44 cm	1 m = 3.28 feet
1 mile = 1.6 km	1 km = 0.621 mile
1 UK pint = 0.56 liter	
1 liter = 1.76 UK pints, and 2.144 US pints	
1 US pint = 0.47 liter	
1 UK gallon = 4.546 liter	
1 US gallon = 3.785 liter	

DIRECTORY

German National Tourist Offices and Representatives

Amsterdam
Duits Verkeersbureau
Hoogoorddreef 76
NL-1101 BG Amsterdam Z.O.
tel. (020) 6978066

Brussels
Duitse Nationale Dienst voor Toerisme/Office National Allemand du Tourisme
54-56, rue A. de Boeckstraat
B-1040 Brussels
tel. (00322) 2459700/2459808

Chicago
German National Tourist Office
c/o German American Chamber of Commerce
Chicago, IL 60603-5978 USA
tel. 312/332-3213

Copenhagen
Tysk Turist-Information
Vesterbrogade 6 D III
DK-1620 Kobenhavn V
tel. (033) 12 70 95/96

Helsinki
DZT-Saksan Matkailutoimisto
c/o Deutsch-Finnische Handelskammer
SF-00100 Helsinki
tel. (080) 6 80 17 74

Hong Kong
German National Tourist Office
c/o Lufthansa German Airlines
Landmark East, 5th Floor
12 Ice House Street
Hong Kong
tel. (052) 8 46 63 88

Johannesburg
German National Tourist Office
c/o Lufthansa German Airlines
22, Girton Road, Parktown
Johannesburg 2000
tel. (011) 643-1615

London
German National Tourist Office
Nightingale House
65 Curzon Street
GB-London W1Y PE
tel. (071) 495 3990

Ljubljana
Predstavnisto DZT
Slowenïjaturist
Titowa 40
YU-610000 Ljubljana
tel. (061) 314 242

Los Angeles
German National Tourist Office
444 South Flower Street, Suite 2230
Los Angeles CA 90071
tel. 213/688-7332

Madrid
Oficina Nacional Alemana de Tourismo
San Agustin 2, Plaza de las Cortes
E-28014 Madrid

tel. (091) 4 29 35 51

Mexico City
Oficina Nacional Alemana de Tourismo
c/o Lufthansa German Airlines
Av. de Las Palmas 239,
Col. Lomas de Chapultapec
11000 Mexico D.F.
tel. (025) 202 3535

Milano
Ente Nazionale Germanico per il Turismo
Via Soperga 36
I-20 127 Milano
tel. (02) 26 111 598

Moskow
German National Tourist Office
c/o Lufthansa German Airlines
Hotel Olympic Penta
Olimpinski Prospekt 18/1
120110 Moskwa/Rossija
tel. (095) 975 3001

New York
German National Tourist Office
Chanin Building
122 East 42nd Street, 52nd Floor
New York, N.Y. 10168
tel. (001212) 308 3300

Oslo
Tysk Turistbyrâ
Klingenberggt. 7
Postboks 1761, Vika
N-0122 Oslo 1
tel. (02) 83 66 20

Paris
Office National Allemand du Tourisme
9, Boulevard de la Madeleine
F-75001 Paris
tel. (31) 40 20 01 88

Sao Paulo
Centro de Tourismo Alemao
c/o Lufthansa Linhas Aéreas Alemas
Av. Sao Luis 71-1 andar
01046 Sao Paulo, SP
tel. (011) 256 1054

Stockholm
Tyska Turistbyrân
Birger Jarlsgatan 11, Box 7520
S-10329 Stockholm
tel. (08) 67 95 095

Sydney
German National Tourist Office
Lufthansa House
9th Floor, 143 Macquarie Street
Sydney 2000
tel. (012) 367 3890

Tel Aviv
German National Tourist Office
c/o Lufthansa German Airlines
1 Ben Yehuda Street
Tel Aviv
tel.(023) 660 558

Tokyo
German National Tourist Office
7-5-56 Asakasa, Minato-ku
Tokyo 107
tel. (013) 35 86 03 80

Toronto
German National Tourist Office
175 Bloor Street East
North Tower, Suite 604
Toronto, Ontario, M4W 3R8
tel. (416) 968 1570

Vienna
Deutsche Zentrale für Tourismus e.V.
Schubertring 12
A-1010 Wien
tel. (22) 513 2791

Zurich
Deutsches Verkehrsbüro
Talstrasse 62
CH-8001 Zürich
tel. (01) 212 0175

Hotels and Restaurants

The following is a small selection of hotels main in the cities and towns mentioned in the text. The establishments have been graded and wherever possible, for each category at least one suggestion is offered. As some are closed on certain days of the week or during winter, a preliminary call is recommended.

Hotels (double room with breakfast):
***luxury and above, more than DM200
**moderate, below DM200

Information after the name of the town includes the postal code (towns in former East Germany are prefixed with an "0"); the number of inhabitants; the telephone code; the address and telephone of the local tourist office – there are various German terms for the latter, so if you write, the most common form of address is *Fremdenverkehrsamt*.

Baden-Baden (7570; 50,000; 07221)
Augustaplatz 8,
tel. 27 52 00
***Brenner's Park-Hotel,
Schillerstr. 6,
tel. 90 00
***Romantik-Hotel Der kleine Prinz,
Lichtentaler Str. 36,
tel. 34 64
**Greiner,
Lichtentaler Allee 88,
tel. 7 11 35

Bamberg (8600; 70,000; 0951)
Gayerswörthstr. 3,

tel. 2 10 40
***St Nepomuk,
Obere Mühlbrücke 9,
tel. 2 51 83
**Romantik-Hotel Weinhaus Messerschmidt,
Lange Str. 41,
tel. 2 78 66

Berlin (1000; 3,200,000; 030; for eastern Berlin 00372)
Europa-Center,
Budapester Straße,
tel. 2 62 60 31
Am Fernsehturm,
tel. 2 12 46 75
***Bristol-Hotel Kempinski,
Kurfürstendamm 27,
tel. 88 43 40
***Seehof,
Lietzensee-Ufer,
tel. 32 00 20
***Riehmers Hofgarten,
Yorckstr. 83,
tel. 78 10 11
**Rheinsberg am See,
Finsterwalderstr. 64,
tel. 4 02 10 02
**Atrium-Hotel,
Motzstr. 87,
tel. 2 18 40 57

Bonn (5300; 296,000; 0228)
Münsterstr. 20,
tel. 77 34 66
***Bristol,
Prinz-Albert-Str. 2,
tel. 2 69 80
***Rheinhotel Dreesen,
Rheinstr. 45,
tel. 8 20 20
**Schaumburger Hof,
Am Schaumburger Hof 10,
tel. 36 40 95
**Haus Hofgarten,
Fritz-Tillmann-Str. 7,
tel. 22 34 82

Bremen (2800; 530,000; 0421)
Am Bahnhofsplatz,
tel. 30 80 00
***Park-Hotel,
Im Bürgenpark,
tel. 3 40 80

**Mercure-Columbus,
Bahnhofsplatz 5,
tel. 1 41 61
**Landhaus Louisenthal,
Leher Heerstr. 105,
tel. 23 20 76

Cologne (5000; 992,000; 0221)
Am Dom,
tel. 2 21 33 40
***Excelsior Hotel Ernst,
Trankgasse 1,
tel. 27 01
***Dom-Hotel,
Domkloster 2a,
tel. 2 02 40
**Haus Lyskirchen,
Filzengraben 28,
tel. 2 09 70
**Königshof,
Richartzstr. 14,
tel. 23 45 83

Dessau (O-4500; 96,000;
003747)
Friedrich-Naumann-Str. 12,
tel. 46 61

Düsseldorf (4000; 570,000;
0211)
Konrad-Adenauer-Platz/
Heinrich-Heine-Allee 24,
tel. 35 05 05
***Nikko,
mmermannstr. 41,
tel. 83 40

***Schnellenburg,
Rotterdamer Str. 120,
tel. 43 41 33
**Astor, Kurfürstenstr. 23,
tel. 36 06 61
**Domo,
Scheurenstr. 4,
tel. 37 40 01

Frankfurt/Main (6000; 627,500;
069)
Hauptbahnhof,
tel. 21 23 88 49
Römer,
tel. 21 23 87 08
***Hessischer Hof,
Friedrich-Ebert-Anlage 40,

tel. 7 54 00
***Pullman Hotel Savigny,
Savignystr. 14,
tel. 7 53 30
**Westend,
Westendstr. 15,
tel. 74 67 02
**Diana,
Westendstr. 83,
tel. 74 70 07

Frankfurt/Oder (O-1200;
88,000; 003730)
Karl-Marx-Str. 8a,
tel. 32 52 16
**Stadt Frankfurt,
Karl-Marx-Str. 193,
tel. 38 90
**Kongreßhotel Frankfurter Hof,
Wilhelm-Pieck-Str. 1,
tel. 38 70

Freiburg (7800; 179,000; 0761)
Rotteckring 14,
tel. 3 68 90 90
***Colombi-Hotel,
Rotteckring 16,
tel. 2 10 60
**Zum Roten Bären,
Oberlinden 12,
tel. 3 69 13

Garmisch-Partenkirchen (8100;
26,500; 08821)
Dr. Richard-Strauß-Platz,
tel. 18 06
***Posthotel Partenkirchen,
Ludwigstr. 49,
tel. 5 10 67
**Reindl's Partenkirchner Hof,
Bahnhofstr. 15,
tel. 5 80 25
**Berggasthof Panorama,
St Anton 3,
tel. 25 15

Hamburg (2000; 1,650,000;
040)
Flughafen,
Terminal 3,
tel. 30 05 12 40
Burchardstr. 14,
tel. 30 05 10
***Prem,

An der Alster 9,
tel. 24 17 26
***Vier Jahreszeiten,
Neuer Jungfernstieg 9,
tel. 3 49 40
***Abtei,
Abteistr. 14,
tel. 45 75 65
**Hafen Hamburg,
Seewartenstr. 9,
tel. 31 11 30
**Baseler Hof,
Esplanade 11,
tel. 35 90 60

Hanover (3000; 510,000; 0511)
Ernst-August-Platz 8,
tel. 1 68 23 19
***Kastens Hotel Luisenhof,
Luisenstr. 1,
tel. 3 04 40
***Schweizerhof Hannover,
Hinüberstr. 6,
tel. 3 49 50 (with +++ restaurant)
**Loccumer Hof,
Kurt-Schumacher-Str. 16,
tel. 1 26 40
**Intercity-Hotel,
Ernst-August-Platz 1,
tel. 32 74 61

Heidelberg (6900; 132,000;
06221)
Pavillon am Hauptbahnhof,
tel. 2 13 41
***Hirschgasse,
Hirschgasse 3,
tel. 4 03 21 60
***Alt Heidelberg - Restaurant
Graimberg,
Rohrbacher Str. 29,
tel. 91 50
**Parkhotel Atlantic,
Schloß-Wolfsbrunnenweg 23,
tel. 16 40 51
*Kohler,
Goethestr. 2,
tel 16 60 88

Kiel (2300; 245,000; 0431)
Sophienblatt 30,
tel. 9 01 23 05
***Maritim-Bellevue,

Bismarckallee 2,
tel. 3 89 40
***Kieler Yacht-Club,
Hindenburgufer 70,
tel. 8 50 55
**Kieler Kaufmann,
Niemannsweg 102,
tel. 8 50 11
**Astor,
Holstenplatz 1,
tel. 9 30 17

Koblenz (5400; 107,000; 0261)
Pavillon am Hauptbahnhof,
tel. 3 13 04
***Scandia Crown Hotel,
Julius-Wegeler-Str. 6,
tel. 13 60
**Brenner,
Rizzastr. 20,
tel. 3 20 60
**Kleiner Riesen,
Kaiserin-Augusta-Anlagen 18,
tel. 3 20 77

Konstanz (7750; 75,000; 07531)
Bahnhofplatz 12,
tel. 28 43 76
***Steigenberger Insel-Hotel,
Auf der Insel 1,
tel. 2 50 11
**Stadthotel,
Bruderturmgasse 2,
tel. 2 40 72
**Goldener Sternen,
Bodanplatz 1,
tel. 2 52 28
**Schlössli (2 miles S, in Switzerland), CH-8598 Bottighofen,
Seestraße, tel. (072) 75 12 75

Leipzig (O-7010; 530,000; 003741)
Sachsenplatz 1,
tel. 7 95 90
***Merkur,
Gerberstr. 15,
tel. 79 90
***Gästehaus am Park,
Schwägrichenstr. 14,
tel. 3 93 90
**Stadt Leipzig,
Richard-Wagner-Str. 1,
tel. 28 88 14

Lübeck (2400; 216,000; 0451)
Markt,
tel. 1 22 81 06
Beckergrube 95,
tel. 1 22 81 09
***Scandic Crown Hotel,
Gustav-Radbruch-Platz,
tel. 3 70 60
***Kaiserhof,
Kronsforder Allee 13,
tel. 79 10 11
**Jensen,
Obertrave 4,
tel. 7 16 46
**Alter Speicher,
Beckergrube 91-93,
tel. 7 10 45

Mainz (6500; 180,000; 06131)
Bahnhofstr. 15,
tel. 28 62 10
***Hilton International,
Rheinstr. 68,
tel. 24 50
***Europahotel,
Kaiserstr. 7,
tel. 97 50
**Dietrich (in 6501 Nieder-Olm,
6 miles S),
Maler-Metten-Weg 20,
tel. (06136) 50 85
**Hammer,
Bahnhofsplatz 6,
tel. 61 10 61
**Moguntia,
Nackstr. 48,
tel. 67 10 41

Mannheim (6800; 310,000; 06572)
Kaiserring 10,
tel. 10 10 11
***Augusta-Hotel,
Augusta-Anlage 43,
tel. 41 80 01
**Am Bismarck,
Bismarckplatz 9,
tel. 40 30 96

Meißen (O-8250; 36,000; 003753)
An der Frauenkirche 3,
tel. 44 70

**Hamburger Hof,
Dresdner Str. 9,
tel. 21 18
**Sächsischer Hof,
Hahnemannplatz 17,
tel. 30 28

Munich (8000; 1,300,000; 089)
Hauptbahnhof,
tel. 2 39 12 56
Pettenbeckstr. 3,
tel. 2 39 12 72
***Vier Jahreszeiten Kempinski,
Maximilianstr. 17,
tel. 23 03 90
***Bayrischer Hof,
Promenadeplatz 6,
tel. 2 12 00
***Rafael,
Neuturmstr. 1,
tel. 20 09 80
**An der Oper,
Falkenturmstr. 10,
tel. 2 90 02 70
**Consul,
Viktoriastr. 10,
tel. 33 40 35

Münster (4400: 252,000; 0251)
Berliner Platz 22,
tel. 51 01 80
***Schloß Wilkinghege,
Steinfurter Str. 374,
tel. 21 30 45
***Romantik-Hotel Hof zur
Linde (4¹/₂ miles NE),
Handorfer Werseufer 1,
tel. 32 50 02
**Central,
Aegidiistr. 1,
tel. 4 03 55
**Feldmann,
An der Clemenskirche 14,
tel. 4 33 09

Nürnberg (8500; 478,000; 0911)
Hauptbahnhof,
tel. 23 36 32
Am Hauptmarkt,
tel. 23 36 35
***Altea Hotel Carlton,
Eilgutstr. 13,
tel. 2 00 30

***Maritim,
Frauentorgraben 11,
tel. 2 36 30
**Burghotel-Großes Haus,
Lammsgasse 3,
tel. 20 44 14
**Weinhaus Steichele,
Knorrstr. 2,
tel. 20 43 78

Oberammergau (8103; 4,600;
08822)
Eugen-Pabst-Str. 9a,
tel. 10 21
**Böld,
König-Ludwig-Str. 10,
tel. 30 21

Passau (8390; 50,000; 0851)
Rathausplatz 3,
tel. 3 34 21
***Holiday Inn,
Bahnhofstr. 24,
tel. 5 90 00
**Wilder Mann,
Am Rathausplatz,
tel. 3 50 71
**Laubenwirt,
Bräugasse 27,
tel. 3 34 51

Potsdam (O-1500; 140,000;
003733)
Friedrich-Ebert-Str. 5,
tel. 2 11 00
***Schloß Cecilienhof,
Neuer Garten,
tel. 2 31 41
**Touristen- und Congreßhotel,
Otto-Grotewohl-Str. 60,
tel. 8 60

Rostock (O-2500; 252,000;
003781)
Schnickmannstr. 13,
tel. 2 52 60
***Warnow,
Hermann-Duncker-Platz 4,
tel. 3 73 81
**Hotel am Bahnhof,
Gerhart-Hauptmann-Str. 13,
tel. 3 63 31

Rostock-Bad Doberan (O-2560;

9 miles W; 0037 8193)
Markt 5,
tel. 30 01
**Kurhaus,
August-Bebel-Str. 2,
tel. 30 36

Rostock-Warnemünde (O-2530;
7 miles NW)
Heinrich-Heine-Str. 17,
tel. 53 11/5 11 42
***Neptun, Seestr. 19,
tel. 53 71
**Eurotel am Leuchtturm,
Am Leuchtturm 16,
tel. 5 25 43

Rothenburg ob der Tauber
(8803; 11,000; 09861)
Rathaus,
tel. 4 04 92
***Eisenhut,
Herrngasse 3,
tel. 70 50
**Goldener Hirsch,
Untere Schmiedgasse 16,
tel. 70 80
**Glocke,
Am Plönlein,
tel. 30 25

Rüdesheim (6220; 9,600;
06722)
Rheinstr. 16,
tel. 29 62
***Krone Aßmannshausen (3
miles NW),
Rheinuferstr. 10,
tel. 40 30 (with ++ restaurant)
***Jagdschloß Niederwald (3
miles NW), tel. 10 04 (with ++
restaurant)
**Rheinstein, Rheinstr. 20, tel.
20 04

Saarbrücken (6600; 200,000;
0681)
Hauptbahnhof,
tel. 3 65 15
Rathausplatz,
tel. 3 69 01
***Pullman Kongreß-Hotel,
Hafenstr. 8,
tel. 3 06 91

**Meran,
Mainzer Str. 69,
tel. 6 53 81

St Goar (5401; 3,500; 06741)
Heerstr. 120, tel. 3 83
**Schloßhotel auf Burg
Rheinfels,
Schloßberg 47,
tel. 80 20

St Goarshausen (5422; 2,000;
06771)
Rathaus,
Bahnhofstr. 8,
tel. 4 27
*Erholung,
Nastätter Str. 15,
tel. 26 84 (with + restaurant)

Schwerin (O-2750; 130,000;
003784)
Am Markt 11,
tel. 81 23 14
**Niederländischer Hof,
Karl-Marx-Str. 12,
tel. 8 37 27
**Weinhaus Uhle,
Schusterstr. 15,
tel. 86 44 55

Stuttgart (7000; 559,000; 0711)
Königstr. 1a,
tel. 2 22 82 40
***Am Schloßgarten,
Schillerstr. 23,
tel. 2 02 60
***Royal,
Sophienstr. 35,
tel. 62 50 50
**Azenberg,
Seestr. 14,
tel. 22 10 51
**Am Feuersee,
Johannesstr. 2,
tel. 62 61 03

Trier (5500; 99,000; 0651)
An der Porta Nigra,
tel. 97 80 80
**Dorint-Hotel,
Porta-Nigra-Platz 1,
tel. 2 70 10
**Petrisberg,

Sickingenstr. 11,
tel. 4 11 81
**Villa Hügel,
Bernhardstr. 14,
tel. 3 30 66

Ulm (7900; 110,000; 0731)
Münsterplatz,
tel. 6 41 61
***Stern,
Sterngasse 17,
tel. 6 30 91
**Goldener Bock,
Bockgasse 25,
tel. 2 80 79
**Ulmer Spatz,
Münsterplatz 27,
tel. 6 80 81

Weimar (O-5300; 62,000;
0037621)
Marktstr. 4,
tel. 53 84
**Elephant,
Markt 19,
tel. 6 14 71 (with + restaurant)
**Russischer Hof,
Goetheplatz 2,
tel. 6 23 31

Wiesbaden (6200; 260,000;
0611)
Hauptbahnhof,
tel. 1 72 97 81
Rheinstr. 15,
tel. 1 72 97 80
***Nassauer Hof,
Kaiser-Friedrich-Platz 3,
tel. 13 30
***Schwarzer Bock,
Kranzplatz 12,
tel. 1 55-0
**Urbis,
Kranzplatz 10,
tel. 3 61 40

Würzburg (8700; 124,000;
0931)
Pavillon vor dem Hauptbahnhof,
tel. 3 74 36
Marktplatz,
tel. 3 73 98
***Maritim Hotel Würzburg,
Pleichertorstr. 5,

tel. 3 05 30
***Walfisch,
Am Pleidenturm 5,
tel. 5 00 55
**Zur Stadt Mainz,
Semmelstr. 39,
tel. 5 31 55

PHOTO CREDITS

Randa Bishop : 4/5, 42, 44, 68, 72 (top, left), 76, 84 (top,left), 272, 273, 275, 284, 294, 297, 298, 301, 345

Glaser : 12, 13 (bottom), 22, 23, 27, 39, 43, 80 (top, left & right)89, 95 (top, left & bottom, right), 123, 125, 128, 129, 141, 142, 156, 165, 171, 174/175, 215, 216/217, 219, 221, 230, 240, 242, 258, 259, 260, 270, 276, 277, 282, 283, 286, 302, 304, 305, 309, 325, 327, 342, 356, 367, 384, 386, 390, 392, 394, 401, 404 (bottom), 405 (bottom)

Greg Evans : 56, 58, 60 (bottom, right), 120, 130, 131, 136/137, 139, 144/145, 148/149, 210, 214, 218/219, 236/237, 248, 278/279, 292/293, 258, 402/403, 405 (top), 406, Backcover (left & right)

Greg Evans/Richard Balley : 34, 126

Greg Evans/T J Barclay : 376

Greg Evans/Paul Cullen : 353, 359

Greg Evans/Mike Davis : 324

Greg Evans/Reiner Elsen : 24, 96/97, 105, 134/135, 138, 140, 142/143, 146, 150/151, 152/153, 162/163, 172/173, 194/195, 288/289, 321, 322, 361, 364

Greg Evans/Mike Englefield : 29, 30

Greg Evans/Walter F Joseph : 101

Greg Evans/Mikoako : 226

Greg Evans/Heinz Mollenhauer : 8, 53, 59, 70/71, 104, 168, 170, 182, 187, 193, 198, 203, 224, 274, 290, 320/331, 370, 372

Greg Evans/Renier Van Randers : 20

Lee Foster : 2/3, 7, 14 (bottom), 50, 81 (top, right), 92, 98, 239 (top), 246/247, 268/269, 295, 296, 306, Backend paper

Image Bank/Werner Bokelberg : 6, 13 (top)

Inter nationes : 16/17, 32/33, 54/55, 166, 185, 188, 232, 267, 314, 316, 323, 339, 360 (top)

Stefan B. Polter : 60 (top, left), 88, 93, 187, 192, 201, 202, 204, 317, 318, 378, 379

Roland and Karen : 14 (top), 15, 40, 41, 46/47, 50/51, 52, 63, 64/65, 66, 72 (bottom, right), 75 (top, left), 81 (bottom, left), 83, 84 (bottom, right), 90/91, 100, 102, 110, 113, 114, 116/117, 118/119, 239 (bottom), 250, 251, 252, 254, 257, 261, 265, 392, 395, 396, 400 (top & bottom), Backcover (bottom)

Pankaj Shah : 31, 36, 38, 74, 75 (bottom, right), 102, 106/107, 108/109, 233, 234, 235, 238 (top, left & right), 243, 244, 245, 264, 320, 329, 330/331, 352, 357 (bottom), 385, 387, 393, 398, 399, 404 (top)

Morten Strange : 61 (top, right & bottom, left), 62 (top, left & bottom, right), 63 (left)

Doug Traverso : Front end paper, x, xi (top & bottom), 1, 10, 19, 21, 28, 48, 82, 86/87, 132, 155, 157, 159, 160/161, 174/175, 189, 191, 197, 334, 337, 340, 344, 345, 346, 349, 360 (bottom), 363, 366, 368, 374/375, 375

INDEX